D0070668

# PUBLIC SCHOOLING IN AMERICA

## A Reference Handbook

# PUBLIC SCHOOLING IN AMERICA

## A Reference Handbook

Richard D. Van Scotter

CONTEMPORARY WORLD ISSUES

**ABC-CLIO**
Santa Barbara, California
Denver, Colorado
Oxford, England

Copyright © 1991 by Richard D. Van Scotter

All rights reserved. No part of this publication may be reproduced, stored
in a retrieval system, or transmitted, in any form or by any means, electronic,
mechanical, photocopying, recording, or otherwise, except for the inclu-
sion of brief quotations in a review, without prior permission in writing from
the publishers.

**Library of Congress Cataloging-in-Publication Data**

Van Scotter, Richard D.
  Public schooling in America : a reference handbook /
Richard D. Van Scotter.
    p.  cm. — (Contemporary world issues)
    Includes bibliographical references and index.
    1. Public schools—United States—Handbooks, manuals, etc.
    2. Education—United States—Handbooks, manuals, etc.
    I. Title.  II. Series.
    LA217.2.V36  1991    371'.01'0973—dc20    91-28497

ISBN 0-87436-595-3 (alk. paper)

98 97 96 95 94 93 92 91    10 9 8 7 6 5 4 3 2 1 (hc)

ABC-CLIO, Inc.
130 Cremona Drive, P.O. Box 1911
Santa Barbara, California 93116-1911

This book is printed on acid-free paper ∞ .
Manufactured in the United States of America

371 010973
V278p

*For my children Shannon, Philip, and Caitlin,*
*who each in a special way*
*make the most of their*
*schooling and education*

# Contents

# Preface

Let us now ask how in our system of education are we to guard
against dryrot [inert ideas]. We enunciate two educational com-
mandments, "Do not teach too many subjects," and again, "What
you teach, teach thoroughly."

Alfred North Whitehead[1]

A FRIEND, WHO HAD SPENT MANY YEARS in the classroom, once
remarked that the zenith of American public schooling was
reached in 1969. Since that year, it has been downhill. By this she
meant students have become more distracted, the curriculum
more fragmented, teachers more beleaguered, and administrators less courageous. In retrospect, I find it difficult to quarrel
with her generalizations. To my mind, the 1960s were the "education decade."

The spirit of this book, however, is one of optimism. Not
since entering teaching a quarter century ago have I been so
enthusiastic about the prospects for public schooling in the decade ahead. I sense that in the 1990s, society—government,
business, and education—is poised for a *fundamental* change that
is long overdue. And the nature of this restructuring, renewal,
and reform, as it is variously called, is hardly a mystery. We simply
have to meet at the crossroads of the insightful reports that

1. Alfred North Whitehead, *The Aim of Education* (New York: The Macmillan
   Company, 1929), 14.

emerged during the 1980s. More than a good start could be made if we were to marshal support behind the leadership and proposals of Ernest Boyer, Al Shanker, and Ted Sizer.

Yet, never have I been so acutely aware of the perils en route. Another message within these pages is that we need to "cast a wide net" if we are to get to the root of the public school crisis. Indeed, the culprits in society are many: they include socio-economic transformations that, to be countered, will require nothing short of a national education policy. I'm referring to the expansion of global corporate enterprises with their declining support of the public interest; the growth of sprawling metropolitan environments at the expense of community integrity in our nation's cities; video technology that quietly undermines the cognitive curriculum; student employment in low-wage fast-food restaurants and shopping malls that are what Mary Bicouvaris labelled "silent killers of education"; and finally, dual-income and single-parent families that are too preoccupied to tend to their children's learning.

Likewise, educators need to shoulder their share of the blame and make an about face. Here I'm referring to an educational political structure (made up of 50 state departments and over 15,000 school districts) that is too fragmented to mobilize a national policy; public school officials too willing to take on broad social responsibilities; administrators unwilling or unable to assume academic leadership; and finally, teachers too dispirited and unsupported to be innovative.

Then there is the detached, often arrogant, position of the nation's leading colleges and universities toward teacher education. The unofficial position of, in particular, the public and private "Ivies" is one of *noblesse oblige*. Their primary interest appears to be balancing the demands of civic duty against academic image. Most cherish their image as society's "last bastion of liberal studies" and "islands of intellectual activity," but diligently keep a scorecard on the number of graduates who go on to such professions as medicine, law, engineering, and finance. They dare not ponder for long the proposition that *few liberal arts graduates make more moral use of their rigorous education than those who become teachers of our nation's children.*

From their visible and powerful positions, business and government leaders can be very influential. While the decline of public schooling is a complex issue, reform calls for fundamental, rather simple solutions. Too often, however, the proposals

offered by our national leaders outside education are frustrat-
ingly simpleminded.

Granted, more money for schooling isn't the answer to focusing on core learning, fostering higher-level thinking, or raising
expectations for students. Nevertheless, it can reduce the number of overcrowded, deteriorating schools and provide teachers
with a more dignified work environment and status. Money also
has helped such institutions as business, medicine, and the military take advantage of the latest technological advances. As is
pointed out in several chapters of this book, increased school
funding over the past few decades has not been spent frivolously,
but rather to support the increasing number of social and cultural demands communities have placed on schools. To put the
money issue in perspective: the average cost of providing a full
year's education for each student in U.S. public schools has
edged up to nearly $5,000—roughly the cost of one day in a U.S.
hospital for what medical authorities call minor surgery.

The fascination of many national spokespeople with local
control of schooling is peculiar given the thousands of educational jurisdictions that pepper the American landscape. It is the
specter of decentralization—in which the many states and local
school districts attempt to reinvent program models and curriculum—that creates turgid bureaucracies. As John Goodlad and
other thoughtful educators have exclaimed in various ways, it is
high time policymakers formulate national goals, learning standards, and curriculum frameworks for all public schools to
follow. Such a mandate would free local districts from tasks most
are ill-prepared to accomplish, trim administrative staff, and
permit schools to concentrate on what they do best—the creative
implementation of goals, standards, and curriculum in ways that
fit the local situation.

Public school choice is welcomed by families who find a
school nearby with an educational philosophy and learning environment suited to their child or children. If choice also is
extended to teachers, it becomes all the more inviting. To leap
from these modest benefits, however, and herald choice as the
key to educational reform (as some government officials and
business leaders do) stretches credibility.

As Gallup surveys reveal, American families believe their
neighborhood school is just fine. The claims many advocates of
school choice make remind me of economist Charles Schultz's
quip about the exaggerations of supply-side economics: "There's

nothing wrong with [it] that division by 10 couldn't cure."

School reform, as Ernest Boyer warns, will stall and ultimately fail unless classroom teachers are involved. Many proposals during the 1980s, however, viewed teachers as part of the problem but not the solution. Providing teachers with more authority to accompany their added responsibilities would help redress this.[2] Restructuring the functions of teachers to recognize those with special interests and to take advantage of particular talents (as Al Shanker recommends) would not likely require more money. However, providing teachers with the technical training and professional recognition that their counterparts in other careers receive would not come cheaply. Nevertheless, teachers are the linchpin to addressing the more difficult issues and most vexing problems of school reform.

The present time in public schooling, unlike earlier periods of crisis, has the feel of urgency and looming catastrophe that didn't exist before. Our public schools are in jeopardy. Yet, despite all the talk about failed monopolies, privatization, school choice, vouchers, tuition tax credits, and the superiority of private schooling, people seem to understand how fundamental public schools are to our democratic way of life. They know, for example, the importance of John Egerton's message when he writes, "Public education, for all its flaws and shortcomings, is the nearest thing we have to a publicly-owned and operated institution devoted to the general welfare." If our public school system is allowed to deteriorate, the quality of education for many will sink to the same inadequate level as the health care, legal services, transportation, insurance, and retirement benefits they now receive.[3] While we might be able to make do with such inadequacies and injustices in some areas, it is intolerable when applied to our most precious resource—the education of our children.

Richard D. Van Scotter
Colorado Springs, Colorado

2. The Carnegie Foundation for the Advancement of Teaching, *The Condition of Teaching: A State-by-State Analysis,* with foreword by Ernest Boyer (Princeton, NJ: Princeton University Press, 1990), vii–x.

3. John Egerton, "Can We Save the Schools?," *Progressive,* 46:3 (March 1982), 27.

# Acknowledgments

WRITING A BOOK CAN BE A TRYING, exhausting, not to mention time-consuming experience without the benefit of a sabbatical or even an academic schedule. It also can be a lonely experience without the interaction of fellow teachers taken for granted in academia. Nevertheless, I'm grateful for the enduring friendships and intellectual relationships with John Haas, Richard Kraft, and Jim Schott of Boulder, with whom I've collaborated on other works and whose thinking has helped me shape the structure and ideas for this book. I also value the stimulating dialogues on educational issues with Pete Harder, David Earle, and Nancy Brown, three former classroom teachers among the growing number with whom I now work at Junior Achievement.

I also appreciate the patience and kindness of my editor at ABC-CLIO. Laurie Brock has the ability to gently remind me that above all else this is a reference book. Nevertheless I make no apologies for the passages that reveal the heart and soul as well as the mind in my writing. I trust you will find this makes the book more interesting, informative, and perhaps inspiring.

Throughout the many evenings, weekends, and even vacation time that writing often demands, I could always count on the understanding and comfort, along with the measured responses and superb editing, of my wife, Pamela. Perhaps these abilities and skills have something to do with the fact that she graduated from high school in 1969.

I would like to thank Allyn and Bacon for permission to reprint selections from *Social Foundations of Education*, Third Edition, by Van Scotter, Haas, Kraft, and Schott, copyright © 1991 by Allyn and Bacon.

# 1

# Reviving the Spirit of American Education

Two simultaneous developments dominated the American education scene during [this century]: the first was the steady expansion and extension of schooling—in mission scope, intensity, and clientele; the second was the revolution outside the schools—the revolution implicit in the rise of cinema, radio, television and in the transformation of the American family to which they contributed.[1]

OUTCRY OVER THE QUALITY OF PUBLIC SCHOOLS did not originate in the 1980s. The history of American education reads as a stream of reform movements. Liberal critics tend to claim that schools must respond more to the needs of individual students and a changing world; conservatives, in contrast, want to emphasize discipline, basic learning, and traditional values. Intermittent turmoil should come as no surprise. For most of the twentieth century, schools have been charged with educating all children and carrying out many of society's goals.

"If a nation expects to be ignorant and free," wrote Thomas Jefferson, "in a state of civilization, it expects what never was and never will be."[2] This connection between education and the realization of democracy in America would grow stronger as the culture changed. For the first 100 years or so, universal education meant the elementary school years. During what R. Freeman Butts called the republican era (roughly from the 1770s to 1870s), the ideal was *some* education for all, and *much* education for a few.[3] The nation's focus on the twin goals of *excellence* and *equity* was under way but on divergent paths: Excellence in classical studies was emphasized for future business, professional, and political leaders; equity in the basics for others.

The economic landscape changed dramatically during the late 1800s, from an agrarian society to an emerging industrial society. The demands of economic life dictated that more education be provided for a growing number of young people. In the democratic era (from the 1870s to 1970s), the goal was as *much* education as possible for *all*. During this period, the common school movement expanded to the secondary schools. By the 1970s every youngster was afforded a public school education through high school. The quests for excellence and equity had been merged in the same classrooms for the same students, creating discernible tension.

As the nation embarks on its third century, the industrial period is giving way to an era defined by an information- and service-oriented society. Even entry-level jobs now require more skill and training than they did a generation ago. Juxtaposed to this, a growing number of students attending public schools from so-called minority groups—largely blacks, Latin-Americans, and Asian-Americans—are becoming the majority. And a disproportionate number of students from minorities perform poorly academically or drop out of school. The tension between providing a quality education (excellence) and educating everyone (equity) has taken on a new dimension.

For more than two centuries, the animating spirit of American education has been its commitment to popularization. The need for this commitment to succeed has never been as strong as today, but the difficulty of achieving it is equally great.

## The Need for Hard Heads and Soft Hearts

Educational reform for most of the twentieth century can be likened to a swinging pendulum. Before this century, the history of education in the United States followed a relatively steady course that gradually made schools accessible to more and more children. The efforts of such political and educational giants as William Penn and Benjamin Franklin during the colonial period, Thomas Jefferson in the early days of the republic, and later Horace Mann, defined the aims and shape of American schooling. While the progress of common schooling advanced the goal of equity, the elite sectors of society consistently supported schools—both private and public—that focused on excellence. Until the 1900s, these twin goals served separate needs that seldom were in conflict.

FIGURE 1-1    The Growth of the American High School

## The Growth of the American High School

| YEAR | 14- TO 17-YEAR-OLDS IN SCHOOL | HIGH SCHOOL GRADUATES AGE 25-29 | MEDIAN YEARS OF SCHOOLING IN THE U.S. |
|------|------|------|------|
| 1890 | 6.7  | 3.5  | —    |
| 1900 | 11.4 | 6.3  | —    |
| 1910 | 15.4 | 8.6  | 8.1  |
| 1920 | 32.3 | 16.3 | 8.2  |
| 1930 | 51.4 | 28.8 | 8.4  |
| 1940 | 73.3 | 38.1 | 8.6  |
| 1950 | 76.8 | 52.7 | 9.3  |
| 1960 | 86.1 | 60.7 | 10.5 |
| 1970 | 92.0 | 75.4 | 12.2 |
| 1976 | 91.4 | 83.1 | 12.5 |
| 1980 | 90.8 | 85.4 | 12.6 |
| 1988 | 92.8 | 86.1 | 12.9 |

Adapted from *Digest of Education Statistics 1988* (Washington, D.C.: U.S. Government Printing Office, 1988), pp. 15, 60.

For a full half century from 1890 until 1940 (see Figure 1-1), the number of 14–17-year-olds attending high school virtually doubled every decade. In 1900 approximately 10 percent of the high school–age population was in school; by 1930 this figure had reached 50 percent and by 1960 nearly 90 percent. Then it began to level off.

During the early decades of the twentieth century, the progressive reform movement added a new dimension to the United States' persistent search for a way to educate its diverse population. In a stable agrarian society, traditional education, with its teacher-centered emphasis on subject matter that supplemented learning in the central culture, was appropriate. John Dewey, who spearheaded the progressive movement, and others saw that an increasingly industrial and urban society, characterized by sprawling cities, mass immigration, ethnic ghettos, and factory labor, needed a new type of education. For the growing number of children from diverse backgrounds, who would have to cope with a complex social and economic environment, progressive education emphasized applying knowledge to the "real world" and "learning by doing."

William Burt Lauderdale points out that representatives of the two dominant philosophies influencing education were not blind to the merits of each other's aims. Those who supported the Western European tradition of classical education wanted to serve the "common people" as well as the academically elite and economically powerful. In turn, the progressives were not out to corrupt classical studies by advocating a broader, more practical education.[4] The goal of American education is to assimilate both positions and forge curricula appropriate for a wider audience of American youth. No one exemplified this understanding more than John Dewey, who went to great lengths to integrate subject matter with the learner's experiences.

Nevertheless, it is not surprising that as the mass of educational reform increased during the 1900s, it began to resemble a swinging pendulum. The common school, designed to meet the needs of virtually all students through the secondary years, had become reality. Heretofore, the two major traditions in educational reform were at least compatible if not unified. One, based on a quest for equity, opened opportunities to varied constituents of an immigrant nation and addressed the school curriculum to the needs of the whole child in an industrialized society. The other, based on the pursuit of academic excellence, has championed education for literacy that is rooted in the knowledge accumulated through centuries of Western civilization.

By the 1930s, and particularly in the 1940s, traditionalists became alarmed at what they perceived as a severely listing educational ship, dangerously weighted in favor of student interests and nonacademic subjects. The assault was led by *essentialists* William Bagley, Arthur Bestor, Mortimer Smith, Hyman Rickover, and Max Rafferty. During the 1950s, critics such as Robert Hutchins and James Conant offered

FIGURE 1-2   Educational Reform

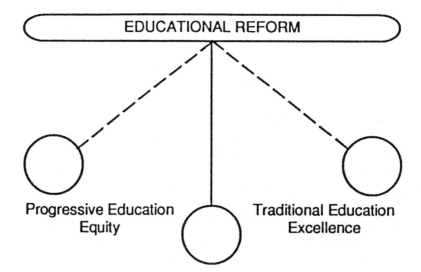

*balanced* proposals to guide the school curriculum. But the barriers were erected, and most educational reformers chose sides in this dualistic environment.

Reform in American education has been jerked from side to side, rather than guided down a rational path, during the greater part of the 1900s. Proponents of the two reform traditions today appear to wear blinders that provide them but a narrow view of what makes for an appropriate education. On one hand, modern traditionalists in their pursuit of high standards, achievement, literacy, and accountability display justifiably *hard heads* when they demand that schools offer a solid academic curriculum. Unfortunately, many traditionalists display equally *hard hearts* when they neglect to consider the strides public education has made in opening school doors to a wide range of students from different ethnic backgrounds, intellectual abilities, and socioeconomic levels. Progress toward standards of excellence is painfully slow when schools and teachers work with all children, not just the academically talented. Still, schools do neglect to serve some students when they frame policies and curricula that treat all students as if they were equal in their ability to handle academics and freedom. And they fail to challenge many when they don't demand competency.

On the other hand, progressive educators have had both the good sense and the compassion to display *soft hearts* in opening educational opportunities to disadvantaged students while helping to craft curricula that address the interests and needs of all students. Despite the pitfalls sometimes encountered, these efforts adapt the educational legacy of Jefferson, Mann, and Dewey to modern times. Unfortunately, in their humanistic zeal, some advocates in this tradition display *soft heads* when they act as if what students learn is unimportant so long as they enjoy the experience.

A commitment to either equity or academic excellence by no means excludes the other. Yet those who speak for one goal tend to favor it at the expense of the other. The point is that national leadership is needed to show the way toward educational policy that integrates excellence and equity—that is both hard-headed and soft-hearted. As with the two ideals of democracy—liberty and equality—these often clash. And there is no tidy recipe for just the right blend in any given situation.[5]

## The Conflict in Education

The dichotomy between those who advocate equity and others who demand excellence is vividly illustrated by two recent benchmark events in American education: the passing of the Elementary and Secondary Education Act (ESEA) in 1965 and the publication of *A Nation at Risk: The Imperative for Educational Reform* in 1983. As Lauderdale writes, "These two events—occurring less than two decades apart—symbolically represent the polarity of views on what should be the national priorities for education."[6]

## Era of Softness

The ESEA was a significant departure in educational policy and a major effort to serve the underprivileged. The five parts of ESEA (which substantially increased federal spending for schooling) provided funds to help school districts develop libraries, purchase instructional materials, set up reading programs, conduct research, and train teachers to work with children who came from culturally different and economically deprived environments.

This act was passed at a time of keen interest in the quality of elementary and secondary school education. To start, university scholars in the physical sciences, history and social sciences, mathematics, and English took a hand in reshaping the school curricula to convey the basic structure of learning and the science of teaching. As Jerome Bruner wrote, "Any subject can be taught effectively in some intellectually honest form to any child at any stage of development."[7] Discovery learning was the underlying theme of these "new math," "new science," and "new social studies" curricula. A few projects, such as Man, a Course of Study, which Bruner directed, cut across disciplines.

Another group of romantic and radical critics took aim at schools for failing to teach the underprivileged and understand the emotional needs of middle-class students while breaking the spirits of nearly all youngsters. Authors such as John Holt, *How Children Fail* (1964); Paul Goodman, *Compulsory Mis-education* (1964); Jonathan Kozol, *Death at an Early Age* (1967); and Herbert Kohl, *36 Children* (1967) were just a few who defined this spirit and message. It was also a period when some reformers were calling for alternative schools, usually "free school" alternatives to the prevailing "order and control" of conventional schools. A few scholars, most notably Ivan Illich, *Deschooling Society,* and Everett Reimer, *School Is Dead,* both written in 1971, said that the people will be genuinely educated only when formal schooling is eliminated and education is designed around convivial and incidental learning.

In arguably the most important work of the period, Charles Silberman, *Crisis in the Classroom: The Remaking of American Education* (1970), explained that it was time educational reformers understood the teachings of John Dewey and took them seriously. Many progressive educators earlier in the century were preoccupied with child-centered curricula and school environments at the expense of intellectual content. In reacting to the softness and vulgarities of curricula, particularly "life-adjustment" curricula, Silberman explained, reformers from the academic community made the same mistake, except they opted for the other side of the dichotomy. If educational reform is to be purposeful and succeed, it needs to address the question of what methods of instruction and classroom organization are effective as well as what subject matter is worth knowing.[8]

## Desegregation

One way public schools addressed the cultural demands for equity was through extensive school desegregation in the 1970s; another was through "mainstreaming" of children with disabilities. Perhaps the most historic landmark in American education is the U.S. Supreme Court's *Brown v. Board of Education* decision (1954) which struck down the "separate-but-equal" doctrine that had justified racially segregated schools. Change was not immediate. Most communities did not favor integrating blacks and other minorities with the dominant Caucasian school population, so schools found ways to avoid desegregation orders. This practice ended in 1971 when the Supreme Court in *Swann v. Charlotte-Mecklenburg Board of Education* directed district courts to set down specific ways schools were to desegregate. The results were sweeping and striking, particularly in the South: By 1980 only about one out of every four black students attended nearly all-minority schools; two decades earlier the vast majority had attended such schools.

This transformation had significant disruptive effects on schools: Redistricting and busing led to violence and strong measures to control it, disintegration of school spirit, white flight to suburban and private schools, and teacher resignations. Segregated schools were the result of housing patterns based on socioeconomic factors and an underlying racism in communities. But, because they were unable to affect the root causes of this inequality, courts placed the burden of redress on schools. Not surprisingly, the strains of integration took their toll on both the culture of schools and the quality of the curriculum. Any reform proposal that expects to have credibility must acknowledge the increased responsibility and burden that desegregation placed on schools.

## Mainstreaming

The Education for All Handicapped Children Act of 1975 (Public Law 94–142) has been hailed as the Bill of Rights for disabled children and their parents. The law requires that all disabled children, depending on how severe the disability, be placed in whatever school setting is the "least restrictive" and comes closest to the climate of the "regular classroom." The effect is that virtually all disabled students are mainstreamed, or instructed in the same class with everyone else. Schools also are required to provide programs individually tailored for the disabled, though in *Board of Education of the Hendrick Hudson Central School District v. Rowley* (1982) the U.S. Supreme Court said the intent of P.L. 94–142 was "more to open the door of public education . . . than to guarantee any particular level of education once inside."

In some classrooms mainstreaming has been a significant help to the disabled without distracting other students, and has even benefited the nondisabled. In other classrooms, however, it has put tremendous strain on the teachers. Some students need a great deal of attention and disrupt the class to get it. On the balance, including the disabled student in the mainstream classroom has improved education by advancing the goal of equity. Any reform proposal demanding excellence, however, must consider the constraints of this responsibility.

In the wake of events in the larger society and efforts to provide opportunities for low-ability, disabled, and non–English speaking students, schools attempted to accommodate all students. As David Cohen points out in *The Shopping Mall High School* (1985), they did this in three broad ways: by increasing the number of courses offered, thereby fragmenting the curriculum; by deemphasizing academic work and increasing remedial courses; and by relaxing course standards and requirements. "This flexibility," Cohen remarks, "is in one sense deplorable because students have been shortchanged. But in another it is admirable, because the schools have faced so many demands from so many quarters, and have tried to respond helpfully and in a certain sense humanely—even though they do not have the resources to do the many jobs they have embraced or have been assigned."[9] In the process more than a few educators and schools lost sight of a primary purpose of schooling: to ensure that all students come away with the basic skills and knowledge to prepare them to be capable citizens and workers in society.

## Era of Hardness

The swing to the essentials of learning in the 1940s and 1950s was a response to excesses of progressive educators in the preceding decade. Critics such as historian Bestor and Admiral Rickover, albeit hard-headed and hard-hearted, were justified in throwing the spotlight on the weakness in child-centered methods, permissive attitudes, and life-adjustment education. Many of those progressive educators, with whom John Dewey disagreed sharply, were guilty of carrying a soft head atop their soft hearts.

Less than two decades after the ESEA, *A Nation at Risk,* a report from the National Commission on Excellence in Education, revived the spirit of the 1950s and again set off a lively discussion on the potentially fatal shortcomings of public schools. The commission loaded its message with inflammatory passages such as:

> If an unfriendly foreign power had attempted to impose on America the mediocre educational performance that exists today, we might well have viewed it as an act of war. As it stands, we have allowed this to happen ourselves. We have squandered the gains in student achievement made in the wake of the Sputnik challenge. . . . We have, in effect, been committing an act of unthinking, unilateral educational disarmament.[10]

The commission fired a salvo of ammunition to support its claim: American students fare poorly in international comparisons of achievement; 40 percent of minority youths are functionally illiterate; average achievement of high school students on standardized tests is lower than a generation earlier; gifted students are not performing to their ability; average SAT scores fell between 1963 and 1980; achievement scores in science by 17-year-olds have declined since 1969. The list goes on and concludes by citing the need for business and the military to increase spending on costly remedial education in reading, writing, spelling, and computation.

Lost in the tough talk of the *At Risk* report was its awareness of the environmental context of education. The commission writes:

> It is important, of course, to recognize that the *average citizen* today is better educated and more knowledgeable than the average citizen of a generation ago—more literate, and exposed to more mathematics, literature, and science. The positive impact of this fact on the well-being of our country and the lives of our people cannot be overstated. Nevertheless, the average graduate of our schools and colleges today is not as well-educated as the average graduate of 25 or 35 years ago, when a much smaller proportion of our population completed high school and college. The negative impact of this fact likewise cannot be overstated.[11]

More importantly, the report makes a pitch for creating a "learning society"—one in which educational opportunities extend beyond schools and colleges into "homes and workplaces; into libraries, art galleries, museums, and science centers; indeed, into every place where the individual can develop and mature in work and life." This is a genuine plea for lifelong learning that not only contributes to a person's career goals but also to the general quality of life.[12]

## Back to the Basics

*A Nation at Risk* came on the heels of the back-to-basics movement in the latter part of the 1970s. "Back-to-basics" was a bumper-sticker phrase that had more political than pedagogical significance. The tack taken in the back-to-basics movement had at least two serious flaws: It didn't really teach reading or math, and it ignored other learning.

Reading, writing, and arithmetic are not self-contained skills like wallpapering and tennis. They are cognitive skills that are inseparable from subject matter and content. Remedial programs are little more than drills when isolated from purposeful literature and real issues. English teachers, for example, are obliged to spend valuable time gearing students for tests at the expense of other learning. Reading is most effectively taught in the context of academic subjects, including not only literature but history, social studies, and science. Reading, or any intellectual skill, does not exist in a vacuum.

Experienced teachers know how to raise students' test scores if that's what carrot-and-stick incentives demand. Timing and drill are everything if you're not concerned about depth of understanding and retention.

Despite rising test scores in recent years, research by the National Association for Educational Progress (NAEP) indicates that high school graduates do not possess the reasoning power they need to function as citizens and workers in an information society. Fewer than half can draw inferences from written material; only one-fifth can write persuasive essays; and only one-third can solve math problems requiring several steps.

Students do not develop intellectual qualities—the ability to think rationally and logically, do problem-solving tasks, evaluate issues, and use different modes of inquiry—because that is not what is taught in most classrooms. One of John Goodlad's salient conclusions in *A Place Called School* is that the curriculum is dominated by "the persistent and repetitive attention to basic facts and skills." The schools, he adds, are failing to develop intellectual qualities: "the ability to think rationally, the ability to use, evaluate, and accumulate knowledge, a desire for learning."[13]

It's not surprising that "critical thinking" is one of latest buzz terms in educational reform circles. Emphasis on the "basics" today has nothing to do with returning anywhere; rather it demands a leap forward to the fundamentals of higher-order thinking.

## Essentialism Revisited

More than anything, the back-to-basics movement signaled a return to traditional values and was but a stepping stone to the stronger swing to conservative educational thought in the 1980s. Several other assessments and reports followed *A Nation at Risk* and reinforced its message: E. D. Hirsch, Jr.'s *Cultural Literacy: What Every American Needs To Know* (1987) with Diane Ravitch and Chester Finn's *What Do Our 17-Year-Olds Know?* (1987) fall into this portion of the reform continuum. These reformers represent an extension of the essentialist position of a generation earlier when they advocate a return to academic studies and essential knowledge.

The similarity between the reform literature of the 1980s and that of the 1940s and 1950s is uncanny: The earlier essentialists' works include Idding Bell's *Crisis in Education* (1949), Arthur Bestor's *Educational Wastelands* (1953), Albert Lynd's *Quackery in the Public Schools* (1953), and Mortimer Smith's *The Diminished Mind* (1953).

Perhaps the most vocal critic of all was President Reagan's Secretary of Education, William Bennett, who conveyed a similar theme in his many public speeches and reports: The quality of American schools is deteriorating while the basic competency and knowledge of students are eroding. Bennett recommended a course of study that would emphasize history, literature, and the humanities. During the high school years, students in the English curriculum would study literature, including American, British, and world literature, for four years. Social studies would consist of three required years of history, including U.S. history and Western civilization. Both the science and mathematics curricula would require three years of solid academic offerings. All students would be required to take two years of a foreign language.[14] Bennett's *James Madison High School* (1987) curriculum forms a bridge to the classical dimension of traditional education. (See Figure 1-3.)

An essentialist curriculum represents one view of the traditional agenda; perennialism is the other. In the 1940s and 1950s, Robert Hutchins, then president of the University of Chicago, was its primary spokesperson. The message of Allan Bloom's best-seller, *The Closing of the American Mind* (1987), although not aimed at precollegiate schooling, is couched in the perennialist's tradition. In his book Bloom, a professor of philosophy and political science at the University of Chicago, uses eloquence, humor, and sarcasm to plead for a return to the classics. He simply wants to restore the humanities to what he regards as their rightful position in the liberal arts curriculum. As the subtitle of his book reveals, "Higher education has failed democracy and impoverished the souls of today's students." The answer to this malaise,

FIGURE 1-3    James Madison High School, a Four-Year Plan

| SUBJECT | 1st YEAR | 2nd YEAR | 3rd YEAR | 4th YEAR |
|---|---|---|---|---|
| ENGLISH | Introduction to Literature | American Literature | British Literature | Introduction to World Literature |
| SOCIAL STUDIES | Western Civilization | American History | Prin. of American Democracy / American Democracy & the World | |
| MATH | Three years required from among the following: Algebra I, Plane & Solid Geometry, Algebra II & Trigonometry, Statistics & Probability (1 sem.), Pre-Calculus (1 sem.), and Calculus AB or BC | | | |
| SCIENCE | Three years required from among the following: Astronomy/Geology, Biology, Chemistry, and Physics or Principles of Technology | | | |
| FOREIGN LANGUAGE | Two years required in a single foreign language from among offerings determined by local jurisdictions | | **ELECTIVES** | |
| PHYSICAL EDUCATION/ HEALTH | Physical Education/ Health 9 | Physical Education/ Health 10 | | |
| FINE ARTS | Art History / Music History | | | |

Source:    William J. Bennett, *James Madison High School: A Curriculum for American Students* (1987).

according to Bloom, is as basic and perennial as Western thought and the Great Books: a liberal arts curriculum based on reading classic texts as their authors intended them to be read, letting these works dictate the big questions to discuss.[15]

The perennialist or classical tradition has been related to elementary and secondary education through the work of Mortimer Adler, architect of *The Paideia Proposal*. Adler is chairman of the Paideia Project, made up of university scholars and public school administrators who generated ideas for it. Taking its name from the Greek word meaning "the upbringing of a child," this position is built on the ideas of Hutchins, Adler's former colleague at the University of Chicago, and other classical scholars who share this pedagogical position. Hutchins captured the essence of the position when he wrote that since "democracy makes everyone a ruler, and a liberal education is the education that rulers need, then every citizen should have a liberal education."[16]

The Paideia Proposal is based on several assumptions about learning; a main one is that all children are educable, regardless of background or ability. The central feature of Paideia is 12 years of the same course of study for all children, beginning at age four. As Adler explains, the Paideia curriculum uses three teaching styles to achieve the three educational goals: lecturing, to transfer fundamental knowledge; coaching, to teach basic intellectual skills; and Socratic questioning, to enlarge understanding.[17]

Adler also believes that "all genuine learning is active, not passive. It involves the use of the mind, not just the memory. It is a process of discovery, in which the student is the main agent, not the teacher." Adler, an admirer of Dewey's work, takes care to clarify Dewey's oft-quoted maxim that genuine "learning is by doing."

> What John Dewey had in mind was not exclusively physical doing or even social doing—engagement in practical projects of one kind or another. The most important kind of doing, so far as learning is concerned, is intellectual or mental doing. In other words, one can learn to read or write well only by reading and writing. . . . To learn how to do any of these things well, one must not only engage in doing them, but one must be guided in doing them by someone more expert in doing them than oneself.[18]

Given the wide range of children that teachers work with in many classrooms, the goal of the Paideia Proposal, while admirable, is utopian. Adler is on firm ground, however, when he explains that an overarching goal of schooling is to create lifelong learners who have the ability to learn on their own. To accomplish this, learning must be challenging, meaningful, and enjoyable.

> There is little joy in most of the learning they are now compelled to do. Too much of it is make-believe, in which neither teacher nor pupil can take a lively interest. Without some joy in learning—a joy that arises from hard work well done and from the participation of one's mind in a common task—basic schooling cannot initiate the young into the life of learning, let alone give them the skill and incentive to engage in it further. Only the student whose mind has been engaged in thinking for itself is an active participant in the learning process that is essential to basic schooling.[19]

# A Delicate Balance

It may come as a revelation that the objectives of hard-headed schooling can be combined with those of the soft-hearted thinkers. That we can have schools with high academic standards while meeting the comprehensive needs of the wide variety of students is not only feasible but imperative. Such a synthesis, in fact, has been available throughout most of this century. Today, blueprints for this education exist in several works.

The Carnegie Council on Adolescent Development set forth plans to reconstruct and revitalize middle-grade schools in its 1989 report, *Turning Points: Preparing American Youth for the 21st Century.* Earlier, the Carnegie Foundation, in *High School: A Report on Secondary Education in America* (1983), written by the foundation's president, Ernest Boyer, constructed a plan to overhaul the high school curriculum. In *A Place Called School: Prospects for the Future* (1984), John Goodlad proposes to refashion both elementary and secondary school programs. Goodlad's work, based on an extensive study of schools across the United States, is being implemented through the Center for Educational Renewal, which he directs.

Unfortunately, simplistic and sensational measures in educational policy tend to gain public support. Responses to *At Risk* and other reform reports of the 1980s testify to this. Recommendations have led to increased academic requirements—more credits required for graduation and more required courses, especially in science, mathematics, history, and English. Ironically, this has encouraged more students to drop out of school—a result that comes as no surprise to keen observers of the connection between school and society. As Cohen points out, "A large fraction of students now in high school seem quite immune to such requirements. These students are educationally purposeless"—and with justifiable reason.[20]

Students, like most adults, Cohen explains, do not regard academics as the primary purpose of schools. For most students, staying in school serves to keep them off the streets, delays entry into a crowded labor market, permits them to socialize with friends, and provides a convenient place to teach many life skills such as driving a car and avoiding the hazards of sexual contact. Students know that, if they are armed only with a high school diploma, most available jobs will be on assembly lines, in supermarkets, with fast-food restaurants, and at shopping malls—jobs that require minimal skills and knowledge. Students who plan to attend college to avoid this fate also know that being admitted to most colleges requires modest academic achievement.

In 1953, Bestor warned, "The idea that the school must undertake to meet every need that some other agency is failing to meet, regardless of the suitability of the schoolroom to the task, is a preposterous delusion that in the end can wreck the educational system."[21] In *High School* Boyer outlined a core curriculum that weaves together an academic and a practical course of study, grounded in genuine "learning by doing" for students from diverse backgrounds and abilities. (See Figure 1-4.)

FIGURE 1-4    Carnegie High School Curriculum

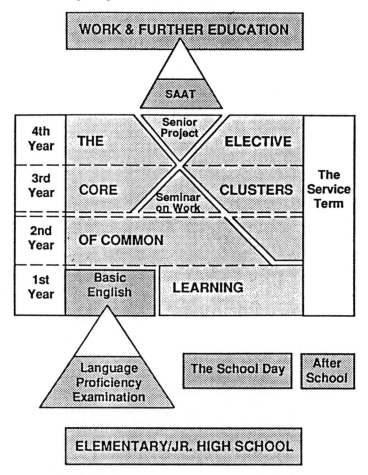

Source:    Ernest L. Boyer, *High School: A Report on Secondary Education in America.* Copyright 1983 by The Carnegie Foundation for the Advancement of Teaching. Reprinted by permission of HarperCollins Publishers.

In Boyer's proposal for the Carnegie Foundation, the first priority is language—oral and written. Mastery of the English language is a prerequisite to all other learning in school and is developed throughout the core curriculum. In turn, writing, which may be the most difficult area of the language curriculum to master, is the most critical. "Clear writing," Boyer explains, "leads to clear thinking; clear thinking is the basis for clear writing. Perhaps more than any other form of communication, writing holds us responsible for our words and ultimately makes us more thoughtful human beings."[22]

The second priority in the Carnegie proposal is a core of common learning made up of several components:

Cultural Literacy—including the study of literature, the arts, and a foreign language.

The Perspective of History—highlighting themes in U.S. history, Western civilization, and non-Western studies.

Civics—emphasizing the traditions of democratic thought, structures of our government, law, social and global issues.

Science—introducing all students to the processes of discovery in the biological and physical sciences.

The Study of Mathematics—developing the ability to solve practical problems, structure them systematically, and find appropriate solutions.

The Impact of Technology—including the history of man's use of tools, how science and technology have been joined, and the ethical and social issues technology has raised.

Health—focusing on the functions and changes in the human body and lifetime fitness.[23]

To help them make the transition from school to the world of work or higher education, students could take courses during the last two years of schooling from an "elective cluster" in which they could explore career options or do further study in selected academic subjects.[24] All students also would take a "seminar on work" that would examine how attitudes toward work have changed over the years, how they differ from one culture to another, and how changes in the economy affect careers and job opportunities. The Carnegie Foundation's curriculum is topped off with a "senior independent project" that focuses on a significant contemporary issue and draws on various fields of study that have made up the student's program. To enrich students' understanding of the adult world they are entering and to impress on them the value of social and civic obligations, Boyer would establish a "new Carnegie unit" in service to the community.[25]

This type of curriculum, when properly implemented, combines academic, vocational, and cultural understandings appropriate for a postindustrial age. It also has the potential to reveal the richness of literature and history, science and technology. In the hands of skilled teachers, it can show students how to apply knowledge to the lives they lead in our society and help them develop the desire and capacity to learn for themselves as well as to judge what is worth learning. Ultimately, this curriculum, to use words from Silberman, promises to "prepare people not just to earn a living but to live a life—a creative, humane, and sensitive life." In other ways, it is designed to meet the requirements of *excellence* and *equity.*

Will a framework such as this capture the attention of all students? The distractions and temptations of our consumption- and entertainment-oriented culture are many. And conditions in the vast corporate world or in higher education are not likely to change significantly. It has become fashionable for business executives to decry the "shoddy products" turned out by schools; but businesses mostly need workers with steady work habits and modest intellectual skills. A few colleges and universities maintain high academic standards, but the salient goal for most is to fill classrooms and dormitories.

As pointed out in *The Shopping Mall High School,* there are ways to cope with potential dropouts and those who languish in secondary schools. These include a national youth service for high school–age youth and those not yet ready for the intensity of demanding college studies, lifetime educational entitlements for people to return to high school at any time, lowering the school-leaving age, and eliminating twelfth grade.[26] Given the elusiveness of effecting change in business, higher education, and other institutions, schools are an easy target for reform.

Nevertheless, if students are to be prepared for the modern world, reformers will need to create configurations of learning among diverse organizations and businesses that are appropriate for urban, suburban, and rural communities. The schoolhouse is just one learning place in this arrangement.

## Notes

1. Lawrence A. Cremin, *Public Education* (New York: Basic Books, 1976), 51.

2. Gordon C. Lee, ed., *Crusade against Ignorance: Thomas Jefferson on Education* (New York: Publications Bureau, Teachers College, Columbia University, 1961), 18–19.

3. R. Freeman Butts, "Search for Freedom—The Story of American Education." *NEA Journal* (March 1960): 42.

4. William Burt Lauderdale, *Educational Reform: The Forgotten Half,* Fastback 252 (Bloomington, IN: Phi Delta Kappa Educational Foundation, 1987): 20.

5. I'm indebted to economist Alan Blinder for the metaphoric use of *heads* and *hearts* that he insightfully applied to economic policy and its twin pillars, efficiency and equity,

in *Hard Heads, Soft Hearts: Tough-Minded Economics for a Just Society* (Menlo Park, CA: Addison-Wesley, 1987).

6. Lauderdale, *Educational Reform*, 24.

7. Jerome Bruner, *The Process of Education* (New York: Random House, 1960), 33.

8. Charles E. Silberman, *Crisis in the Classroom: The Remaking of American Education* (New York: Random House, 1970), 178–180.

9. Arthur G.Powell, Eleanor Farrar, and David Cohen, *The Shopping Mall High School: Winners and Losers in the Educational Marketplace* (Boston: Houghton Mifflin, 1985), 295–297.

10. National Commission on Excellence in Education, *A Nation at Risk: The Imperative for Educational Reform* (Washington, DC: U.S. Government Printing Office, 1983), 5.

11. Ibid., 11.

12. Ibid., 13–14.

13. John I. Goodlad, *A Place Called School: Prospects for the Future* (New York: McGraw-Hill, 1984), 236.

14. William J. Bennett, *James Madison High School: A Curriculum for American Students* (Washington, DC: U.S. Department of Education, 1987), 9–12.

15. Allan Bloom, *The Closing of the American Mind: How Higher Education Has Failed Democracy and Impoverished the Souls of Today's Students* (New York: Simon and Schuster, 1987), 344.

16. Robert J. Hutchins, *The Conflict in Education in a Democratic Society* (New York: Harper & Row, 1953), 84.

17. Mortimer Adler, *The Paideia Proposal: An Educational Manifesto* (New York: Macmillan, 1982), 21–32.

18. Ibid., 50.

19. Ibid., 52.

20. Powell et al., *The Shopping Mall High School*, 303.

21. Arthur Eugene Bestor, *Educational Wastelands: The Retreat from Learning in Our Public Schools* (Urbana: University of Illinois Press, 1953), 75.

22. Ernest L. Boyer, The Carnegie Foundation for the Advancement of Teaching. *High School: A Report on Secondary Education in America* (New York: Harper & Row, 1983), 85–93.

23. Ibid., 94–113.

24. Ibid., 128–130.

25. Ibid., 113–116, 209–215.

26. Powell et al., *The Shopping Mall High School*, 304–305.

# 2

## Issues Confronting Schools

Today's high school is called upon to provide the services and transmit the values we used to expect from the community and the home and the church. And if they fail anywhere along the line, they are condemned. What do Americans want high schools to accomplish? Quite simply we want it all.[1]

IN THE MID-1800s, SCHOOLS CONCENTRATED ON TEACHING the three R's to pioneers. Later in the century, schools were charged with assimilating immigrants from diverse countries into the American culture. With the shift from an agrarian-based economy to an industrial one, schools taught knowledge, skills, and attitudes to prepare young people for a changing working world.

In those early days, educational leaders such as Thomas Jefferson and Horace Mann expected schools to carry out the reforms of society. With the influence of progressive education in the 1900s, John Dewey and others called on schools to impose higher ideals or to help reform society. Both traditions influence education today.

Schools have been the medium with which the American way of life is transmitted to its citizens. The American way has been a grand political and economic experiment, and U.S. schools have been a bold educational experiment. The emerging electronic, information-based culture in the final decades of the twentieth century is testing the influence and limits of schools in our society.

# The School as a Crucible

As social problems surface, Americans often turn to schools for solutions. This is particularly true in times of major crises, or events that are perceived as such.

When the cold war heated up in the 1950s and the Soviet Union launched Sputnik into space, leaders called for more rigor in the school curriculum. The public, politicians, and business leaders saw a direct connection between the nation's lagging military technology and power, and the quality of mathematics and science in the schools.

In the 1980s, the United States' primary concern shifted to economic productivity and the country's ability to compete in the international trade arena with Japan. The conventional view held that a direct link existed between students' learning basic skills and knowledge, and the nation's economic capability. In response, business's interest in schooling intensified during the 1980s.

The drive to educate everyone led to some unintended effects: Schools provided more and more aspects of children's education. The United States has attempted to prepare each person for a life as a producer, consumer, worker, parent, and citizen. Understandably, the results have fallen short of the goals.

## Schooling and Education

The goals society has set for schools remain out of reach for several reasons. To start, society confuses education and schooling, and places the whole burden of education on schools. As historian Henry Steele Commager points out, the responsibility for educating citizens, since the days of ancient Greece, belonged with every institution in a society: the family, church, business, and community. Today, these institutions include the press, labor unions, sports, medicine, law enforcement, the media, and community organizations. Few of these institutions, however, include education as one of their functions.[2]

The family and the church, once pillars of society, no longer function as the primary source of moral guidance for most people. Other institutions, whether they produce goods, services, information, or entertainment, are essentially self-serving. In simpler times, before the corporate landscape dominated our economic society, incidental education through a variety of institutions played a central part. Education today has fallen largely on the schools, both an imprudent and an infeasible assignment.

In an educative society the efforts of schools, television, other media, and institutions would be coordinated. School can effectively play only a part in the overall educational picture. Other agencies are needed to complement and supplement its role.

## An Eclectic Agenda

The task of schools is made more difficult, if not impossible, because they have been assigned or have assumed responsibilities that belong to other agencies—mainly because these agencies fail to perform these tasks today. Schools impart a host of vocational-technical skills, driving instruction, and character development, as well as teaching about health, drugs, alcohol, AIDS, sex, child abuse, nutrition, family life, careers, energy, nuclear weapons, the environment, law, and more.

Why, for example, don't police departments and insurance companies assume the function of driver's education? They have much to gain from good driving and should be able to instruct more effectively. Where are the medical community and the food industry when it comes to teaching health-related topics, or business and industry in teaching job-related skills? Computer technology, for example, could be taught in virtually any community today by experts from the communications and information industry. How involved are the media in school journalism and theater? These potential agencies of education now serve only those who can afford to pay for their services.

Home economics, far from teaching traditional housekeeping, is a catchall for teaching about health, nutrition, sex, drugs, personal conflict, and social relations. Not long ago, these topics were responsibilities of the family.

There are other areas: Physical education and participatory sports are vital for developing children, but in American schools they take a backseat to entertainment provided by interscholastic football, basketball, and other spectator sports. A more sensible model would be community-supported club teams for many sports at various levels of competency, coached by adults in the community.

## The Television Curriculum

In our postindustrial culture, children, like adults, receive much of their education from movies, video, radio, advertising, popular magazines, and particularly television. In the words of Neil Postman, television constitutes the major educational enterprise undertaken in the United States, which is why he calls it the first curriculum; school is the second.[3] In this sense much learning today is incidental. The problem is that too much of it is "miseducative."

Postman wrote this before television programs such as CNN Newsroom and Channel One were ushered into classrooms. Most of the furor surrounding Whittle Communications' Channel One dealt with its advertising content.[4] An equally serious question, however, concerns the nature of the medium itself: Is television an appropriate way to educate students on complex national and global issues?

Skepticism about classroom television programs comes from two fronts. First, critics, particularly of Channel One, observe that such programs are fast-paced and essentially entertaining. In defense of the programs, teachers are likely to comment that many politically apathetic students at least become aware of events such as the changes in Central and Eastern Europe after viewing the short and snappy television pieces. Few observers argue, however, that student learning goes beyond the superficial.

In turn, educators point out that unless the format of these television lessons is incorporated into teachers' curricula, they will not result in deeper knowledge and a serious understanding of issues and events. Given the more than 15,000 school districts, and their patchwork of curriculum frameworks, this is a tall order.

Beyond this, as Postman explains, the TV curriculum is in conflict with the school curriculum. The structure of television is based on *images,* which are concrete, specific, and immediate. In short, the content of the TV curriculum consists of picture stories. The school curriculum, on the other hand, is based on *words,* which tend to be abstract, conceptual, and translatable. Whereas the TV curriculum appeals directly to emotional and largely unreflective responses, the school curriculum requires sophisticated cognitive processing.[5]

Because the present culture is so dominated by the information environment (shaped by television, telecommunications, and computers), it is imperative that schools emphasize the written word and conceptual thinking. Postman recommends that they serve as a countervailing force, or "thermostatic device," to provide balance in the culture. In our "culture of high volatility and casual regard for the past," he adds, "schools stand as the only mass medium capable of putting forward the case for what is not happening in the culture." They need to maintain an intellectual focus and to offset the biases of the larger society.[6]

# Schools Serve the Melting Pot

*The Melting Pot* is the title of a 1909 play that captured a popular ideal: that diverse national and ethnic peoples who come to the United States to live would, over time, lose their distinctive qualities of national origin and become Americans. The play, written by Israel Zangwill, also showed that the United States represented hope and a better future for the many immigrant groups. Schools have been a pivotal institution for fulfilling the promise of the melting pot—to Americanize or acculturate new citizens and provide everyone the opportunity for a better life.

The glory of the United States, however, has been denied to many who live here. People in all societies tend to view others from an ethnocentric frame of reference; Americans are no exception. Those from ethnic groups whose values, religious beliefs, and ways of living differ much from the dominant American culture have suffered from prejudice and discrimination. At one level, discrimination may simply mean avoidance, but it can escalate to the level of denial and deprivation. During the history of the United States, for example, Orientals have been denied the right to immigrate here; blacks were denied the right to vote and sit where they pleased on buses; Native Americans and Mexican-Americans were deprived of their land.

When discrimination is institutionalized, segregation occurs and contact between groups is restricted. De jure, or legal, segregation has been practiced throughout much of U.S. history in housing, hospitals, and churches, as well as in schools. Because of the complexity of relationships in our society and economy, de facto segregation, that is, occurring in practice, has existed voluntarily or in the absence of laws. In either case, ethnic discrimination has denied some people the opportunities provided others. The strong American faith in education as the vehicle for achievement and success has made schools a hotbed of racial and ethnic controversy, despite the fact that racially imbalanced schools are largely the result of segregated housing patterns.

## Desegregation and Integration

In *Brown v. Board of Education* (1954), the U.S. Supreme Court declared it unconstitutional for states to assign children to schools on the basis of race. The Civil Rights Act of 1964 added that desegregation means assigning students to public schools "without regard to their race, color, religion, or national origin" but not in order to overcome racial imbalance.

When communities and schools were slow to desegregate, the courts demanded specific remedies and described what was meant by integration with "all deliberate speed." They specified how to define school attendance areas, how to reassign faculty members, what remedial programs were needed, and where to locate new schools.

## Busing

A controversial tool employed by the courts to achieve racial integration has been the practice of busing students from their neighborhood schools to schools in other areas of the city. The opposition to busing for racial balance has been strong. In cities where minority populations were smaller and integration resulted in Caucasian-dominant student bodies, busing has been effective, though not necessarily without disruptions. In those cities with large minority populations, citizens battled busing in the courts. They said that, faced with already segregated populations, they could not draw boundary lines that fostered integration without sacrificing benefits of the neighborhood school.

When courts responded that all segregation, including de facto segregation, is the result of state action and therefore can be remedied by the state, many families fled urban school districts. *White flight* became a popular term to describe the movement of white families out of largely urban districts to suburban communities or private schools to avoid court-ordered busing. Families who moved included both those who wanted to be separated from minority groups and those who sought what they perceived as better quality schools. Generally, it was the higher-income families who moved from the urban centers to more affluent residential communities surrounding the city. As a result, four decades after the *Brown* decision, integration has been uneven, and a majority of black and Hispanic students in large metropolitan areas still attend schools where they make up more than 50 percent of the student body.

Given the improbability of busing having much effect in urban school districts where most students are from minority groups, the courts have turned to incentives to integrate schools. Several big-city systems, for example, have established magnet schools, which specialize in the performing arts, math and science, computer technology, languages, business, and the like, to attract students from across the metropolitan area. Few cities, however, have any illusions that such measures will bring about substantial change in the short run. Most court orders acknowledge that integration is likely to be more deliberate than speedy.

# Equality of Educational Opportunity

In 1966 James S. Coleman conducted a study, authorized by the Civil Rights Act of 1964, that examined the status of educational opportunity in the United States. It documented that racial segregation in education was very high nationwide and nearly absolute in the South. Eighty percent of all white pupils in the first and twelfth grades attended schools that were 90 to 100 percent white. Sixty-five percent of all black students in the first grade attended schools that were 90 to 100 percent black; in the twelfth grade, 48 percent attended schools in which half or more of the students were black.[7]

The findings, published as *Equality of Educational Opportunity (EEOR)*, or the Coleman Report, also pointed out that the meaning of "equal educational opportunity" had been modified as a result of the *Brown v. Board of Education* Supreme Court decision a decade earlier. Here the court ruled that separate-but-equal facilities were not enough. Implicit in this argument, Coleman pointed out, was the need to assess the effects of schooling on the student. In other words, equal school resources were no guarantee of equal school effectiveness. This salient finding of the report was overshadowed by its racial implication that our schools needed to be integrated.

The Coleman group also found that achievement in school, for both white children and black children, was most effected by the educational backgrounds and aspirations of fellow students. The next most important factor was the quality of teachers, and the least important were the school facilities and curriculum materials. These findings, not surprisingly, led school policymakers and judges to argue that through integration, black students would benefit from attending school with achievement-oriented white students. Coleman, however, never drew the conclusion that busing students was the appropriate way to accomplish this integration.

## Financing Schools

"The contrast in money available to the schools in a wealthy suburb and to the schools in a large city jolts one's notions of the meaning of equality of opportunity," wrote James Conant.[8] Since Conant made these observations, nearly a generation ago, steps have been taken to reduce this disparity. The federal government has mounted small-scale but vigorous efforts to increase educational resources for children of inner cities. State governments also have worked to close the gap in financial resources among communities, but substantial inequities remain.

In California, for example, the wealthiest district has 50 times as much local wealth per pupil as the poorest, and about triple the total revenue per child after state and federal grants. In New York the richest district in per pupil wealth has approximately 14 times as much local wealth as the poorest, and the revenue disparity is about two to one. In Texas, the richest district is 700 times richer than the poorest; the local revenue is more than twice as much.

Inequities among school districts were even greater before the California Supreme Court, in *Serrano v. Priest* (1971), declared that the state's funding system was unconstitutional. In this landmark case, the court found that communities relied heavily on the local property tax to finance their schools; this tax, in turn, is tied to property values, which vary widely among school districts. This is unfair, the court ruled, because it discriminates among classes of people and thereby violates the equal protection clause of the Fourteenth Amendment to the U.S. Constitution. The court then told the state that school funds must be distributed equitably among districts.

The only school finance case to make it to the U.S. Supreme Court involved a Texas lawsuit. In *San Antonio v. Rodriguez* (1973), the high court held in a 5–4 decision that disparities in school spending among districts did not violate the Fourteenth Amendment's equal protection clause because education is not a fundamental right guaranteed by the Constitution.

After the Rodriguez decision, state courts heard numerous school finance cases during the 1970s and 1980s. Only about half the decisions, however, overturned existing, inequitable funding systems. For example, New York state's high court, in *Levittown v. Nyquist* (1982), said that education is not a fundamental right protected by either the state or federal constitution, and that attempts to equalize educational opportunities across districts would undermine local control of schools. In 1989, the Wisconsin Supreme Court declared that the state's funding system is a matter for the legislature, not the courts, to handle.

In contrast, the Texas Supreme Court, in *Edgewood v. Kirby* (1989), said that the state's school finance system did violate the Texas Constitution's equal rights guarantee. The justices issued a strong statement citing "glaring disparities" among rich and poor districts and explained that "property-poor districts are trapped in a cycle of poverty from which there is no opportunity to free themselves." The court told the state that school districts that make similar tax efforts should have similar revenues per pupil.

Over the past couple of decades, the revenue gap among school districts has been reduced, but not nearly eliminated. As Figure 2-1 helps to illustrate, this is largely the result of the fact that an increasing share of school money comes from state funds. The obstacles to approaching equity among districts within a state, not to mention among states, are many.

FIGURE 2-1   Trends in Revenue Sources for Public Elementary and Secondary
                   Schools: 1920–1987

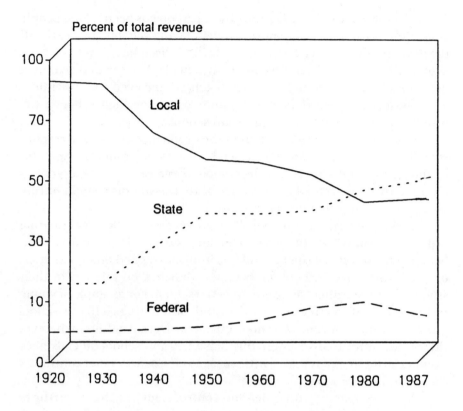

Sources:   National Center for Education Statistics, 1988. National Education
                 Association, *Estimates of School Statistics, 1986–1987*

To start, when schools depend for much of their revenue on the local tax base, there is a tendency (as Texas recognized in *Edgewood v. Kirby*) for the "rich to get richer, and the poor to get poorer." Industry and homeowners are attracted to prosperous areas with well-funded schools. Next, the courts from state to state are divided on how much authority they have to address inequities in school financing systems. Finally, though most states have adopted methods and formulas to redistribute state funds among local districts, rarely are the plans carried out vigorously. School finance decisions often are highly political issues for state legislatures, and wealthier districts apply substantial pressure to reduce the redistribution of funds.

# Safety and Order

For nearly two decades the Gallup Organization has been asking people what they consider the foremost problem facing schools. In nearly all those years, the answer has been "a lack of discipline." Actually, the problem is not insufficient discipline in schools, but the undisciplined behavior of some students. Students, teachers, and even administrators are physically attacked in many junior or senior high schools; the problem is particularly acute in urban schools.

School officials have not created the problem, but they are responsible for controlling it. Most antisocial behavior of students originates in the homes and streets, not in schools. Because nearly everyone is required to attend school until the age of 16, classrooms contain unruly youngsters with little interest in studies.

Unfortunately, some school officials overreact in their zeal to bring order and control to the classroom and surrounding environment. School officials often suspend students from classes and other activities, or expel them from school for behavior that has no relation to their studies or the learning environment of the school. For example, a young person's use of cigarettes, alcohol, and other drugs off the school grounds is not relevant to school business. Decent adults, whatever their roles, want to discourage this behavior, and school officials have avenues to do so, but it makes little sense to choose ways that contradict the central educational purpose of schools.

A preoccupation with order and control is no less characteristic of schools today than it was in 1970 when Charles Silberman wrote *Crisis in the Classroom*.[9] When managed with an eye toward the greater purpose of education, this quality can provide the structure necessary for productive and enjoyable learning environments. In too many schools, however, such a preoccupation leads to oppressive and petty regulations that make them grim and joyless places.

Creating healthy, orderly schools need not be an overwhelming task. Schools might follow a simple but fair maxim to ensure and maintain this order: A child's right to an education should only be terminated when that child interferes with the right of other children to have one. Teachers must have the power to dismiss students who disrupt learning in the classroom, and administrators should suspend students who violate the greater school environment. Such a policy also sends a clear message to students and parents about the school's paramount purpose.

Schools are responsible for providing engaging academic learning, but educators should be neither jailers nor entertainers. The fact that many students are not intellectually motivated need not alter the central purpose of schooling. As Postman remarks, "The school is not an extension of the street, the movie theater, a rock concert, or a playground, and certainly not an extension of the psychiatric clinic." The school may be the only remaining public situation in which traditional rules control group interaction, and it would be a grave mistake to change the rules because some students cannot function within them.[10]

## Conflicting Values

Values bombard young people from many sources—television, magazines, music, corporations, religious groups, as well as churches and families. Schools are only one more voice in the dark. Many observers correctly argue that promiscuous drug use and sex are essentially moral dilemmas. Some critics, however, add that schools have been stripped of any moral dimension to deal with the problems of adolescents by social and educational activists who have driven prayer from the classroom and religion from textbooks while promoting value-free curricula.

Contrary to this view, schools have sufficient moral authority to teach values that are valid to a democratic society and other universal principles that have helped guide human conduct for centuries. These include principles established in the Constitution, rational thinking, and ultimately the appeal of human dignity. Such values may or may not coincide with religious beliefs, but holding a certain religious belief is not a condition of moral authority.

Schools convey ethical and democratic values daily throughout their corridors. In the classrooms of capable teachers, values also are taught through the study of history, government, economics, world studies, literature, and the sciences. Indeed, schools can teach about religion, as the Supreme Court has made clear; they just cannot promote religion in any form. Religious freedom is a cornerstone of our nation, and the courts wisely prohibit public schools from undermining this civil right.

The problem is not that schools have become value-free, but that they are expected to teach values that society subscribes to but does not consistently practice. In trying to do so, teachers often appear foolish, idealistic, or romantic.

Society requires schools to teach the Bill of Rights and respect for law, but elects to office people who ignore the Constitution when they find it convenient to do so. The work ethic and craftsmanship are espoused, but society showcases those who lead extravagant lives regardless of how their affluence was obtained. Children are taught the virtues of honesty, fairness, and cooperation, but a competitive economic environment often rewards those who are cunning. Children are told to "say no to drugs" but can obtain nicotine from vending machines and consume caffeinated soda, while their parents abuse alcoholic beverages. Schools are encouraged to teach that the United States is a peace-loving nation, while the military establishment is generously funded. Schools are asked to foster sportsmanship, but society rewards and reveres the winner.

These conflicting lessons are not lost on the young. Unfortunately, many either accept the contradictions and hypocrisy or come away feeling negative and distrustful.

In the early days of American schooling, as Commager reminds us, the beliefs of society were, by and large, harmonious with the lives people led. A growing child saw cultural values displayed daily in the home, workshop, and community. Schools served merely to reinforce the dominant morality displayed throughout society. Statesmen such as Thomas Jefferson and James Madison were seen as genuinely being in pursuit of the public welfare. By contrast, many public figures today appear corrupt, incompetent, or opportunistic.[11] This view, unfortunately, casts a shadow of cynicism that tends to obscure the dedicated, even noble, efforts of some government, business, and labor officials.

Values exist, both implicitly and explicitly, in society and schools. Underlying much of the current goals of reform, from restoring basics to regaining the United States' competitive business edge, is a quest for traditional values—including politeness, obedience, discipline, hard work, loyalty, and respect for authority. Many people view the past several decades as a period when secular humanism undermined traditional values.

Emphasis on religious values has surfaced in efforts to revive prayer and scientific creationism in schools, to ban certain books, and to revamp "affective-education" programs. Schools that take seriously the charge to be a "thermostatic force" or "island of intellectual activity" do not adhere to particular political, economic, or religious positions.

## Creationism and School Prayer

Historically, schools have served to convey popular beliefs and values of society and the community. U.S. Supreme Court decisions related to Bible reading, school prayer, aid to parochial schools, and creation theory have reduced the influence of religious values in schools. As the effect of churches in society waned over the past several decades, some people looked to the schools for help. This has led to appeals for teaching creationism and installing voluntary prayer.

*Creationism* is essentially a moral statement or position and not a scientific theory. It is based on the faith in and omnipotent power of a supreme being and is not rooted in empirical science. The theory of evolution, in contrast, is strongly supported by the scientific community. The theory of creation is deeply ingrained in the culture of conservative religious groups. Liberal and humanistic religious groups, in turn, treat creationism as part of historical lore and seek to reconcile lessons from religion and science.

Teaching creationism in public schools clashes with at least two fundamental cultural values: respect for the religious values of individuals and recognition of the value of scientific inquiry to understanding the physical and social universe. In *Edwards v. Aguilard* (1987), the U.S. Supreme Court ruled that a Louisiana law requiring public schools to give a balanced treatment to the theories of creation and evolution in science classes violated the First Amendment prohibition of the government's establishing any religion. The court in effect said that creation theory is a religious doctrine that is supported by certain sects.

Creation theory is rightfully learned in the church or at home. Teaching about creationism is appropriate in, for example, world history but not in biology. Schools serve individuals and society best when they serve foremost as places to examine ideas and beliefs while teaching cultural knowledge and universal values. As such, the historical relevance of creationism deserves to be taught in the humanities, and evolution taught in the sciences.

*Prayer,* once a common practice in schools, was declared unconstitutional by the U.S. Supreme Court in 1962. During the 1980s, advocates of school prayer, buoyed by the Reagan administration, attempted to establish voluntary prayer in the schools. They argued that no one would be forced to pray. Participation in an official prayer, however, often is not a free choice. The minority student or teacher, whether agnostic, atheist, Catholic, Jewish, Moslem, or whatever, faces pressure to conform to the majority. This is the essence of the Supreme Court's interpretation of the First Amendment, which guarantees free expression of religion.

The real issue is not voluntary versus required prayer, as the rhetoric implies. Voluntary prayer in school as an individual expression is clearly permissible by any interpretation of the Constitution. One would hope that individuals come to school with ethical understandings learned in the home, church, or other community organizations. Individuals who find inspiration or comfort in prayer can exercise this right at home, at church, or wherever they have a moment of peace—

including the study hall, classroom, and athletic playing field. In the words of an insightful high school student, "As long as there are tests in school, prayer will also be there."

## Censorship

Most attempts at censoring schoolbooks come from political and religious groups. Would-be censors, for the most part, claim that certain texts, library books, and other reading materials are anti-Christian or anti-American.

The right to read falls under the rights guaranteed to all Americans by the First Amendment. This amendment states that Congress may pass no law that abridges freedom of speech or the press, and the courts have interpreted this to include freedom to read for adults. The extent of this freedom is less clear for minors, who are more impressionable than adults and must be protected. However, the U.S. Supreme Court, while recognizing that a school board has reasonable control over the content of school libraries, has ruled that the board may not ban books because it dislikes the ideas—political, religious, social, and cultural—contained in them.

Parents and others in the local community have a right to help with, but not to control, the selection of schoolbooks. Although citizens must be careful not to exclude a book merely because it doesn't fit the local viewpoint, schools are obliged to reject irresponsible or imprudent reading material. Attempts at censorship are rarely directed at books that appeal strictly to prurient interests or have no socially redeeming value. For the most part, conscientious librarians and teachers have screened out such material. Nevertheless, one out of every three book-banning efforts is effective. The book in question is either removed or access to it is limited. Three of the most censored books have been Plato's *Republic*, Melville's *Moby Dick,* and Steinbeck's *The Grapes of Wrath.*

According to the People for the American Way, a lobbying group, attempts to censor instructional material increased more than 150 percent during the 1980s. Those books most challenged included *Finding the Way,* a health book; several books by Judy Blume; *The Catcher in the Rye,* by J. D. Salinger; *Of Mice and Men,* by John Steinbeck; Mark Twain's *The Adventures of Huckleberry Finn*; *Cujo,* by Stephen King; *The Diary of Anne Frank*; and Harper Lee's *To Kill a Mockingbird.*

Censorship also occurs in less overt ways: Twenty-two states have textbook-selection policies involving committees that include public citizens. Publishers exercise prior restraint to head off controversy and to enhance chances that their books will be adopted by schools. The adoption of textbooks, particularly in California, Texas, and Florida, is very competitive. History texts, for example, tend to play down slavery and civil rights, the Vietnam War, Watergate, and other unflattering national issues. Biology, health, and social studies generally are subjects targeted for scrutiny.

Because they have a young and captive audience, teachers must choose reading materials and learning activities in a responsible way. They need to ensure that ideas, concepts, and viewpoints are accurately presented. The teacher is in a critical position and must recognize the fine line between an educative experience and indoctrination. This doesn't mean that one should avoid controversy; rather, treat it in a fair and, if possible, objective way.

## Affective Education

Affective education encompasses a variety of values-related programs and learning objectives. "Values clarification" and "moral reasoning," for example, were two popular approaches to affective learning in the 1960s and 1970s. In various ways both programs drew fire from conservative political and religious groups and from civil rights and libertarian groups. The critics said either that these programs didn't teach the "right" values, or that their approach was a form of indoctrination.

The latest values program to surface is "character education." Its aim has been to develop moral strength and attitudes through teaching traditional American values, which include altruism, loyalty, compassion, obedience, courage, punctuality, courtesy, generosity, honesty, responsibility, integrity, tolerance, self-discipline, self-respect, industriousness, and respect for authority.

Character education is also not without critics. Civil libertarians are quick to point out that in the wrong hands it risks serving as a Trojan horse to usher religious values into the school. Various exercises also border on indoctrination and an invasion of privacy.

Although character education earmarks values indigenous to the American experience, it omits other, sometimes conflicting, values. Independence, inquiry, justice, disobedience, and intolerance are also part of the American tradition. Needless to say, acting on these values will likely conflict with the more conventional values on the character-education agenda. Then again, some values may conflict with each other—honesty and loyalty, industriousness and punctuality, or respect for authority and self-respect. Conflict, however, is hardly inappropriate in values education or in any part of the intellectual curriculum. On the contrary, it is a necessary ingredient in the struggle to understand history, science, economics, and public policy—in short, to act as astute citizens. Any curriculum that purports to deal with a subject as sensitive and complex as values must be prepared to confront conflict.

# Restructuring Schools

Schools are essentially political institutions, the chief instrument for reproducing society in a desired image. And they have consistently served this purpose. Not everything society demands of its schools, however, is in the best interests of education. In the past few decades, schools have been asked to educate everyone in virtually all aspects of living. Try as hard as they might to meet this demand, schools are unable to deliver. As a result, public education today is in jeopardy.

Schools, Postman explains, should not attempt to accomplish goals that other institutions serve. The family, religious institutions, health professions, communications media, and community groups all have specific functions. Schools do not have the time to assume these functions, nor are teachers competent to serve as therapists, psychologists, priests, social workers, or parents. It may be tempting to assume these responsibilities when they are not performed by other institutions, but nothing in the training of teachers prepares them to do what others are supposed to do. The task of teaching the academic curriculum is challenging enough without trying to do everyone else's work.[12]

American schools last underwent fundamental change approximately 100 years ago. This period near the turn of century was one of restructuring in our society: The changing economic base no longer depended on adolescent labor, but it demanded different workplace skills and attitudes, while mass immigration prompted the need to "Americanize" the many new citizens. City school systems grew rapidly.

A number of educators, business leaders, and government officials sense that now is the time for another fundamental change in the structure of American schooling. The transformation of our economic society and the wave of new immigrant groups from Third World countries beg for a reshaping of school organization and curriculum. Many national leaders argue that the United States is in a competitive race for its life. And schools are seen as the fulcrum to the economic and political well-being of our nation.

## A Longer School Year

Over the past few decades, many courses have been added to the school curriculum, but school time remains almost constant: 8:00 A.M.–

2:30 P.M., Monday through Friday, September through May. Alongside the bloated curriculum, school buildings across the land, some magnificent structures, sit idle about 180 days a year.

This half-year school calendar, which holds a tight grip on the attitudes of Americans, has recently shown signs of loosening. Contrary to the belief that the 180-day school year is a legacy from the time when the academic calendar followed the agricultural cycle, this tradition is more a product of the industrial age. As Michael Barrett reminds us, public schooling only came of age in the United States during the twentieth century. From 1890 to 1974, school enrollment among American 14- to 17-year-olds grew from 7 percent to 92 percent. During this same period, the average length of the school year increased from 135 days to 179.[13]

According to the Education Commission of the States (ECS), 46 states mandate a minimum school year of 175 to 180 days. One state requires just over 180, and three require less than 175. Compared to other industrialized nations, the United States ranks at the bottom in the number of required school days.[14]

FIGURE 2-2    Number of School Year Days around the World

| | |
|---|---|
| Japan | 243 |
| West Germany | 226–240 |
| South Korea | 220 |
| Israel | 216 |
| Soviet Union | 211 |
| Netherlands | 200 |
| England/Wales | 192 |
| Hungary | 192 |
| New Zealand | 190 |
| Finland | 190 |
| France | 185 |
| Ireland | 184 |
| Canada | 180–185 |
| Spain | 180 |
| Sweden | 180 |
| **United States** | **179** |

Source:    Michael J. Barrett, "The Case for More School Days." *The Atlantic* 266, no. 5 (November 1990): 80.

A major obstacle to increasing the traditional nine-month school calendar is the leisure-time agenda of families. Summertime invokes images of camps, uninterrupted fun for younger children, full-time jobs for teenagers, and family vacations.

These leisure demands of families appear to be augmented by the general complacency of Americans toward the quality of education. In his study of three countries a decade ago, Harold Stevenson found that American mothers were considerably more content with their children's performance in school than Japanese and Taiwanese mothers were with their children's performances. About 40 percent of the American mothers said they were "very satisfied," compared to 5 percent of Japanese and Taiwanese mothers. Nearly one-third of the Japanese and Taiwanese mothers, in turn, were "not satisfied" with their children's performance, but only 10 percent of the American mothers expressed dissatisfaction. Likewise, American parents indicated much more satisfaction with the quality of their schools than did their counterparts in Japan and China. Some 91 percent of the American parents responded that the school was doing an "excellent" or a "good" job, but only 42 percent of the Taiwanese mothers and 39 percent of the Japanese mothers were so positive.

In a recent study comparing the attitudes of American and Japanese teenagers, conducted for Junior Achievement by the Gallup Organization, pollsters found that American students share their parents' sanguine view of schooling. For example, 56 percent of the American students surveyed indicated that they placed "a great deal" or "quite a lot" of confidence in public schools, compared to 44 percent of the Japanese students. This confidence in schools, incidentally, was higher than their confidence in any of the other institutions surveyed, which included banks (51 percent), Congress (46 percent), big business (45 percent), and television (31 percent). American students were also more complementary of their school courses than were Japanese students. Contrary to public perceptions, more than two-thirds of the Americans said they received good training in each of the academic areas tested (mathematics, English, science, social studies/history, foreign languages, business, economics, arts, and music); in Japan, math and Japanese were the only subjects in which more than two-thirds of the students said they would get good training before leaving high school. Typical of this comparison is the finding that 90 percent of the American students gave high marks to mathematics, compared with 70 percent of the Japanese students.[15]

Teachers are no more enthusiastic about an extended school year than are families, and many have nine- or ten-month union contracts as a buffer again legislative change. These classroom practitioners, in turn, are buttressed by time-and-learning theorists who contend that the road to increased student achievement is better paved by more efficiently managing smaller units of classroom learning, or "scheduled time," "instructional time," "engaged time," and "time-on-task." Extending the school year (a "global-time measure") won't help much, these researchers argue, if things such as classroom disruptions, inattentiveness, and absenteeism inhibit engaged learning.

Despite such admirable yet esoteric efforts to improve classroom productivity, the appeal of a longer school year is gaining ground. As Barrett explains:

> A longer school year, while hardly sufficient in itself to reclaim quality in American education, is a superstructure under which other changes can be made. A school year of, say, 220 days will serve as a big tent. A number of things may go into the tent to make it a better place: to accommodate them all and to arrange them in proper order requires the space the tent provides.[16]

Americans appear to understand that the public schools' expanded comprehensive curriculum requires a much larger tent than was needed just a couple decades ago. In 1959, even in the wake of Sputnik, 67 percent of the public polled by the Gallup Organization opposed "increasing the number of days per year in school" for high school students, while only 26 percent were in favor. By the 1980s the mood had shifted: When Gallup asked interviewees in 1984 if the school year should be extended by 30 days to 210, more respondents still opposed (50 percent) than approved (44 percent), but the gap was narrowing. Then in 1989, Gallup, in its annual poll of attitudes toward public schooling with *Phi Delta Kappan,* asked: "In some nations students spend about 25% more time in school than do students in the U.S. Would you favor or oppose increasing the amount of time that students in this community spend in school?" A majority of 48 percent said they were in favor; 44 percent were still opposed, and 8 percent were undecided.[17]

Then again, a longer school year, particularly for younger children, may have more practical than educational appeal for many families. An increasing percentage of children are being reared in single-parent homes or families in which both parents work. To these parents, more school days mean lower day-care expenses and fewer worries about where the kids are.

## Reorganizing the Learning Place

In this high-technology world dominated by electronic media and multinational enterprises, the role of schooling also has changed. Competency in basic skills (math, reading, and writing) and basic knowledge (literature, history, and science) is only a start. It is just as important to teach critical thinking and problem-solving across the curriculum: These intellectual abilities apply equally to core subjects, vocational studies, citizenship, and values.

Despite experiments with flexible scheduling, informal class-rooms, and open campuses, the school environment has changed little over the years: Secondary schools operate on fixed schedules of six or seven periods, each nearly one hour long, with a set time between classes—just enough for students to make the next class.

Albert Shanker, president of the American Federation of Teachers (AFT), believes that public schools have a golden opportunity to become much more effective, but that the moment won't last long. If governors, businesses, and organizations don't see results from the resources they have begun to provide, their support will be withdrawn.

Schools, Shanker explains, must seize the initiative if they are to carry out their intellectual agenda and survive. He recommends that schools restructure themselves by organizing teaching staffs into teams of six or seven instructors. Each team would be responsible for the learning of a group of about 120 students in all subjects throughout their elementary, middle, or high school grades. This team approach could be implemented differently from school to school, but essentially it is a "school within a school." Each team would be headed by at least one lead or master teacher and include some combination of parapro-fessionals, student or intern teachers, administrative assistants, and regular teachers. Each team would decide how it will organize itself to carry out the many tasks that go on in classrooms. There would be no department heads, assistant principals, or guidance counselors; these people would be part of the instructional team. A team would plan and organize instruction, implement the curriculum, advise students, be mentor to new teachers, coach the less competent, and weed out the incompetent.

Learning would take place in small groups with a stress on cooperative learning and little or no lecturing. Instruction would be based on active learning—problem-solving, simulations, interactive computer programs, oral and written reports. Each activity would be given as long as needed to accomplish the task, so bells would be eliminated. The intent, needless to say, is for students to become intellectually involved and enjoy school, but they also would be re-sponsible for what they learn. Students could no longer sit back and be passive, but in various ways must demonstrate what they are learning.

One member of each team would serve on a faculty senate to help forge school policy, and another would work on the curriculum com-mittee. In cooperation with a master planner (principal) who would oversee school operations, teaching teams would run the school.[18]

# Reorganizing the Curriculum

Like school structure, the curriculum has remained remarkably unchanged. Teaching is centered on lessons from the text, lectures with some discussion led by the teacher, and emphasis on facts, skills, and drills. As John Goodlad describes in *A Place Called School*, teachers and administrators, by and large, are uncomfortable with hands-on activities or learning by doing, while those who plan field trips, community-based projects, workshops, and small conferences encounter logistical hurdles. In his words, "Teachers may start out 'fighting the system,' but it is easier, ultimately, to settle down into conventional ways of teaching. And one tends to look more normal doing so. The cards are stacked against innovation."[19]

The impediment to stating a clear mandate for all schools lies in the political structure of education. The U.S. Constitution gives states the overall responsibility for education. Consequently, any government or national task force recommendations must be interpreted and enacted by states and local school districts. Federal laws, funds, and persuasion at times do effect changes in state educational policy, but Goodlad has found no clear aims for education and schooling. After examining state guides to education, his major conclusion is that the area is a "conceptual swamp." The time is long past due, he says, for "the 50 states to articulate, as basic policy, a commitment to a broad array of educational goals . . . that have emerged in this country over more than three hundred years."[20]

In his report on secondary education in the United States, Ernest Boyer set forth four essential goals that, with minor adjustments, could also serve elementary and middle schools.

First, according to Boyer, "schooling should help students develop the capacity to think critically and communicate effectively through a mastery of language." Second, "it should help all students learn about themselves, the human heritage, and the interdependent world." Third, Boyer would have high schools "prepare all students for work and further education through a program of electives that develop individual aptitudes and interests." Fourth, schools "should help all students fulfill their social and civic obligations through school and community service."[21]

Goodlad also proposed a set of comprehensive goals that define the role of schools in the larger educational context. Goodlad's extensive research and policy recommendations, which complement Boyer's work, provide a clear guide for schools as they wade through the quagmire of educational reform proposals of recent years. His goals encompass four areas: academic goals—including mastery of basic skills and intellectual development; vocational goals—emphasizing skills related to careers and attitudes toward work; social, civic, and cultural goals—developing interpersonal understandings, citizenship participation, and values characteristic of the common culture; and personal goals—focusing on emotional and physical well-being, creativity, and aesthetic expression.[22]

Unlike some reform ideas that surfaced during the 1980s, Boyer's and Goodlad's proposals are rooted in an understanding of the historical function of schools in American society. Reform ideas that focus exclusively on the basics; or on history, literature, math, and science; or on classical studies, define the role of schools too narrowly. On the other hand, educational policy must guard against assuming a too ambitious role for schools.

While these goals would provide young people with the knowledge, skills, and attitudes that are reasonable to expect of schools, they leave a strategic role for other agencies in completing the "whole education" of students.

## Reformulating the Essentials

Ted Sizer, former Harvard dean and Phillips Academy headmaster who is now at Brown University, is putting into practice ideas consistent with the quest to blend excellence and equity. Through the Coalition of Essential Schools, which he also directs, Sizer's group is helping schools change in fundamental ways. Small schools, big schools, even private and parochial schools, he explains, share the basic problem of "trying to do too much."

Sizer's answer is to simplify what schools do and concentrate on the "essentials." One path to simplification is to "restructure overloaded and ineffective schools." In the rapidly growing number of coalition schools, teachers form science, social studies, and humanities teams in which they can pool their expertise and spend more time with a smaller number of students. A counterpart to this focusing is that greater academic demands are placed on students. The theme sees the "student as worker," accountable for a high level of intellectual performance.

A second essential to change is simplifying the smorgasbord curriculum of schools and focusing a particular course on critical themes and higher-level thinking. The message is "less is more," and schools must make tough decisions about what is most essential to know, then teach it thoroughly. Sizer calls this the "politics of subtraction." There is no quibbling over what is more important—subject matter or thinking skills, knowledge or critical thinking. One does not truly exist without the other.[23]

# Public School Choice

Choice has become a popular avenue of school reform in recent years. While the broad term *restructuring* can be vague or confusing, *choice* conveys a sense of freedom and power. Being able to choose among options appeals to Americans because choice is at the heart of the U.S. democratic system and market economy.

Historically, choice has been available to many American families. Some families, for example, have chosen whether to have their children attend public or private (parochial or independent) schools. Families also have decided in what neighborhoods to live and, therefore, what schools to attend. Dating back to the early decades of this century, many high school students have opted to attend specialized technical schools that most city school districts created.

During the 1960s and 1970s a host of alternative schools emerged across the national landscape. The first alternatives were associated with free schools—mostly the Summerhill type that represented an alternative to the traditional school. In fact, most of these schools grew up outside the public school system. The goal of these schools was to "humanize learning" by creating environments where the innate goodness and curiosity of children could emerge, and thereby to restore joy to learning.

Lawrence Cremin points out that the free school movement, and the educational reform movement of the 1960s in general, had their roots in the progressive education movement of the 1920s and 1930s.[24] Alongside free schools, the open school—also referred to as the informal or open classroom—became a popular alternative a couple of decades ago. Buoyed by Silberman's pivotal book, *Crisis in the Classroom* (1970), open schools and classrooms provided "progressive" educators with a golden opportunity to reestablish the theory and practices of John Dewey, from a generation earlier. This alternative developed almost wholly within the system.[25]

The flurry of experimentation within communities and schools tended to produce explosive educational environments. Efforts to revive fundamental and back-to-basics schools flourished alongside the counterculture and progressive varieties. It was in this context that alternative schooling came to mean choice. In an attempt to avoid the crossfire created by reformers of different beliefs, advocates for alternatives substituted the less emotionally loaded and controversial term *options,* or public options in education. Mario Fantini's *Public Schools of Choice: Alternatives in Education* (1973) provided an historical and theoretical rationale for this transformation.

Fantini and other proponents of alternatives envisioned a rational structure of school options—free, open, modified, continuous-progress, standard, and fundamental schools—each supported by its conceptual framework. What resulted instead was a proliferation of choices—outside the public school system, inside the system, and within schools. These choices included free schools, fundamental schools, open classrooms, schools without walls, vocational programs, dropout programs, unwed mother programs, back-to-basics, career education, special education schools, magnet schools, gifted and talented programs, schools within schools, and voucher plans. Few of these options, however, were based on clear, distinct principles related to school organization, learning theory, and teaching strategies. Frankly, to many communities, the alternative school meant a dumping ground for disruptive students.

During the latter years of the 1970s and much of the 1980s, interest in school options waned. Still, distinct alternatives or choices prevailed. Magnet schools, particularly in urban centers, attracted students with special interests and talents. Some cities, frustrated with turgid bureaucracies, turned to decentralization or community control of neighborhood schools. In the late 1980s this trend took the form of site-based management and individual school accountability committees. A few communities also experimented with educational vouchers, which provided families with the purchasing power to select the school they desired.

Although the voucher system created more heated theoretical discourse than it did viable achievement, it was the antecedent of the "school choice plans" being implemented today. The term *public schools of choice* has been used for about two decades, but the concept has acquired a new meaning in today's political-economic environment. The choice concept now embraces the original alternative-school reformers, who typically were perched on the progressive or liberal side of the political spectrum, and advocates from the fundamental or conservative side, who lobby for a return to the essentials of learning.

Perhaps most significantly, the business community, motivated by economic fears of declining productivity and intense competition in world markets, is leading the charge to decontrol the educational marketplace and force schools to compete for students. David Kearns, chairman and CEO of Xerox, writes, "By any measure, today's educational system is a failed monopoly." What's required, he explains, is an economic model for schools that brings willing buyers (families and students) together with sellers (schools) in a market where they can deal with each other. As a result, the public school monopoly would be dismantled and replaced by a choice system. He adds:

> In a choice system, the state would fund individual children, rather than individual schools or school districts. Money earmarked for education would reach the public school *only* when the student elected to enroll. The school would lose its guaranteed income, and would be forced to provide offerings that meet the needs and interests of the community it proposed to serve.[26]

By 1990 ten states had approved open-enrollment or choice plans, and several more are considering the concept. These plans vary from allowing students to transfer freely from school to school within the state (Minnesota, Idaho, Utah) to allowing transfers only within a school district (Colorado). The most controversial program is Wisconsin's, where the legislature adopted a voucher-type plan that allowed up to 1,000 Milwaukee public school students to enroll in private nonsectarian schools at state expense, beginning in the fall of 1990.

FIGURE 2-3   States with Choice Plans

| | |
|---|---|
| Arkansas | Nebraska |
| Colorado | Ohio |
| Idaho | Utah |
| Iowa | Washington |
| Minnesota | Wisconsin |

Source:   Information for this figure from William Snider, " 'Choice' Proposals Make Headway in Statehouses in 1990," *Education Week* 10, no. 26 (September 5, 1990): 26, 33.

Opposition to choice is similar to the skepticism voiced about vouchers a decade or more ago. Opponents state that students who choose to migrate are likely to go from poorer districts and neighborhoods to the more affluent schools. This will leave schools that are already at a disadvantage in an even worse position. This shift also will tend to skim the most informed, most mobile, and best students from some schools, and it will encourage ethnically, racially, and socioeconomically homogeneous schools.

Many students who transfer, the critics argue, will do so because of the competitiveness of athletic teams rather than the quality of academic programs, which in turn will raise player recruitment issues.

At another level, intelligent choice assumes that parents and children can identify the best or most appropriate type of instruction for them. Because they lack experience, young students select largely according to what "feels right," and many parents lack the necessary knowledge, interest, and time to make a wise choice. The point is that far from all families would choose a school for academic reasons.

Others explain that education is a public good and not merely a private one. The individual student and family are not the only bene-factors of a sound education (or the only victims of an inadequate education); society has a stake in the schooling of each child. Choice presupposes that one form of educational experience is potentially as good as another. In effect, the critics say, schooling is not a commodity in the way that a computer, an automobile, or a television set is, and it matters a great deal whether a student's education is inappropriate or inferior. Society has a right, they argue, to demand that schools set forth learning goals and objectives that apply to all students.

A choice system, in theory, also does not address two major short-comings of schooling today, critics add. It neither assures that the smorgasbord curriculum will become more intellectually focused and engaging nor that teaching will foster rational thinking, imaginative powers, and competencies.

As in the debate over vouchers, the broad coalition of choice advocates brings together supporters with divergent positions: On one hand the laissez-faire group would impose few if any restrictions on schools and parents, and let the marketplace determine which schools will prevail and what shape their curricula will take. In contrast, the educational planners would build in provisions to ensure high curric-ulum standards, access to information, provisions for transportation, and policies to prevent the discriminatory selection of students.

## School Reform in Focus

Much educational reform during the 1980s has moved from the top down—from state legislatures and departments of education down to the classroom. Instead of working with principals and teachers to renew school learning environments, reformers focused on regulations. They erected more and higher hurdles for students to scale, including an increase in academic courses required for graduation. And students as early as first grade are being assigned letter grades from A to F. Although this served to stimulate some students, it further demoralized many it was intended to help—those "at risk." As a result, the number of dropouts increased.

Teachers also have been less than enthusiastic about the national school-reform movement. When the Carnegie Foundation for the Advancement of Teaching interviewed more than 13,500 teachers in 1988, 70 percent said the reforms since the 1983 *At Risk* report deserved no more than a C rating, and 20 percent gave them a failing grade. Half of the teachers surveyed said morale within the profession had declined in the last five years. A majority pointed out that political interference, state regulations, and bureaucratic paperwork had increased. On a positive note, teachers said that "goals at their schools are more clearly defined" than they were five years earlier; "student achievement has gone up in . . . math, reading, and writing"; and instructional materials, including textbooks, have improved.[27]

In a similar study conducted three years later, the Carnegie Foundation found that teachers' views on school reform continued to darken: Only 18 percent gave the movement an A or a B, compared to 31 percent in 1987. Teachers were less satisfied with the degree of control they had over their jobs, were more pessimistic about curbing the incidence of dropouts, and felt less respected in their communities.[28]

Despite gains, many teachers are disenchanted with the reforms because they have not been involved. This approach to reform sent a clear signal that teachers were part of the problem, not the solution. Boyer pointed out in the introduction to the Carnegie report that, "Teachers have remained dispirited, confronted with working conditions that have left them more responsible, but less empowered." As most educators realize, educational excellence cannot be legislated but must be patiently nurtured within the school and the classroom.[29]

## Notes

1. Ernest L. Boyer, The Carnegie Foundation for the Advancement of Teaching, *High School: A Report on Secondary Education in America* (New York: Harper & Row, 1983), 57.

2. Henry Steele Commager, *The People and Their Schools*, Fastback 79 (Bloomington, IN: Phi Delta Kappa Education Foundation, 1976), 28–33.

3. Neil Postman, *Teaching as a Conserving Activity* (New York: Dell, 1979), 50.

4. Channel One is a 12-minute news and information show, designed to bring national and world events to the classroom, that includes two minutes of commercials (four 30-second spots). It was introduced to schools in 1990 by Whittle Communications of Knoxville, Tennessee. Because of its advertising content, California and New York State educational officials took steps to bar Channel One programming in its schools. Other educational officials have criticized its slick format, questioning its value in learning. With part of the proceeds from the advertising, Whittle provided participating schools with a satellite dish, videocassette recorder, and a 25-inch color television monitor for designated classrooms.

5. Postman, *Teaching as a Conserving Activity*, 52–56.

6. Ibid., 19–24.

7. Fredrich Mosteller and Daniel P. Moynihan, eds, *On Equality of Educational Opportunity* (New York: Random House, 1972), 7.

8. James B. Conant, *Slums and Suburbs* (New York: McGraw-Hill, 1961), 10.

9. Charles E. Silberman, *Crisis in the Classroom: The Remaking of American Education* (New York: Random House, 1970), 122–126.

10. Neil Postman, "Order in the Classroom." *The Atlantic* 244, no. 3 (September 1979): 35–38.

11. Henry Steele Commager, "The School as Surrogate Conscience." *Saturday Review* 2, no. 8 (Jan. 11, 1975): 54–55.

12. Postman, *Teaching as a Conserving Activity*, 113–115.

13. Michael J. Barrett, "The Case for More School Days." *The Atlantic* 266, no. 5 (November 1990): 90–91.

14. Ibid., 80–81.

15. These findings are from the analytic report of *The Junior Achievement/Gallup International Youth Survey.* The Gallup Organization is located at 100 Palmer Square, 47 Hullfish Street, Princeton, NJ 08542. Copies of the report are available from Junior Achievement, Inc., 45 E. Clubhouse Drive, Colorado Springs, CO 80906. Phone: (719) 540-8000.

16. Ibid., 100.

17. Stanley M. Elam and Alec M. Gallup, "The 21st Annual Gallup Poll of the Public's Attitudes toward the Public Schools," *Phi Delta Kappan* 71, no. 1 (September 1989): 48–49.

18. I've elaborated on Mr. Shanker's proposal that he delivered in a talk on restructuring schools for the Association of Supervision and Curriculum Development (ASCD).

19. John I. Goodlad, *A Place Called School: Prospects for the Future* (New York: McGraw-Hill, 1984), 237.

20. Ibid., 48–50.

21. Boyer. *High School: A Report on Secondary Education in America*, 66–67.

22. Goodlad, *A Place Called School*, 51–56.

23. Ron Brandt, "On Changing Secondary Schools: A Conversation with Ted Sizer," *Educational Leadership* 45, no. 5 (February 1988): 30–36.

24. Lawrence A. Cremin, *Public Education* (New York: Basic Books, 1976), 9–11.

25. Silberman, *Crisis in the Classroom*, 265–322 (chap. 7).

26. David T. Kearns and Denis P. Doyle, *Winning the Brain Race: A Bold Plan To Make Our Schools Competitive* (San Francisco: ICS Press, 1988), 15, 18–19.

27. *Report Card on School Reform: The Teachers Speak* (Princeton, NJ: The Carnegie Foundation for the Advancement of Teaching, 1988), 1–11.

28. The Carnegie Foundation for the Advancement of Teaching, with a Foreword by Ernest Boyer, *The Condition of Education: A State-by-State Analysis* (Lawrenceville, NJ: Princeton University Press, 1990), 3–5, 12, 29, 76.

29. *Report Card on School Reform*, 11.

# 3

# Chronology

Military history has its campaigns and battles, political history its presidents, prime ministers, and kings. History other than military and political
often lacks such frameworks.[1]

THANKS TO THE WORK OF ECONOMISTS such as Robert Heilbroner,
the so-called "dismal science" has its historical framework and
"worldly philosophers" to help us understand economic society.[2] And
despite his disclaimer above, historian Edward Krug left us with a
guide to educational movements. The following is a chronology of
significant events, state and federal legislation, Supreme Court decisions, proposals, and publications that have shaped American public
schooling from colonial times to the present.

**1635**    **The Boston Public Latin School.** The present-day Public Latin
School of Boston traces its ancestry to the United States' oldest
school, which came about as a result of a public meeting on April
13, 1635. Those attending the meeting appointed a schoolmaster to
teach the children of the city.

The Boston school followed the model of grammar schools in
England, meaning they taught the grammar of Latin. Other communities in the Massachusetts Bay Colony, as well as some in Plym-
outh and Connecticut, also set up grammar schools. By 1700, there
were 26 schools of Latin grammar in New England.

The main curriculum was Latin and Greek, but many American
schools also taught reading and writing in English. What students
learned about history, philosophy, natural science, and even mathematics came through their study of the classics.

**1635**
*cont.*

As Krug points out, these were not secondary schools as we know them today. All of the students were boys, typically ages 8 to 15, and the course of study lasted seven years. Not all the students who attended grammar schools went on to college, nor had all college students gone to a grammar school. Many boys at this time were prepared for college through tutoring or studying on their own.[3]

In the early colonial period, college for many meant crossing the ocean to attend Oxford or Cambridge in England. In 1636 the General Court of Massachusetts Bay Colony (the colonial legislature) voted to provide funds for a college. A year later the next court ordered the college to be located in Newtown across the Charles River from Boston. In 1638 the name of Newtown was changed to Cambridge, and the United States' first college had students, a professor, and a building. That same year a clergyman named John Harvard died and left the college a sum of money nearly double that allocated by public authorities. In March of the following year, the General Court named the college Harvard.

**1642** **Massachusetts Bay Law of 1642.** The colonial legislature of Massachusetts passed a general education law requiring all parents to see that their children were taught to read, to understand the major laws of the colony, to know the catechism, and to learn a trade.

**1647** **Old Deluder Law of Massachusetts Bay Colony.** Apparently not satisfied with the 1642 law, the Massachusetts legislature required all towns with at least 50 families to appoint an elementary teacher for reading and writing who would be paid from municipal taxes. Towns of 100 or more families also were to appoint a teacher of Latin grammar, in modern terms a secondary-school teacher.

The 1647 law was labeled the Old Deluder Law because, as those who drafted it warned, communities need schools to counter that "old deluder, Satan himself," who works to keep the young from learning proper language and ways of living.

All children, girls as well as boys, could now be taught by the schoolmaster, or receive instruction in school. Although the law required towns to appoint teachers, it did not compel school attendance. Compulsory schooling was still 200 years away. After all, according to this law, the function of grammar schools was preparation for attending a university, as Krug explains.[4]

**1749** **Franklin's Philadelphia Academy.** In a pamphlet titled *Proposals Relating to the Education of Youth,* Benjamin Franklin proposed a new kind of school—an academy. Designed to prepare youth for the practical affairs of life, namely business, vocation, and leisure, the academy was a major departure from the Latin grammar school.

**1749**
*cont.*
English replaced Latin and Greek as the primary curriculum. Some of the studies were optional; for example, students were not required to study Latin and Greek.

The academy started in Philadelphia in 1751. Among the subjects of study were arithmetic, geometry, astronomy, modern languages, the classics, history, agriculture, and gardening. One division of the academy, which emphasized the practical studies, would later be called a secondary school.[5]

In 1755, the name was changed to the College and Academy of Philadelphia, and the institution was given the authority to grant degrees. Although the college charter was subsequently revoked, the enterprise was reorganized in 1791 as the University of Pennsylvania. Thus, Franklin's academy led to the development of a major university.

**1778**
**The Phillips Academy, Andover, Massachusetts.** Franklin's academy was the first major departure from the classical curriculum, but it was not the forerunner of the U.S. academy that we associate with elite independent schools today. This development is credited to Samuel Phillips, who founded Phillips Academy of Andover in 1778. Five years later his uncle opened a sister school, Phillips Academy of Exeter, in New Hampshire.

Although Andover and Exeter were private schools, they had a public purpose. While many of their students went on to college, the aim of the schools was considerably broader. Along with English, mathematics, logic, writing, music, geography, and other subjects, students learned the values and morality of the "great end and real business of living."

During the 1800s, from New England to the farthest frontiers, thousands of academies were started by many different individuals and groups, including churches. Although known by a variety of names, such as seminaries, institutes, and colleges, Krug explains, they were what we would identify as secondary schools. Most were private ventures, though many received public funds.

In general, these assorted academies opened up educational opportunities for girls. Most schools, however, were criticized for having low academic standards and scholarly ideals. By 1900 most of the old-time academies ceased to exist. Those that remained are associated with status and wealth and with preparation for college, though this elitist image is a recent phenomenon. During the nineteenth century, academies were vehicles of popular education.[6]

**1779**
**Jefferson's School Plan for Virginia.** As a member of the Virginia legislature, Thomas Jefferson submitted a "Bill for the More General Diffusion of Knowledge." In it, he proposed that all children of the

**1779**
*cont.*
state receive three years of free elementary schooling in reading, writing, arithmetic, and history. The bill carefully spelled out the locations of and requirements for elementary schools.

In addition, he proposed that grammar schools be constructed in specific areas of the state to accommodate a select group of the best male students from the elementary schools for further studies. The brightest graduates of these secondary schools were then to be granted scholarships for study at the William and Mary College in Williamsburg.

Jefferson conceived his plan as a way to provide a broad base of intelligent citizens who could judge important issues and combat potentially tyrannical leaders, as well as to develop enlightened leaders. The plan was ideologically and economically radical for the times.

Although Jefferson's bill was defeated in the Virginia legislature, it influenced the thinking of political officials and educators. The bill was awesome in its comprehensiveness, fascinating in its detail, and unique in its structure.[7]

**1787**  **The Northwest Ordinance.** When Virginia and other states ceded their western lands to the United States in the ordinance for the territory northwest of the Ohio River (known as the Northwest Ordinance), its authors encouraged the development of "schools and means of education forever."

The Land Ordinance of 1785 had outlined a plan to survey the new federal territory. According to this ordinance, the land was to be segmented into townships six miles square, each containing lots or sections of one square mile, or 640 acres. To encourage the development of schools, lot number 16 in each township was reserved for a public school.

The Northwest Ordinance did not lead directly to the development of public schools. Nevertheless, as new states were admitted to the Union, sections were designated for school districts.[8]

**1789**  **Massachusetts Law on School Districts.** This law "to Provide for the Instruction of Youth, and for the Promotion of Good Education" updated the 1647 law. Where the earlier law had stipulated instruction in reading and writing for the early grades, the new one added the English language, geometry, and "decent behavior."

More importantly, it authorized towns to do what many already were doing, to define within their boundaries a new political unit—the school district. In turn, school districts became corporations with the power to sue and be sued.[9]

The concept of the school district became popular during the 1800s as states joined the Union and assumed overall responsibility for education. Except in the South, where the county became the

**1789**
*cont.*
dominant form of school organization, most districts were quite small. The school district, particularly in the Midwest, has remained a major instrument of local control and a symbol of decentralized power.

During the early decades of the 1900s, there were well over 100,000 school districts in the nation. Since the 1950s, in an effort to make school organizations more efficient and improve the curriculum, many smaller districts have been consolidated into larger ones. Today, there are about 15,000 school districts among the 50 states.

**1805**   **The New York Free School Society.** The Society for Establishing a Free School in the City of New York was formed by De Witt Clinton and others to provide education for the poor who were not otherwise provided for by a religious society. The Free School Society began operations with money from private sources, but by 1809, with funds from the state legislature and a grant of land from the city, the society built its own schoolhouse. And public schooling in the United States was under way.

Within 15 years, the Free School Society was well established with six schools, about 5,000 students, and funding from the state. By 1840, however, the society had become embroiled in a controversy involving the efforts of religious groups, including the Roman Catholics, to seek state funds to help finance their schools. In 1842, the legislature created a Board of Education for New York City to develop and administer a system of free and common schools. This did not shut off funds to the Free School Society, but set up a parallel, wholly public system that led to the society's decline.[10]

The Free School Society, as Michael Katz explains, was conceptually a much different system from the "incipient bureaucratic" model that subsequently emerged in New York City and other urban areas. Katz describes the society as an example of "paternalistic voluntarism," in which schools were administered by distinguished, capable, but largely disinterested men who gave rudimentary training in literacy and morals to lower-class children. It was a form of noblesse oblige, in which one class helped to civilize another.[11]

**1821**   **The Boston English Classical School.** Citizens of Boston assembled in Faneuil Hall on January 15 to authorize a new major school to function alongside the Latin School. The school committee explained that too many parents had to spend large sums of money to send their children to private academies outside the city, and too many children were separated from their families.

This committee outlined a three-year curriculum and approved salaries for a principal and support staff. Three years after the school began, the committee opened a new building and changed the name to the English High School. Both Boston Latin and the English High

**1821** School developed strong academic reputations; perhaps because of
cont. this, enrollments increased only modestly during most of the 1800s.
With the rapid increase in the number of high school students after
1890, both schools grew substantially, particularly the English High
School. By 1920, enrollment at English High was about 2,200, while
just over 1,000 students attended Boston Latin.[12]

**1827** **Massachusetts Law on High Schools.** The Commonwealth of
Massachusetts passed the first law mandating a state-supported
secondary school in communities of 500 or more families. By 1840
Massachusetts had 26 such schools; most of them were called high
schools.

Nevertheless, high schools were slow to develop in other states
before 1850. Administrative policies and the curriculum were quite
inflexible, until Lowell, Massachusetts, set up a dual course of study,
one called classical, the other English. After 1850, the number of
high schools increased significantly.

Most high schools were found in large cities: Philadelphia set
up Central High School in 1837; Chicago started its first one in 1856,
with three courses—English, classical, and normal, the latter for
training teachers. New York, however, did not have a public high
school until 1897. By the time of the Civil War, the United States
had approximately 300 public high schools, of which more than
one-fourth were in Massachusetts.[13]

**1836** **McGuffey's Eclectic Readers.** The United States' most widely
known schoolbooks were written by William Holmes McGuffey, a
professor of ancient languages at Miami College in Ohio, professor
of natural philosophy at the University of Virginia, and the president
of Cincinnati College and Ohio University.

McGuffey's *First Eclectic Reader* and the second reader were
published in 1836. A year later, he completed the third and fourth
readers, along with a primer for beginning readers. His fifth reader
appeared in 1844, and the sixth in 1857. He completed the series in
1863 with a reader for high school students. The readers were revised
several times through 1901. By 1920, an estimated 122 million copies
had been sold.

The readers contained a combination of prose and poetry; the
fourth, fifth, and sixth readers, for older children, featured antholo-
gies of work by American and British writers including Hawthorne,
Whittier, Byron, and Shakespeare. McGuffey's strong convictions
on the aims of education were vividly illustrated in the readers, which
were laced with messages on morals and manners. McGuffey died
in 1873.[14]

**1837**    **Horace Mann and Massachusetts Board of Education.** On April 20, 1837, the Massachusetts legislature created the first state board of education. As secretary of the board, the legislators named Horace Mann, a successful lawyer with a promising political career, who turned out to be a superb choice.

Mann traveled and labored tirelessly to promote public schooling in the state. During his 12 years as head of the board, he produced annual reports on timely aspects of education. In them, Mann hammered away relentlessly at the responsibility of communities to support good, free schools. To this theme he added messages on school discipline, classroom teaching, and the training of teachers.

In his *Seventh Annual Report,* published in 1843 after a tour of Europe, he wrote admiringly of the Prussian schools that had adopted the teaching methods of Johann Pestalozzi. This Swiss educator emphasized love and patience for the young and used real objects in teaching. Mann's praise for the progressive teaching methods and absence of harsh discipline in Prussian schools was not welcomed by Boston educators.[15]

Mann was sensitive to the poverty and injustices in society, and he saw education and schools as a lever to ameliorate these conditions. In his twelfth and final report (1848), he wrote that education "is the great equalizer of the conditions of men—the balance wheel of the social machinery. . . . It does better than disarm the poor of their hostility toward the rich; it prevents being poor."[16]

Woven through his tough-minded political philosophy and educational goals was a humanitarian spirit. Mann succeeded in leaving his society a better place.

**1839**    **First Normal College.** During the early 1800s, teachers in public schools came mostly from academies. The idea of a state institution dedicated to educating teachers, based on teacher seminaries in Prussia, was encouraged by several Massachusetts educators including Mann, clergyman William Brooks, and James Carter, a teacher and prominent writer.

The first normal school opened in Lexington, Massachusetts, site of a famous Revolutionary War battle. Although these teachers' schools grew slowly at first, the movement developed rapidly after the Civil War. By 1890, there were 135 public normal schools with more than 26,000 students. To upgrade the image of normal schools, Massachusetts in 1895 required entrants to be high school graduates.

Eventually, the one- and two-year normal school courses were expanded to three- and four-year programs. By the 1920s, some major universities accepted transfer credits from normal schools toward bachelor's degrees. As the normal schools grew into state teachers' colleges, they also offered such degrees.[17] Subsequently,

**1839**  teachers' colleges throughout the country offered a general curricu-
*cont.*  lum and became state colleges. By the latter decades of the 1900s,
many of these schools had opened other colleges on their campuses
and added graduate programs to become state universities.

**1848**  **New Quincy School, Boston.** The traditional school facility in the
early United States, even in big cities, usually was a large room or
hall that housed several hundred students. Sometimes the school
building had two stories with large halls on each level.

One of the many messages in Mann's *Seventh Annual Report* dealt
with the structure of schools. In Prussia he found students classified
according to ages and attainment, with a single teacher in charge of
a single class. In 1848, the city of Quincy erected a building to
accommodate this new type of school organization. It was four stories
high with 12 classrooms, each holding 56 "scholars," plus a hall large
enough for 700 people. It also had six smaller recitation rooms. Each
teacher had a separate room, and each student a desk.

By the late 1860s, graded schools had become popular. Students
moved from one grade to the next annually or were held back for
more study. After the Civil War, the pattern of an eight-year elementary school and a four-year high school (the 8–4 plan) prevailed. By
1900, elementary schools were being reduced to six grades with
secondary education beginning in grade seven. In 1910 Berkeley,
California, ushered in the introductory high school, later known as
the junior high school. Subsequently, most schools were organized
according to a 6–3–3 or 6–2–4 plan.

**1852**  **Massachusetts Law on Compulsory Schooling.** Many states had
passed laws requiring communities to provide public schools, but
not until 1852 were parents required to send children to school. By
1890, 27 states and territories had enacted compulsory-attendance
laws. When Mississippi passed its legislation in 1918, compulsory
schooling was on the books of every state. Later, a few states repealed
their laws. Provisions in the early law in Massachusetts and other
states permitted parents to send children to private schools or educate them at home.

**1857**  **Organization of the National Teachers' Association.** From modest beginnings, the United States' first national organization for
teachers grew rapidly during the late 1800s. The NTA changed its
name in 1870 to the National Educational Association, which was
trimmed to National Education Association in 1908 and referred to
as the NEA.

During the mid-1900s, the American Federation of Teachers
(AFT), which is an affiliate of the AFL-CIO, challenged the domi-
nance of the NEA. The AFT's success, particularly in urban school
districts, forced the NEA to move from its more conservative policies.

**1857**
*cont.*

Although the NEA has attempted to maintain the image of a "professional" organization, as opposed to the AFT's trade unionism, the two organizations today are similar in principles and practices. Like the AFT, the NEA supports collective bargaining, election of bargaining agents in schools, sanctions against districts that oppose or violate contracts, and even strikes—euphemistically termed withdrawal or withholding of services. In effect, the NEA and the AFT are both unions and professional organizations.

**1867** **U.S. Department of Education.** On March 2, 1867, President Andrew Johnson signed a bill that established the federal Department of Education. The law established an office of the Commissioner of Education, but it was not a cabinet position. The first commissioner was Henry Bernard, who had been the chief education official for Connecticut.

The purpose of the department was to collect statistics and facts in order to show the condition and progress of education throughout the country, and to dispense this information to promote an efficient and effective educational system.

In short order, the name was changed to the Office of Education and the office was placed in the Department of Interior. In 1870 its name was changed to the Bureau of Education, only to be switched back to the Office of Education in 1929. In 1953 it became part of the newly created Department of Health, Education, and Welfare— a cabinet position.[18] After many years of lobbying by the NEA and other supportive organizations, in 1979 President Carter created a cabinet-level Department of Education and changed the commissioner's title to Secretary of Education.

**1874** **Public Support for High Schools Authorized.** Several states had laws requiring or authorizing communities to establish and support schools with public funds. By 1874, more than 100 high schools had been established in Michigan before complainants in Kalamazoo charged that the district had not put the issue of public-supported high schools to a vote in the district.

In a decision that proved a boost for free high schools, the Michigan Supreme Court ruled that people of a state could start and support public high schools with tax funds. A year later the Wisconsin legislature authorized public high schools in that state; Minnesota followed in 1881.

The Kalamazoo decision is often credited with starting the precipitous growth of high schools that began in the late 1800s. More accurately, it coincided with the economic transformation of U.S. society from an agrarian into an industrial base, and with public opinion. High school was becoming an economic and educational imperative.

**1892**  **Committee of Ten on Secondary School Studies.** The NEA formed the Committee of Ten on Secondary School Studies to standardize the high school curriculum and to secure uniform college-entrance requirements. The committee, chaired by Charles Eliot, president of Harvard University, also set out to "broaden the channel" from high school to college. At that time, the classical course, with four years of Latin and two or three years of Greek, was the standard for college preparation. An English course was accepted for high school students who did not plan to go to college. President Eliot and a few other committee members sought to make the English course acceptable for college entrance.

The result was a compromise outlining four courses of study: classical (including Latin and Greek), Latin-scientific (with no Greek required), modern language (requiring neither Latin nor Greek), and English (requiring only one foreign language). The Committee of Ten also held that secondary schools existed primarily to prepare students for life and secondarily to prepare them for college.

The plan established English, one foreign language (either modern or ancient), history, mathematics, and, in some cases, science as the core high school curriculum. The committee recommended that students be permitted a few electives and that the Carnegie unit (one course taken daily for one year) be established as the standard of measurement. To Eliot's delight, the committee recommended that colleges accept students who had completed any one of the four courses. Latin and Greek were no longer the foundation for college preparation.[19]

**1901**  **North Central Association's Commission on Accredited Schools.** During the late 1800s, the universities of Michigan, Wisconsin, and Illinois developed programs to evaluate high schools. The graduates of schools "accredited" by these programs could be accepted by the universities without an examination. State departments of education in Indiana and Minnesota conducted similar accreditation plans.

In 1901 the North Central Association of Colleges and Secondary Schools established its own Commission on Accredited Schools to coordinate the existing efforts and extend accreditation to the entire area from Ohio to Colorado. The North Central action became the "western system" of college admission by certificate or diploma, as opposed to the "eastern system" by examination.

In 1912, the commission also began to accredit colleges, mainly for granting transfer of student credits. In 1916, the commission was divided into two, one for high schools and one for colleges.[20]

**1917**  **Smith-Hughes Act for Vocational Education.** By 1900 many elementary schools included manual training, and the technical or

**1917**
*cont.*
manual-training high school had appeared. Momentum grew to establish technical and vocational education as part of the mainstream curriculum in all high schools. Much of this emphasis came from the National Society for the Promotion of Industrial Education, a group comprised of educators, social workers, manufacturers, and civic leaders.

In 1914 Congress authorized the Commission on National Aid to Vocational Education, which in turn recommended federal support for vocational teachers. That same year Congress passed the Smith-Lever Act, providing for a federally assisted agricultural extension program. This campaign to provide technical education in high schools was seen as a logical extension of the Land Grant College Acts of 1862 and 1890, which provided resources to promote agricultural and technical studies in higher education.

With much support from President Woodrow Wilson, the Smith-Hughes bill was passed in 1917. This legislation provided several million dollars a year from the federal government for schools to train and pay the salaries of teachers in agriculture, trade, industrial arts, and home economics. All funds were to be matched by the states.

**1918**
**Cardinal Principles of Secondary Education.** Around the turn of the century, high school enrollments began to increase substantially. A growing number of students did not continue on to college, so preparation for college was not a high priority for many. The NEA appointed another committee to examine this transformation of the high school. In 1918 the committee published a 32-page pamphlet called *The Cardinal Principles of Secondary Education,* a modest publication that influenced secondary education for several decades.

In recommending that all "normal boys and girls" attend school until the age of 17 or 18, the *Cardinal Principles* was the first proposal for universal secondary education. It also called for comprehensive high schools that would include a variety of programs guided by the seven aims of education: health, command of fundamental processes, worthy home membership, vocation, citizenship, worthy use of leisure time, and ethical character.

The Seven Cardinal Principles, as they were popularly called, inspired educators and shaped the pattern of U.S. education for the next 50 years.[21] *Cardinal Principles* reflected the confidence of professional educators and others who shared the spirit of progressivism that schooling could ameliorate social ills. It was the classic statement of the possibility of social engineering through education.[22]

**1919**
**Progressive Education Association.** Progressivism in American education is associated with the child-centered and activity-based learning of the 1920s and 1930s. Progressive ideas had been filtering through the schools at least since Horace Mann wrote about the

**1919**   informal methods he observed in Europe. Still, by 1920 traditional
*cont.*   education prevailed in American schools. In 1919, the Progressive
Education Association, made up of leading university educators but
largely teachers in private and public experimental schools, organized to counter the lockstep methods, mindless drill, and harsh
discipline characteristic of traditional classrooms.

Although the association's program was diverse, it clearly stood
for individuality and more freedom—for the child to develop natu-
rally; for the teacher to be a guide to learning, not a taskmaster; and
for cooperation between the school and the home. During the next
two decades, few schools escaped the program's influence: Desks
were unbolted from the floors, learning centered around small-group
activities, playgrounds and gymnasiums became commonplace, and
curriculum materials were more engaging.

The association and progressivism declined by the mid-1940s,
in part because of the inordinate demands that informal methods
placed on teachers. Progressive classrooms required extremely dedicated teachers and supportive administrators. Perhaps more telling
was the mood of the nation, which had shifted to an uneasy con-
servativism with the advent of War World II. In 1955 the Progressive
Education Association disbanded.

**1945**   **Life-Adjustment Education.** Charles Prosser captured the spirit
of a two-day conference on vocational education, sponsored by the
U.S. Office of Education, when he remarked in his closing statement
that schools, through vocational programs, are serving the 20 percent of their youth who desire to enter skilled professions, and high
schools continue to prepare another 20 percent for college. But the
remaining 60 percent who languish in school, many dropping out,
are not receiving the "life adjustment" training they need and are
entitled to as U.S. citizens. Prosser went on to recommend that the
federal education commissioner take steps to solve this problem that
affected so many young people.

In some respects, the subsequently formed Life Adjustment
Commission attempted to put some teeth into the Seven Cardinal
Principles promulgated several decades earlier, by urging schools to
experiment with programs to help prepare average students to become competent homemakers, workers, and citizens. Because the
aims and resulting curricula of the movement seemed amorphous,
life-adjustment education was poorly understood by the public. Most
felt that the course of study consisted of little more than social
studies, applied science, and letter writing.

When the Soviet Union launched Sputnik I in 1957, an immediate reaction was to blame life-adjustment education for the United
States' lagging behind in the space race. Ironically, though the
movement has been discredited, educators, business leaders, and

**1945**
*cont.*
government officials, when lamenting the ills of public schools, have routinely come back to the essence of Prosser's 1945 resolution. Few criticize and many applaud the college-preparatory and technical-training courses that serve different student populations. Today's concern with dropouts and the mediocre education provided the average high school graduate is a case of "old wine in new bottles."

**1947**
**Everson v. Board of Education.** At the time the Constitution was framed, colonial schools taught the doctrines of the dominant religion, be it Congregational Calvinism in northern schools or orthodox Anglican beliefs in southern schools. It was against this background that Jefferson and others crafted the First Amendment to the Constitution requiring that "Congress shall make no law respecting an establishment of religion, or prohibiting the free exercise thereof."

In 1947, the Supreme Court in *Everson v. the Board of Education* fleshed out the meaning of this amendment to schools. The clause against establishment of religion, the high court said, was intended to erect a "wall of separation between church and state." Nevertheless, it ruled that New Jersey was not violating this separation when the state legislated that public school buses could be used to transport children to parochial schools. This augmented an earlier decision, *Cochrane v. Louisiana State Board of Education* (1930), in which the court upheld the right of the state to provide textbooks to children in private, including parochial, schools.

Despite the court's holding that religious practices were incompatible with public education, at least until the early 1960s, prayer, Bible reading, and religious observances commonly occurred in many schools. In *Engle v. Vitale* (1962), the U.S. Supreme Court declared that school prayer was inconsistent with the First Amendment's establishment clause. A year later in *School District of Abington Township, Pennsylvania v. Schempp* (1963) the ruling was extended to include required Bible reading. Since 1963, the courts have consistently prohibited any form of state-regulated prayer, including voluntary prayer. However, they have allowed periods of meditation, secular thoughts, or prayer.

Likewise, the courts have been careful to protect the free exercise clause of the First Amendment, which constitutional framers intended to complement the establishment clause. In *Wisconsin v. Yoder* (1972), one of several cases related to this clause, Amish students were excused from attending public schools on the grounds that such compulsory attendance interfered with the practices of their religion.

**1954**
**Brown v. Board of Education of Topeka.** "In the field of public education," declared the U.S. Supreme Court, "'separate but equal' has no place. Separate educational facilities are inherently unequal."

**1954**
*cont.*
Until 1954, racial segregation in schools—whether by legal decree (de jure) or coincidentally (de facto)—was common practice. In order to determine whether an individual had received his or her constitutional guarantee of "equal protection of the laws," the court reasoned, it must look beyond the quality of curriculum materials, teachers, buildings, and other tangible factors to the effects of schooling. And segregated schools, added the court, generate in black children "a feeling of inferiority" that is unlikely ever to be undone.[23]

Despite court orders, busing, and other measures to integrate schools, most black and Hispanic students still attend schools in which they make up more than 50 percent of the student body. Most of these schools are located in the urban centers of the United States where white families have been able to circumvent attempts at integration by moving to more homogeneous suburban communities or sending their children to independent and parochial schools.

**1958**   **National Defense Education Act.** When the Soviet Union launched its space satellite in the fall of 1957, a fallout for American schools was the National Defense Education Act (NDEA), enacted the following September. Initially, it provided financial aid for states to strengthen science, mathematics, and foreign language instruction, as well as loans for students with "a superior capacity or preparation in science, mathematics, engineering, or a modern foreign language."

Subsequent renewals and amendments broadened the provisions of the act to include history, geography, civics, English, and reading. Another feature of the 1964 version was funding for institutes to prepare or upgrade teachers of disadvantaged youth—the culturally, economically, socially, and educationally handicapped.

**1959**   **James Conant's Report on the American High School Today.** The swing of the reform pendulum toward traditional methods, with emphasis on mathematics, science, and the basics, was given a strong push by the report of a study financed by the Carnegie Corporation of New York. This study was conducted by James B. Conant, a former president of Harvard University and the findings reported in his widely read *The American High School Today* (1959).

Conant, however, was not in total agreement with essentialist critics. He argued that in a nation as diverse as the United States, schools must be "comprehensive" if they are to meet the needs of all students. He envisioned the comprehensive high school as a uniquely American phenomenon that must provide a general education for all students, a sound nonacademic elective program for those who will join the work force after graduation, and a solid academic program for those going on to college.

**1959**
*cont.*    Those students he labeled "academically talented," who were not sufficiently challenged, drew the most attention. These students, Conant remarked, were the nation's hope if it was to remain first-rate technologically. He documented shortcomings in programs for the academically talented and specified the number and nature of courses they should take in mathematics, science, foreign languages, English, and the social studies.

The only radical recommendation in the Conant report was to reduce drastically the number of small high schools (those with fewer than 100 students in the graduating class), which he judged inadequate to offer or maintain solid academic programs. This proposal led to a massive consolidation of small districts into larger ones with a substantial decrease in the number of districts nationwide.

**1965**    **Elementary and Secondary Education Act.** Congressional approval of the Elementary and Secondary Education Act (ESEA) broadened the spirit and scope of the NDEA still further. This new act provided funds to help school districts develop libraries, purchase instructional materials, set up reading programs, and train teachers to work with culturally different and economically deprived students.

The ESEA led to a more aggressive role for the federal government in public schooling and became a symbol of our national priorities in education. It was enacted at a time when many schools were being desegregated, programs for the underprivileged launched, and the disabled mainstreamed into regular classes.

**1971**    **Serrano v. Priest School Finance Decision.** Plaintiffs in this landmark case alleged that as a result of the public school financing plan in California they were required to pay higher taxes than residents of other districts in the state to obtain the same or lesser educational opportunities. The California Supreme Court agreed, declaring that the state's funding system violated the equal protection clause of the Fourteenth Amendment to the U.S. Constitution, which prohibits federal and state governments from discriminating unfairly between classes of people.

The California court found that the primary source of money for California schools was the local property tax, which is based mainly on the value of private property within a school district. And the value of private property per pupil varied widely throughout the state. It also found that the methods used to allocate state school funds to districts did little to offset disparities created by local financing, and in some ways widened the gap between rich and poor districts.

The justices ruled that the level of spending on children's education must not be a function of wealth, other than that of the state

**1971**    itself. In a ruling heard across the land, the court ordered legislators
*cont.*    to find an equitable formula to distribute school funds. Not long after
*Serrano,* in *Robinson v. Cahill* (1973), the New Jersey Supreme Court
told that state to revamp its funding system.

**Swann v. Charlotte-Mecklenburg School District.** Despite the
*Brown* decision in the mid-1950s, schools were slow to integrate until
another Supreme Court decision nearly two decades later. In this
North Carolina case, the court set forth strong measures to hasten
integration. It actually directed the district court to provide specific
remedies including student transportation.

As a result, school integration across the nation was set on a
fast track, but not without turmoil and disruption. On one hand,
school systems were redistricted, and many students were successfully bused. In response, however, violence increased, and many
middle- and upper-class families departed urban neighborhoods. All
this tempered the statistical success of desegregation. In many cities
today, schools look anything but integrated as "minority" students
have become the majority.

As the nation entered the 1990s, school integration and finance
efforts took a new turn, in large part due to bold orders from a federal
judge in Kansas City, Missouri. During the mid-1980s, Kansas City
had approved a plan to integrate its public schools by converting a
majority of them to magnets. U.S. District Court Judge Henry Woods
required the state and the school district to share the cost of the plan.

When the school district could not raise its share of the funds,
the judge ordered property taxes in the district to be nearly doubled.
Eventually, the U.S. Supreme Court, in *Missouri v. Jenkins* (1990),
ruled that federal judges do have the authority to order a government
body to raise taxes in order to finance a plan it has approved.

**1983**    **A Nation at Risk Report.** By 1980 the threat of Soviet superiority
in armaments and in space had diminished. However, U.S. schools
did not receive credit for being part of the response to the perceived
Soviet challenge. By then, the United States was faced with a new
threat, this time on the economic front, from Japan and other industrial powers. Not surprisingly, the public schools were judged to have
a major part of responsibility for this national shortcoming.

The sobering story was told in a booklet prepared by the National Commission on Excellence in Education for the U.S. Department of Education and titled *A Nation at Risk: The Imperative for
Educational Reform.* Much of the language of this report is couched in
military terms, but the message is clear: The United States' destiny
is no longer assured by "an abundance of natural resources" and
"only a few exceptionally well-trained men and women." The world
has become a global village, it continues, and "we live among determined, well-educated, and strongly motivated competitors."[24]

**1983**
*cont.*   The commission proceeded to enumerate indicators of our deteriorating educational system—high rates of functional illiteracy, declining test scores, lack of higher-order thinking skills, and a curricular smorgasbord that has "homogenized, diluted, and diffused" learning. The commission's message was a clear indication that the national mood was swinging back to a call for basic learning and traditional methods. The recommendations it offered were by and large a restatement of the Conant report and other calls for reform in the 1950s.[25]

**1989**   **Edgewood v. Kirby School Finance Decision.** Although most states, nearly 20 years after *Serrano v. Priest,* had drawn up plans to share their school revenues among school districts, glaring differences in financial resources among districts remain. While one school district may have $3,000 a year to spend on each child, the one next door may have $5,500.

The state of Texas took an aggressive step to reconcile this discrepancy. The state Supreme Court, in *Edgewood v. Kirby* (1989), cited "glaring disparities" between rich and poor districts and explained that "property-poor districts are trapped in a cycle of poverty from which there is no opportunity to free themselves." Because of an inadequate tax base, poor districts must levy significantly higher rates just to meet minimum accreditation requirements. In turn, the location of new industry, the court argued, is influenced by tax rates and the quality of schools. Thus, property-poor districts, with high tax rates and inferior schools, are unable to attract new industry and thus have little opportunity to improve their tax base.

In a unanimous decision, the justices said the state's existing school finance system did not meet the Texas Constitution's equal-rights guarantee to establish, support, and maintain "an efficient system of public free schools" that provided for "a diffusion of knowledge." The court concluded that school districts must have "substantially equal access to similar revenues per pupil at similar levels of tax effort."

**The Education Summit, Charlottesville, Virginia.** Time will tell just how "historic" this gathering of the White House staff and state governors on the campus of the University of Virginia in Charlottesville was. In this September meeting, President George Bush and the governors set forth national performance goals for education. These were goals, the conference report explained, that would "make us internationally competitive."

If the goals of this Education Summit are accomplished, by the year 2000 all children will start school ready to learn; U.S. students will rank first among nations in mathematics and science; and every adult will be literate and will possess the knowledge and skills necessary to compete in a global economy.

**1989**     These and the other goals outlined by our government leaders
*cont.*      are admirable, yet lofty. Achieving them may require an unprece-
             dented commitment of human and financial resources. Inasmuch as
             little serious science is taught in elementary schools and most high
             school science teachers are poorly prepared to handle the courses
             they teach, reaching this summit promises to be a challenging ascent.

## Notes

1. Edward A. Krug, *Salient Dates in American Education, 1635–1964* (New York: Harper & Row, 1966), ix.

2. Robert Heilbroner, *The Worldly Philosophers* (New York: Simon & Schuster, 1953). Heilbroner revised this immensely popular book several times, and the fifth edition was published in 1980. His *The Making of Economic Society* (Englewood Cliffs, NJ: Prentice-Hall, 1962) also contributes to our understanding of economic history.

3. Krug, *Salient Dates in American Education, 1635–1964,* 1–3.

4. Ibid., 12.

5. Robert Ulich, ed., *Three Thousand Years of Educational Wisdom: Selections from Great Documents,* 2d ed. (Cambridge, MA: Harvard University Press, 1954), 442–448.

6. Krug. *Salient Dates in American Education,* 17–20.

7. Gordon C. Lee, ed., *Crusade against Ignorance: Thomas Jefferson on Education,* Classics in Education no. 6 (New York: Bureau of Publications, Teachers College, Columbia University, 1961), 83–97.

8. Krug, *Salient Dates in American Education,* 30–32.

9. Ibid., 33–35.

10. Ibid., 36–39.

11. Michael B. Katz, *Class, Bureaucracy, and Schools: The Illusion of Educational Change in America* (New York: Praeger, 1975), 7–15.

12. Krug, *Salient Dates in American Education,* 46–48.

13. Ibid., 50–52.

14. Ibid., 58–60.

15. Lawrence A. Cremin, ed., *The Republic and the School: Horace Mann on the Education of Free Men* (New York: Bureau of Publications, Teachers College, Columbia University, 1957), 54–56.

16. Ibid., 87.

17. Krug, *Salient Dates in American Education,* 67–71.

18. Ibid., 87–90.

19. Ibid., 95–99.

20. Ibid., 106–110.

21. Ibid., 117–120.

22. Thomas James and David Tyack, "Learning from Past Efforts To Reform the High School," *Phi Delta Kappan* 64, no. 6 (February 1983): 402–403.

23. *Brown v. Board of Education* was just one of four cases heard by the U.S. Supreme Court on this historic occassion. In addition to this case from Kansas, the Court heard arguments from South Carolina (*Briggs v. Elliot*), Virginia (*Davis v. County School Board*), and Delaware (*Gebhart v. Belton*). Newly appointed Chief Justice Earl Warren, who delivered the opinion, explained that although these cases "are premised on different facts and different local conditions, [their] common legal question justifies their consideration together in this consolidated opinion."

24. National Commission on Excellence in Education, *A Nation at Risk: The Imperative for Educational Reform* (Washington, D.C.: U.S. Government Printing Office, 1983), 6.

25. Ibid., 8–9, 18–21.

# 4

# Biographical Sketches

ALL PHILOSOPHY, REMARKED ALFRED NORTH WHITEHEAD, is a footnote to Plato. And, Neil Postman added, "perhaps all education, as well."[1] Indeed, the theories and practices that guide educators today are rooted in the ideas of Plato, Socrates, Aristotle, and other "grandmasters" of educational thought.[2] Whitehead himself deserves to be included among these Mount Rushmore figures of education. His ideas are as fresh as when they were written a century ago. Likewise, Postman's contributions, whether conventional or radical, have been noteworthy.

This chapter contains short biographies of individuals, some past but most present, who have influenced the course of education and schooling in America over the past 200 years. Had these people not existed, educational theory and practice, as we know them, would be much different.

## Antecedent Thought

The emphasis in our culture and school curriculum on questioning, inquiry, and critical thinking can be traced to the teachings of Socrates (469–399 B.C.). In turn, the idea that education should tap each individual's natural aptitudes and develop the good citizen is a legacy of Plato (427–347 B.C.). And Aristotle (384–322 B.C.) ushered in the rudiments of scientific thought and methodology that have been refined over the years.[3]

Marcus Fabius Quintilian (ca. A.D. 35–95), the foremost Roman writer on education, condemned the use of physical force and emphasized making studies attractive to the learner. Quintilian also stressed the importance of home life and the value of play to learning, as well as the need to understand individual differences. All are critical ideas that educators have yet to master.[4]

Later, a trio of European educators laid the groundwork for humane practices that we find virtually inalienable today. Jean-Jacques Rousseau (1712–1778) explained in *Emile* that learning must grow out of the natural interests and curiosities of the child and involve experiences with the real world through activities. Johann Pestalozzi (1746–1827), in turn, taught that love, empathy, and patience combined with real objects and sensory perception can enhance learning. Many of his ideas were developed in the novel *Leonard and Gertrude*. Friedrich Froebel (1782–1852), remembered as the originator of kindergarten, believed that the primary aim of education is the social and individual development of each child through self-directed activities that emphasize cooperation, spontaneity, and joy.

Many others—Desiderius Erasmus, John Amos Comenius, John Locke, and Johann Herbert, along with Americans Benjamin Franklin and Ralph Waldo Emerson, to name a few—contributed to our educational foundation. Despite their age, these ideas deserve to be resurrected, even reinvented, every generation.

## Thomas Jefferson (1743–1826)

If the inscription on his gravestone is accurate testimony, Thomas Jefferson wished to be remembered more for his work in education than as the third president of the United States. Jefferson was a democratic aristocrat—a unique disposition for the times. While he believed that some people may be more educable than others, he maintained that everyone deserved and required some formal education. Jefferson realized that a free society must have visions of both equity and excellence. Equity without excellence degenerates into mediocrity; excellence without equity becomes privilege.

This quest for a synthesis, which Jefferson began in a relatively uncomplicated United States of America, remains unresolved and presents an even greater challenge in our diverse contemporary society. Although his Bill for the More General Diffusion of Knowledge, introduced in the Virginia legislature in 1779, was defeated, the idea to complement the educational needs of the nation's leaders with those of the people has been an inspiration over the years. While the balance between equity and excellence is still to be achieved, tension between the two goals is healthy. Complacency can easily lead to either a tyranny of the few or a tyranny of the many.

Jefferson conceived a plan to develop enlightened leaders and to provide a broad base of intelligent citizens. He saw tangible results of his labors for education when the University of Virginia, which he initiated, was established in 1819. Fittingly, Jefferson became rector of the Board of Visitors. He supervised the development of the campus, particularly the library, and the selection of the faculty.[5]

## Horace Mann (1796–1859)

Although he had much in common with Thomas Jefferson, Horace Mann was an uncompromising champion of equality in education. Like Jefferson, he argued for the general diffusion of basic skills and knowledge, but he was unconcerned with providing advanced liberal education for the few destined to become leaders. In his words, "The scientific or literary well-being of a community is to be estimated not so much by its possessing a few men of great knowledge, as its having many men of competent knowledge."[6]

Mann sacrificed a promising law and political career to become the first secretary of the Massachusetts State Board of Education in 1837. His presence was felt from the start as he spoke to communities across the state on the imperative of common schooling and delivered messages on a variety of educational topics in his 12 annual reports. Mann, the person, was a curious combination of conservative moralist and political reformist, though he did not fit the popular Jacksonian type. From the start, his legal career, and later his years in education, were marked by service to humanitarian ideals. Like Jefferson, Madison, and others of the time, he understood the integral relationship uniting freedom, education, and republican government.

The two great planks in Mann's educational platform were public support and public control. Society, he argued, is composed of successive generations of people, and it is the duty of each generation to provide quality education for its youth. To do otherwise is to violate a trust. Control of the common school follows from this support. Those who pay are interested in how their tax dollars are spent, and control at the local level, with guidance from the state, will ensure against the heavy hand of central authority.[7]

Mann's educational philosophy was an intriguing blend of progressive teaching methods and what we today call cultural literacy. His attacks on rote learning were sharp and scathing; in one of his highly regarded annual reports, Mann strongly advocated the informal, progressive pedagogy he observed during his European travels. Once children learned the mechanics, however, he recommended a solid curriculum of grammar, literature, history, geography, music, and other subjects. He believed the common school should be devoted to "general education." Specialized vocational training was the responsibility of those in trades and crafts, not of schoolteachers.

After leaving the Massachusetts board, Mann became president of the newly formed Antioch College in Yellow Springs, Ohio. In one of many inspirational messages to the students of Antioch, he asked that they be ashamed to die until they had won some victory for humanity. Mann won his share of victories, including seeing the public school become a characteristic feature of the American landscape. Yet educational battles have a way of resurfacing. Today, urban school bureaucracies, violence and crime, shortages of qualified teachers, alarming dropout rates, sagging test scores, and calls for voucher plans and parental choice threaten to undermine what Mann achieved a century and a half ago.

## Charles W. Eliot (1834–1926)

Charles Eliot, born three years before Horace Mann began his public school crusade, carried forth a reform agenda from his lofty position as president of Harvard University. Eliot had gained national attention as a proponent of modern studies when he published articles on the "new education" in the *Atlantic Monthly* in 1869. At the time he was a professor of chemistry at the Massachusetts Institute of Technology; later that year he became Harvard's president at the age of 35, a position he held until 1909. Although opponents saw his position as an attack on the classics, Eliot's purpose was to strengthen the scientific and technical studies in higher education.

During his tenure at Harvard, Eliot oversaw its growth and ascendancy to a world-renowned university. Even with this responsibility, he took an interest in the "lower schools," joined the National Education Association, and delivered major addresses to this organization on school reform. Eliot's primary aim was to make the public high school a place where the many students not able to afford preparatory schools could be better prepared for admission to reputable colleges. He wanted to enhance the high school curriculum and broaden the channel to college.

In 1892, the NEA's National Council of Education appointed a committee to study the problem of students gaining entrance to colleges and to recommend a standard course of high school study that major colleges would acknowledge. President Eliot was named the chairman of this committee, which included nine other members and was thus labeled the Committee of Ten.[8]

The report of the Committee of Ten addressed the 11 major questions identified by the NEA's executive committee, but not without considerable debate and compromise. Eliot's view, however, did prevail on what he considered the most critical question (number 7): "Should the subject be treated differently for pupils who are going to college, for those who are going to scientific school, and for those who, presumably, are going to neither?" For Eliot the answer was a strong "No."[9]

Eliot's position was that of a democratic idealist with a modern view of schooling at a time when less than 10 percent of the nation's 14- to 17-year-olds graduated from high school.[10] However, it invited much criticism and, despite its democratic appeal, has been abandoned by many school officials. As an increasing proportion of high school–aged young people remained in school, schools have reverted to various forms of explicit and implicit tracking systems.

Much of the report was devoted to four courses of study recommended by the Committee of Ten, all of which would satisfy college admission requirements. The *classical* course was based on Greek, Latin, and German or French, while the *Latin-scientific* course included Latin and German or French. The *modern language* course called for German and French, but no Latin or Greek, and the *English* course included just one foreign language. All of the courses included mathematics and various amounts of history and science, with more of the latter two in the English course. While Eliot had little enthusiasm for these potential tracks, he was pleased with the larger place given modern studies.[11]

## John Dewey (1859–1952)

As a community schoolteacher in his native Vermont, John Dewey saw the inactivity and dullness of traditional classrooms. In 1894 he arrived at the University of Chicago as head of the Department of Philosophy, Psychology, and Pedagogy and began working on new ideas for schools. Two years later he started the Laboratory School in order to test and refine his progressive theories on learning, teaching, and school organization.

Early in his academic career, Dewey departed from traditional philosophy, which he felt had little interest and a weak understanding of how people learn and how knowledge benefits our lives. He was one of the founders of American pragmatism, a major school of philosophy that developed out of the emergence of science and the scientific method, particularly Einstein's theory of relativity and Darwin's theory of evolution. Dewey's pragmatic approach to philosophy, psychology, and politics is developed in *How We Think* (1910), *Reconstruction in*

*Philosophy* (1920), *Experience and Nature* (1925), and *Logic: The Theory of Inquiry* (1938).

The new experimental outlook of psychology, articulated largely by William James, combined with evolutionary theory, shaped Dewey's educational philosophy. He called this experimentalism, and later instrumentalism.[12] In turn, Dewey developed a theory of education based on the idea that people learn best while responding to and acting on their environment—that is by "doing," be it learning to walk, talk, write, swim, draw, and play music, or to solve problems and conceptualize.

Learning, he believed, should involve using not only books but also tools and related materials. In *School and Society* (1899), he examined how people learn most effectively—that is, understand and retain—when they interact in a community or social setting. The basis of education, he added, is the occupations and associations in life that serve human needs. And the most reliable measure of learning is the ability of the individual to act intelligently in new social situations.

In Dewey's most comprehensive work, *Democracy and Education* (1916), he explained that the democratic model is an educative model because people learn as they participate in society, the community, and the classroom. In turn, a democratic society and democratic education are progressive, because they involve people reconstructing the social, political, and economic environment. Living is learning, and education, like democracy, is a way of life.

Dewey elaborated in subsequent writings on this theme of learning through life's experiences. The teacher, he wrote in *Experience and Education* (1938), must know the individual character of a learner (his or her experiences and abilities), organize the present moment in learning, and have a sense of what is to follow. The teacher must also have the intellectual ability to know what information is needed in a learning situation, where to retrieve it, and how to organize this subject matter so that the learner may gain new understandings. Dewey labeled these two interrelated processes the *continuity* and the *interactive* effects.[13]

Dewey's extensive writing and work at the Laboratory School had a profound effect on school environments and teaching methods during the early 1900s. To Dewey the school was an "embryonic community" that included libraries, gymnasiums, art and music rooms, science laboratories, shops, gardens, and playgrounds.

Beyond the classroom wall, he saw the school as a dynamic center in the community. In part, this meant it was to be a lever for social reform in the immediate community and the larger society. Dewey believed that experimental, inquiring, and intelligent behavior is essentially progressive in that it tends to improve the conditions of life for people. He cautioned, however, that the school could not effect this reform alone, for it is only one institution among many that have an educational impact on the community.

## Maria Montessori (1870–1952)

As a young girl Maria Montessori was determined not to become a teacher, the one career suitable for women in her native Italy and most other countries at that time. With fierce independence and determination, in 1894 she became the first woman to receive a medical degree from the University of Rome.

As a physician, Montessori specialized in children's diseases, which led to her interest in the education of "idiot" children. She developed a teaching method emphasizing freedom of expression and initiative, which enabled retarded children to function as well as normal children. She then turned her attention to mentally healthy children and, like John Dewey, saw that the dull and restrictive environment of traditional classrooms was impeding their intellectual and emotional growth.

This curiosity led Montessori to accept a position in charge of children who inhabited a tenement complex in sprawling, fast-growing Rome. Given a room full of 50 children with few toys and little equipment or other learning materials, Montessori simply observed and responded to the children's curiosities as they interacted and played with the didactic materials. Thus her "schoolroom," named Casa dei Bambine, or Children's House, began in 1907. With the success of Casa dei Bambine, other schoolrooms were started in tenements.[14]

In these early Montessori schools, children were allowed freedom of expression, with the teacher acting as a supervisor and observer rather than as an instructor. The Children's Houses were informal and child-centered, but children did not do whatever they wanted. Classrooms were set up by teachers under the direction of Montessori; inconsiderate, abusive, and dangerous behavior was not permitted. Part of the hidden curriculum in Montessori schools was to show children that immobility is not equated with good and activity with evil, as they are in traditional concepts of discipline.[15]

Montessori's pedagogy was influenced considerably by the ideas of Rousseau, Pestalozzi, and Froebel, particularly their emphasis on starting with the nature of the individual child and centering learning on direct concrete experiences with the physical world—in today's terms, hands-on learning. Like these early European educators,

Montessori believed that the teacher's role was to facilitate the process of learning and self-discovery as the child progressed through successive stages of development.[16]

After her success in Italy, word about Montessori's schools spread to educators in other European countries. She set up training institutes in Great Britain and Spain to prepare teachers. Montessori had served as the Italian government's inspector of schools, but when Benito Mussolini learned that she opposed fascism, he closed her schools in 1934. By then Montessori's pedagogy was well known. Prominent American educators visited the European schools and returned with her instructional theory to start Montessori schools in the United States.

Several of Montessori's books have been translated into English. These include: *The Montessori Method: Scientific Pedagogy as Applied to Child Education in the Children's Houses* (1965), translated by Anne E. George; *The Discovery of Childhood* (1967), translated by M. Joseph Costelloe; *The Absorbent Mind* (1967), translated by Claude A. Claremont; *The Child in the Family* (1970), translated by Nancy Rockmore; and *Childhood Education* (1974), translated by A. M. Joosten.

## James B. Conant (1893–1978)

James Conant has been placed in the line of famous educational reformers extending back to Jefferson through Mann, Eliot, and Dewey. The parallel between his career and Eliot's is striking: Both were accomplished chemists (Eliot at MIT and Conant at Harvard) and both were presidents of Harvard University (Eliot from 1871 to 1909 and Conant from 1933 to 1953). From 1947 to 1952, he also served as a member of the General Advisory Committee of the Atomic Energy Commission. In 1953, he was named U.S. High Commissioner to the Federal Republic of Germany and later the ambassador to that country until 1957.

Ten days after performing his last duties as ambassador, Conant was absorbed in a major study of the American high school, funded by a grant from the Carnegie Corporation of New York. The result was his history-making report, *The American High School Today,* published in 1959. This report came on the heels of the Soviet Union's launching of Sputnik I, the first satellite in space. Conant's study reinforced the prevailing wish of the nation to return to basic learning, with an emphasis on mathematics and science. He recommended that the United States' comprehensive high schools develop a solid course of study across the academic disciplines, particularly for those students he labeled the academically talented.

After his study of the American high school, Conant examined the training of public schoolteachers; his findings are captured in *The Education of American Teachers* (1963). While he had spoken with the voice of moderation in the earlier report, he had harsh words in this book for both the education establishment and the academic community, who believe that above all else a teacher must be liberally educated. Conant is the author of several other significant works on education, including *The Child, the Parent, and the State* (1959), *Slums and Suburbs* (1961), *Thomas Jefferson and the Development of American Public Education* (1962), and *Shaping Educational Policy* (1964).

Although his most significant contribution was in education, James Conant also is known for several works on the broader relationship of science to society, particularly *Science and Common Sense* (1951), *Modern Science and Modern Man* (1952), and *Two Modes of Thought* (1964).

## Mortimer J. Adler (1902– )

As the title of his autobiography reads, Mortimer Adler is indeed a philosopher at large. Since leaving the University of Chicago in 1952, Adler has been a modern-day Socrates, moving about the country conducting seminars that prompt students and adults alike to think more carefully.[17]

Adler began his intellectual journey as an editor with the *New York Sun*, then joined the psychology faculty at Columbia University in 1923. There he became a discussion leader in the general honors course under the direction of John Erskine, a renowned scholar of English literature. In this course, students read the Great Books. It was here that a young Mortimer Adler acquired his passion for discussing ideas and asking questions. At Columbia, Adler also met John Dewey and took an interest in the nature of knowledge and learning.

Still early in his academic career, Adler met Robert Hutchins and moved to the Philosophy Department at the University of Chicago in 1930. With President Hutchins, Adler helped develop a Great Books program at Chicago. In 1940, Adler became a best-selling author with the publication of *How To Read a Book* (Simon and Schuster). Eager to take his message and skills in reading, questioning, and Socratic dialogue beyond the walls of academia, Adler conducted adult seminars across the country. Subsequently, he started the Institute for Philosophical Research to establish a home for these seminars. Each summer, Adler still conducts seminars at the Aspen Institute in Colorado.

Adler became a leading spokesperson for the perennialist tradition in education.[18] In 1982, he published *The Paideia Proposal: An Educational Manifesto*, then augmented it with two other short books:

*Paideia: Problems and Possibilities* (1983) and *The Paideia Program* (1984). The Paideia Proposal is a total curriculum for elementary and secondary grades based on three teaching styles: lecturing, coaching, and Socratic questioning.[19] Mortimer Adler now is a professor at the University of North Carolina and chairman of the Board of Editors of the Encyclopaedia Britannica.

Adler's other major books include *How To Think about War and Peace* (1944), *The Idea of Freedom* (two volumes, 1958 and 1961), *The Conditions of Philosophy* (1965), *How To Think about God* (1980), *Ten Philosophical Mistakes* (1985), and *Reforming Education: The Opening of the American Mind* (1977, 1988).

## Paul Goodman (1911–1972)

Paul Goodman made his mark early as a social critic and writer for the off-Broadway stage during the 1950s and 1960s. He also wrote two successful novels, *The Empire City*, a four-volume work (1959), and *Making Do* (1963).

During the 1960s Goodman became a spokesman for the New Left and the counterculture movement with his nonfiction book, *Growing Up Absurd* (1960). He was a leader among the "romantic critics" in education, particularly with the publication of *Compulsory Mis-education* and *The Community of Scholars* (both in one volume, 1964).

Goodman's quarrel with the educational establishment, and most of its critics as well, is that they take schools, in some shape and form, as a prerequisite for education. In his final work, *New Reformation: Notes of a Neolithic Conservative* (1969), Goodman outlined his thoughts on making "incidental education" the chief means of learning. He advocated eliminating most high schools and letting various youth communities assume their social functions; having college education generally follow, rather than precede, entry into the workplace; and designing the education of preschool- and elementary-aged children in such a way as to delay socialization and protect the child's free growth.

## Jerome Bruner (1915– )

Jerome Bruner was thrust onto center stage in the education reform movement of the 1960s when he wrote *The Process of Education* (1961). This small but influential book resulted from the gathering of 34 scientists and scholars at Woods Hole on Cape Cod in 1959 to discuss how science education might be improved in the elementary and secondary schools.

At the time of the Woods Hole conference, major efforts to redesign the curriculum in mathematics, physics, biology, and chemistry were already under way at various universities and curriculum study projects across the country. Bruner's modest book of less than 100 pages not only captured the underlying rationale of these efforts but provided a structure for the subsequent development of other science programs, as well as similar projects in the social sciences. These curricula were popularly referred to as the new math, new sciences, and new social studies.

At the heart of Bruner's rationale for curriculum development was the hypothesis that "any subject can be taught in some intellectually honest form to any child at any stage of development."[20] If a child understood the structure of knowledge, reasoned Bruner, that structure would enable the child to learn on his or her own. These new curricula also were designed to foster "discovery" learning and to encourage students to use intuitive leaps or courageous guesses. Bruner was a leader in developing one of the more innovative curricula of this period, titled Man: A Course of Study.

Bruner began his academic career in 1945 as a professor of psychology at Harvard University, where he founded the Center for Cognitive Studies. During the 1950s, he gradually shifted the emphasis in his work from laboratory research to the more practical issue of improving science education in the schools. He is also the author of *On Knowing* (1964) and *Toward a Theory of Instruction* (1966).

## Maxine Greene (1917– )

Maxine Greene, a professor of English and educational philosophy at Columbia University Teachers College since 1965, is America's leading existentialist educator. Existentialism is a school of philosophy that became popular, particularly in Europe, before, during, and after World War II. Because it lends itself to forms of literary expression, we generally associate it with writers such as Edward Albee, Kurt Vonnegut, Rainer Marie Rilke, Albert Camus, and Joseph Heller, as well as philosophers such as Jean-Paul Sartre, Martin Heideigger, and Maurice Merleau-Ponty.

While it is virtually impossible to base schools or school systems on the philosophy of existentialism, the individual existentialist student and teacher do exist. The existentialist teacher prizes her freedom, respects that of others, and passionately opposes forces that deny that freedom, because individuals ultimately must be able to define who they are and be free to choose what they will be.

Maxine Greene's *Existential Encounters for Teachers* (1967) is a series of excerpts from existentialist writers on different themes (the individual, others, knowing, choosing, and situations) with her comments on the relevance and application of each passage to the life of a teacher. In perhaps her most ambitious work, *Teacher as Stranger* (1973), Greene encourages teachers to examine critically the principles underlying what they think and do in the classroom. The teacher is asked to become more self-conscious about choices and is challenged to commit to those principles. Greene's goal is to persuade teachers to risk taking the existentialist position by clearly understanding what they believe in, then acting on those beliefs in the classroom.

In *Landscapes of Learning* (1978), Greene contends that a person is not endowed with freedom but must achieve it through dialectical engagements with social and economic obstacles. She expands on this theme in her latest work, *The Dialectic of Freedom* (1988).

Greene edited the *Teachers College Record* from 1965 to 1970 and is a past president of the Philosophy of Education Society and of the American Educational Studies Association. She also is the author of *The Public School and the Private Vision* (1965) and *Education, Freedom, and Possibility* (1975).

## John I. Goodlad (1920– )

John Goodlad's career in education brings to mind the versatile ball-player who has played every position. Goodlad began teaching in a one-room rural school and has taught at every level from first grade through graduate school.

Goodlad has spent much of his career on the cutting edge of educational reform. When James Conant was carrying out his study on *The Education of American Teachers* in the early 1960s, Goodlad served as major advisor on the nature of teacher training in colleges and universities. At that time Goodlad was teaching at the University of California, Los Angeles (UCLA), where he later became dean of the Graduate School of Education.

In the late 1960s, Goodlad and his associates conducted a study of the administrative and curricular reforms of the "education decade" (1957–1967)—or what he calls the "golden age of instructional materials." Their findings were reported in *Behind the Classroom Door* (1970). Despite many advances during this period, Goodlad documented that teachers were still very much alone in their work, with little support from principals and little interaction with fellow teachers.[21]

A few years later Goodlad directed a Study of Schooling, one of the nation's most extensive investigations of what goes on in our schools and educational system. In this in-depth inquiry of 1,016 classrooms, 1,350 teachers, 8,624 parents, and 17,163 students were questioned. The results have been reported in *A Place Called School: Prospects for the*

*Future* (1984). It contains a holistic yet detailed assessment of school curriculum and administration, teacher quality, and student tasks.

In the 1990s as director of the Center for Educational Renewal at the University of Washington, John Goodlad continues to be one of the leading figures in educational research and reform. With colleagues at the center, he recently completed the Study of the Education of Educators, the most ambitious assessment of teacher education since Conant's work nearly 30 years earlier. The story of this study is told in his *Teachers for Our Nation's Schools* (1990).

Goodlad has written numerous other books on a range of topics including: *School, Curriculum, and the Individual* (1966), *The Dynamics of Educational Change* (1975), *Curriculum Inquiry: The Study of Curriculum Practice* (1979), and *The Ecology of School Renewal* (1987).

## Lawrence Cremin (1925–1990)

A few years after the journal *Progressive Education* ceased publication in 1957, signaling the end of an era in American pedagogy, Lawrence Cremin produced a definitive history of the movement in *The Transformation of the School: Progressivism in American Education 1876–1957* (1961). "Progressivism," he wrote, "implied the radical faith that culture could be democratized without being vulgarized, the faith that everyone could share not only in the benefits of the new sciences but in the pursuit of the arts as well."[22] For this effort, Cremin was awarded the Bancroft Prize in American history in 1962.

Cremin, who spent his academic career at Columbia University Teachers College, became arguably the nation's foremost educational historian. He served as president of the college from 1974 to 1984 and was the Fredrick A. P. Barnard Professor of Education at the time of his death. Since 1985, he also served as president of the Spencer Foundation. Cremin followed his first major work with a much shorter but equally significant book, *The Genius of American Education* (1965). In it he reminds us that the distinctive purpose and animating spirit of our education lies in its commitment to popularization. In the intellectual tradition of John Dewey, Cremin recognized the expanding role of schools in a society where industrialism was destroying other traditional agencies of education, including the home, shop, neighborhood, and church. Also like Dewey, he argues that while the modern school must educate the whole child, it is sheer folly for it to try to provide the whole education of the child.

In *Public Education* (1976), Cremin recommends an "ecology of education," in which education is provided by a "multiplicity of institutions," including families, churches, synagogues, museums, libraries,

summer camps, agricultural fairs, television networks, as well as jour-
nalists, doctors, dentists, social workers, computer specialists, mechanics, and many others. Together, Cremin explains, these agencies would
interact within the larger society to form "a configuration of education."[23] Whereas in earlier times, this community-based learning
was spontaneous and incidental, today it must be systematic and
intentional.

Cremin won the Pulitzer Prize in history in 1981 for *American
Education: The National Experience, 1783–1876* (1980). He also is the author
of *The Republic and the School: Horace Mann on the Education of Free Men*
(1957), *American Education: The Colonial Experience* (1970), *Traditions of
American Education* (1977), *American Education: The Metropolitan Experience*
(1988), and *Popular Education and Its Discontents* (1990).

## James S. Coleman (1926– )

Section 402 of the Civil Rights Act of 1964 required the U.S. Office of
Education to "conduct a survey and make a report to the President and
the Congress . . . concerning the lack of availability of equal educational opportunities for individuals by reason of race, color, religion, or
national origin in public educational institutions." To carry out this
task, the commissioner turned to James Coleman, then professor of
sociology at Johns Hopkins University.

Two years later, Coleman and his research group produced perhaps the most important social science research report in U.S. history.
Some 570,000 pupils and 40,000 teachers were tested, and information
was gathered on the facilities in over 4,000 schools. The findings of this
report on *Equality of Educational Opportunity (EEOR)*—commonly referred to as the Coleman Report—provided the most powerful critique
of the assumptions and beliefs of American education ever produced.
In the process, James Coleman and his staff redefined the meaning of
equal educational opportunity to include not only inputs, or school
resources, but also outputs, or student achievement.

As a result of the Coleman Report, courts across the land ordered
school districts to integrate their student populations. Although the
Coleman Report did not comment on how schools were to be integrated, people often associate busing and other remedies with this
report. Coleman himself remained skeptical of plans that forced students to attend schools against their will.

Nearly 20 years after the EEOR, Coleman, with coauthors
Thomas Hoffer and Sally Kilgore, published *High School Achievement*
(1982), another controversial report based on comprehensive social
research. Coleman and his associates found that students in private

and Catholic schools consistently outperformed public school students. During the interim, Coleman had joined the Sociology Department at the University of Chicago. Coleman and Hoffer continued this research and published *Public and Private High Schools: The Impact of Communities* (1987), in which they followed students from the earlier study, comparing their progress through high school and into college. Among other findings, the authors show the crucial role of families and community relationships to student success and failure in different types of school settings.

## Ivan Illich (1926– )

Ivan Illich was born in Vienna and came to the United States at age 25, where he served as assistant pastor in an Irish–Puerto Rican Roman Catholic parish in New York City. In 1964 he became cofounder of the Center for Intercultural Documentation (CIDOC) in Cuernavaca, Mexico, where he has directed research seminars on Institutional Alternatives in a Technological Society.

Illich drew the attention of the educational community with the publication of *Deschooling Society* in 1971. He wrote, "The pupil is . . . 'schooled' to confuse teaching with learning, grade advancement with education, a diploma with competence, and fluency with the ability to say something new."[24] Schools base much of their case for existence on the claim that they teach cognitive skills, but their most important functions, Illich argues, include social screening and sorting, teaching values, and state indoctrination—which he labels the "hidden curriculum." Schools, he adds, fail to teach basic literacy to most students of society's lower social classes and fail to nurture all students' authentic talents and lifelong desire to learn. During the twentieth century, formal education has become the state religion, and schools are the New Church.[25]

School is not the only modern institution that educates intentionally, explains Illich. Medicine, social services, the legal system, and the media also have hidden curricula that serve essentially the same purpose as that of schools. However, the school is the most powerful of these agents, for only it is granted the official sanction to shape the beliefs, attitudes, perceptions, and critical judgments of individuals.

People are "schooled" by many institutions, writes Illich, to accept service in place of value: "Medical treatment is mistaken for health care, social work for the improvement of community life, police protection for safety, military poise for national security, the rat race for productive work."

In *Medical Nemesis* (1976), Illich reveals the health hazards and disabling effects of our medical system. *Toward a History of Needs* (1977) is a series of essays that address the institutional harm in modern industrial society associated with the workplace, technology, and energy in addition to schooling and medicine. His most recent book, *ABC: The Alphabetization of the Popular Mind* (1988), with Barry Sanders, examines the threat of modern communications to literacy and the degeneration of language into "information systems."

Illich would replace schooling with "learning webs": networks of people, places, and things. These networks include (1) reference services to educational objects—access to tools, equipment, books, and other functional objects; (2) skill exchanges—convenient means to share skills and information; (3) peer matching—a communications network to help people find partners for desired learning activities; and (4) reference services to educators-at-large—a directory of professionals, paraprofessionals, and freelancers, along with the conditions of their services. His *Tools for Conviviality* (1973) examines how people can gain more control over work, services, information, production, and consumption.

## Ernest Boyer (1928– )

For most of the past two decades, Ernest Boyer has been one the United States' most respected educators. He is a former U.S. Commissioner of Education, who became president of the Carnegie Foundation for the Advancement of Teaching in 1980. Boyer taught at Loyola University in Los Angeles, then served as the head of the Commission to Improve the Education of Teachers for the Western College Association and as director of the Center for Coordinated Education at the University of California, Santa Barbara, before becoming chancellor for the State University of New York in 1970.

Under the auspices of the Carnegie Foundation, Boyer developed *High School: A Report on Secondary Education in America* (1983), a major contribution to the current school reform debate. *High School* analyzes the role that secondary schools have come to assume in society and offers a practical agenda for action. Boyer makes the case that the success of secondary education and the nation's future are intertwined, that the welfare of the nation depends on a firm commitment to public education. He is sensitive to the frustrations teachers experience daily and tells how to improve the situation.

Boyer followed *High School* with a similar work about higher education. The underlying theme of *College: The Undergraduate Experience in America* is that our nation's four-year colleges are academically adrift without clear curricular goals. As a result, students and the public are ill served. After surveying the shortcomings in universities and colleges across the land and noting examples of splendid programs on many campuses, Boyer provides a blueprint to improve undergraduate education.

## Albert Shanker (1928– )

Albert Shanker has been president of the American Federation of Teachers (AFT) since 1974. From 1964 through 1984, he also served as president of New York City's local AFT affiliate. In 1978, he was elected president of the International Federation of Free Teachers' Unions, the first American to hold the post. In addition, he is vice-president of the American Federation of Labor and Congress of Industrial Organizations (AFL-CIO) and chairman of its International Affairs Committee.

Shanker earned a degree in philosophy from the University of Illinois and attended graduate school at Columbia University. He began his education career as a mathematics teacher and later taught at Hunter College. He currently teaches at the Harvard University Graduate School of Education.

His work in behalf of teachers is almost unprecedented in the history of American education. Shanker led the fight to gain collective bargaining rights for teachers and was jailed twice during contract negotiations for New York City public schoolteachers. Collective bargaining is now the norm, rather than the exception, for teachers and other public school employees.

Shanker's influence, however, goes beyond the teachers' union, and he is perhaps the educator most respected by politicians and business executives alike. During New York City's fiscal crisis in the 1970s, he helped the city escape bankruptcy by permitting teachers' pension funds to purchase city securities. He is a long-time advocate of civil and human rights. During the 1960s, he marched in Selma and Montgomery, Alabama, with Martin Luther King, Jr., and participated in the March on Washington, D.C. More recently he marched in Poland with Solidarity leader Lech Walesa to advance the democratic rights of workers.

Since the early 1970s, Shanker has written a weekly column, "Where We Stand," on education, labor, politics, and human rights issues, which appears in the "Week in Review" section of the Sunday *New York Times, Education Week,* and other publications. Even though they are paid advertisements, the articles are considered engaging by publishers and readers alike. As a result of his writings and other work,

Shanker has been a leader in current education reform. He is a strong advocate for fundamental change in the ways that schools are operated and teachers are organized to work with students.

## Neil Postman (1931– )

In 1969, Neil Postman and Charles Weingarten wrote the explosive *Teaching as a Subversive Activity.* In a hard-hitting yet thoughtful and passionate way, Postman declared that the American school system is sick, and its methods are based on fear, coercion, and rote-memory learning. Furthermore, the subject matter it teaches becomes obsolete almost as it is taught. To make matters worse, one of the schools' primary accomplishments is to stifle the intelligence and creativity of students.

The two authors followed this book with several supporting works: *The Soft Revolution: A Student Handbook for Turning Schools Around* (1971) is not about how to overthrow the system, but rather is a collection of homilies, maxims, models, metaphors, case studies, commentaries, and rules to hasten educational change. *The School Book: For People Who Want To Know What All the Hollering Is About* (1973) is a source of information for parents and other concerned citizens. A few years later they wrote *Crazy Talk, Stupid Talk: How We Defeat Ourselves by the Way We Talk and What To Do about It* (1976).

Postman's solution to the counterproductive practices of schools is the inductive method or "inquiry" learning. This approach to learning is consistent with the methods advocated by Jerome Bruner and the leaders of the new sciences, new social studies, and the new English. Postman, a former English teacher in elementary and high schools, faculty member of Harlem Preparatory School, and professor of education at New York University, was a part of the latter movement. His book, again with Weingarten, *Linguistics: A Revolution in Teaching* (1966), illustrates how the processes of inquiry into language can be translated into classroom activities.

Some ten years later, Postman changed direction from his "subversive" teaching days when the *New York Times Magazine* called him a "leading educational radical." The result was *Teaching as a Conserving Activity* (1979), a substantially different though no less passionate and provocative book than his first one. Postman, writing without collaboration of Weingarten, had taken a deep interest in the effects of information, technology, and the media on our culture. He was at that time and still is a professor of communications and media at New York University.

In a cultural sense, both the book and Postman are conservative: The major role of schools in an electronic information age, which stresses pictures, images, and concrete thinking, he explains, must be to emphasize abstract, conceptual, and analogical symbols—in short, words—that require complex cognitive thinking. In another sense, schools must be the intellectual conscience of society and take a radical stance to assume the "thermostatic view." After all, "television . . . constitutes the major educational enterprise now being undertaken in the United States." He calls television the first curriculum; school is the second.

Today Postman continues to examine the effects of culture on learning and the relationship of schools to our technological society. His recent books, *The Disappearance of Childhood* (1982), *Amusing Ourselves to Death: Public Discourse in the Age of Show Business* (1985), and *Conscientious Objections: Stirring up Trouble about Language, Technology, and Education* (1988), illustrate his shift to the role of social analyst and commentator.

## Theodore Sizer (1932– )

"The quintessence of the bureaucrat is accommodation," writes Ted Sizer in the Apologia (Introduction) of *Places for Learning, Places for Joy: Speculations on American School Reform* (1973). Sizer could have taken the bureaucratic conciliatory role himself, first as dean of the Harvard University Graduate of School of Education, then as headmaster of Phillips Academy, Andover, and now as chairman of the Education Department at Brown University. Instead, he has used these positions to encourage educators and the public to reexamine what they want from schools and to foster fundamental change.

In *Places for Learning, Places for Joy,* Sizer explains that, for all their good intentions, Americans are caught in a web of assumptions about the operation of schools that retard imaginative steps.[26] These assumptions, including those that are blatantly false, go unchallenged by all except the intellectual critics, whom the public neither identifies with nor trusts. In short, they constitute a "set of institutional verities." These include a belief that a national consensus on the goals of education exists; that formal education, degrees, and diplomas are good things; that compulsory attendance is desirable; and that schools are to nurture the common culture, or teach the American way, but, ironically, to be governed by local control.

The public hears much criticism about schools, Sizer explains, but generally is satisfied with what schools teach and how they treat children. Any changes people might want are incremental; few believe that schools are in crisis or that they diminish the minds of students. In *Horace's Compromise: The Dilemma of the American High School* (1985), Sizer goes beyond the rhetoric and slogans of reform to help us understand the lives of teachers and what students learn in schools.

Sizer also heads the Coalition for Essential Schools, which is his attempt to define a new set of educational assumptions. Small schools, big schools, even private and parochial schools, he observes, have the basic problem of trying to do too much. Thus, a major theme that cuts across the coalition's nine common principles is to simplify what schools are doing and concentrate on the "essentials." These principles make up the coalition's blueprint for school reform in our information age.

One principle, or path to simplification, is to place specific academic demands on students and hold them accountable for high-level intellectual performances. In this approach, Sizer views "the student as worker."

Another principle is to pare down the smorgasbord curriculum of today's "shopping mall high schools." Secondary schools should teach fewer subjects, cover fewer topics, and concentrate on critical themes and higher-level thinking. In Sizer's words, "Less is more."

Teachers need to work together more, form teams where appropriate, and be generalists willing to teach more than one subject. In the process, teachers can pool their expertise and spend more time with fewer students, explains Sizer.

Sizer's *Horace's School*, a sequel to *Horace's Compromise*, is scheduled to be published in 1992. As the title implies, this book promises to give readers a look inside an essential school.

## Diane Ravitch (1938– )

Diane Ravitch, an adjunct professor of history and education at Columbia University Teachers College, has become a leading proponent of a return to an emphasis on basic studies and subject content in the curriculum. In this respect, she follows in the tradition of educational essentialists who, over the years, have argued that schools erroneously emphasize skills over content and concepts over facts.

Ravitch gained respect as an educational historian when she wrote *The Great School Wars: A History of the New York City Public Schools* (1974, updated and revised in 1988). She established herself as a formidable traditionalist with the publication of *The Revisionists Revised: A Critique of the Radical Attack on the Schools* (1978). She has added to this reputation with *The State of American Education* (1980), *The Troubled Crusade: American Education, 1945–1980* (1983), and *The Schools We Deserve* (1985).

Ravitch and Chester Finn, Jr., codirectors of the Educational Excellence Network, whose goal is to improve schools, teamed up on a study supported by the National Assessment of Educational Progress (NAEP) to find out what high school students were learning. Their findings were published in *What Do Our 17-Year-Olds Know? A Report on the First Assessment of History and Literature* (1987). They concluded that today's students don't know very much, which supports their early observations that historical topics and classical literature are neglected in classrooms. What students know best apparently comes from popular culture, in which historical figures and literary characters have been presented in movies and television shows. Their study went beyond test scores to discover what teenagers read and what influence their home environment has on academic achievement.

## Notes

1. Neil Postman, *Teaching as a Conserving Activity* (New York: Dell, 1979), 32.

2. I borrow the term "grandmasters" from Adolphe Meyer, whose book is an informative guide to educational philosophers. Adolphe E. Meyer, *Grandmasters of Educational Thought* (New York: McGraw-Hill, 1975).

3. Ibid., 5–10, 24–30, 39–44.

4. Ibid., 51–52.

5. Gordon C. Lee, ed., *Crusade against Ignorance: Thomas Jefferson on Education,* Classics in Education no. 6 (New York: Bureau of Publications, Teachers College, Columbia University, 1961), 114–133.

6. Horace Mann, *Lectures, and Annual Reports, on Education* (Cambridge, MA: Published for Mrs. Mary Mann, 1867), 315; in Lawrence A. Cremin, *The Genius of American Education* (New York: Random House, 1965), 41–42.

7. Lawrence A. Cremin, ed., *The Republic and the School: Horace Mann on the Education of Free Men* (New York: Bureau of Publications, Teachers College, Columbia University, 1957), 17–20.

8. The committee included five college presidents: James Angell (University of Michigan), James M. Taylor (Vassar College), James H. Baker (University of Colorado), Richard H. Jesse (University of Missouri), and Eliot; two public school administrators: John Tetlow (headmaster of the Girls' High School and the Girls' Latin School, Boston) and Oscar D. Robinson (principal of Albany High School, New York); a private school headmaster, James C. Mackenzie (Lawrenceville School, New Jersey); a college professor, Henry C. King (Oberlin College); and William T. Harris, U.S. Commissioner of Education. Baker had recently been principal of Denver High School.

9. Edward A. Krug, *Charles W. Eliot and Popular Education* (New York: Bureau of Publications, Teachers College, Columbia University, 1961), 7–10.

10. See Lawrence Cremin's discussion of Milton Mayer's and Mortimer Adler's opposing goals for American education in *The Genius of American Education*, 46ff. Mayer and Adler identify three "irreducible oppositions": aristocratic vs. democratic, realist vs. idealist, and traditionalist vs. modernist.

11. Krug. *Eliot and Popular Education*, 11, 83–99.

12. Martin S. Dworkin, *Dewey on Education: Selections* (New York: Bureau of Publications, Teachers College, Columbia University, 1959), 6.

13. John Dewey, *Experience and Education* (New York: Macmillan, 1938), 25–28, 37–41, 44–45.

14. Rita Kramer, *Maria Montessori: A Biography* (New York: Putnam's, 1976), 107–122.

15. Ibid., 117–119.

16. Ibid., 61–67.

17. Mortimer J. Adler, *Philosopher at Large: An Intellectual Autobiography* (New York: MacMillan, 1977).

18. Stringfellow Barr and Scott Buchanan were president and dean of St. John's College in Annapolis, Maryland, where the entire undergraduate curriculum is devoted to the Great Books. In Adler's view, St. John's is the only college in the United States to offer a true liberal arts education.

19. *The Paideia Proposal* is the product of the Paideia Group, whose members include Ernest Boyer, Theodore Sizer, Ruth Love, and Jacques Barzun. Adler is the chairman of this group.

20. Jerome S. Bruner, *The Process of Education* (Cambridge, MA: Harvard University Press, 1961), 33.

21. John I. Goodlad, M. Frances Klein, and associates, *Behind the Classroom Door* (Worthington, OH: Charles A. Jones, 1970), 94, 98.

22. Lawrence A. Cremin, *The Transformation of the School: Progressivism in American Education, 1876–1957* (New York: Random House, 1961), ix.

23. Lawrence A. Cremin, *Public Education* (New York: Basic Books, 1976), 85–86.

24. Ivan Illich, *Deschooling Society* (New York: Harper & Row, 1971), 1.

25. Ibid., 43–46.

26. Theodore R. Sizer, *Places for Learning, Places for Joy: Speculations on American School Reform* (Cambridge, MA: Harvard University Press, 1973), 17.

# 5

# Reports on
# Public Schooling
# in the United States

The mental nourishment we spoonfeed our children is not only minced
but peptonized so that their brains digest it without effort and without
benefit and the result is the anaemic intelligence of the average American
schoolchild.[1]

SINCE THE DAYS WHEN HORACE MANN TRAVELED the backroads of
Massachusetts to discuss educational issues, Americans have taken a
special interest in their schools. During the 1980s, however, business
leaders, government officials, and the media became especially preoccupied with the quality of the public schools. The result was a
proliferation of studies, reports, and books on schooling.

## Challenges of Popular Schooling

Recent reports on education, of course, are nothing new in the United
States. Roughly 100 years ago, with the nation's transformation from
an agrarian, predominantly rural economic society to an industrial,
urban society, secondary school enrollment began a precipitous rise.
One reason was that young people required more schooling or training
to be prepared for jobs. Fewer 14- to 17-year-olds also were needed on
the declining number of farms, and many could not find jobs in the

industrial workplace. Not surprisingly, high schools began springing up across the American landscape, particularly in the cities.

The change in the U.S. economic society, and with it the change in the schools' mission, prompted the National Education Association (NEA) to convene its famous Committee of Ten on Secondary Studies. In 1892, this group of renowned educators, headed by Harvard president Charles Eliot, issued a report that expanded the high school curriculum to accommodate the increasing number of students. Nevertheless, the core curriculum remained heavily academic. Latin and Greek now shared a dominant place with English, history, science, and modern languages. Only the best students were affected, since in 1900 less than 10 percent of the nation's youth finished high school. Equally important, however, the committee declared that secondary schools existed primarily to prepare students for life, and secondarily to prepare them for college.

High school enrollment doubled during the 1890s and 1900s, then grew at even faster rates during the following decade. Child-labor laws and an influx of immigration increased the number and range of students entering high school. Suddenly a majority of students were not continuing to college; high school would be the end of their schooling. Again the NEA appointed a committee, and in 1918 the Commission on the Reorganization of Secondary Schools published its *Cardinal Principles of Secondary Education*. The committee issued the first call for universal secondary education and the comprehensive high school, guided by its seven aims of education: health, command of fundamental processes, worthy home membership, vocation, citizenship, worthy use of leisure time, and ethical character. These Seven Cardinal Principles, as they were popularly called, inspired educators and influenced school curricula. In short order, curriculum leaders in the sciences, social studies, English, and mathematics established frameworks that, for the most part, still exist today.

During the 1920s and 1930s, secondary school enrollment continued to grow rapidly. Still, many students did not complete high school for either economic or academic reasons. Many dropped out of school to help support their families during the Depression, while others failed in school, did not perceive they had the ability to succeed, or were dissatisfied with the curriculum.

At the height of its influence in 1930, the Progressive Education Association (PEA) proposed an experiment to test its underlying principles and practices. This experiment, called the Eight-Year Study because it ran from 1932 to 1940, was carried out by the PEA's Commission on the Relation of School and College in 30 leading secondary schools, public and private. Each school was invited to design its curriculum around six principles: (1) greater mastery of learning, (2) more continuity in learning, (3) the release of creative energies of students, (4) a clearer understanding of the problems of contemporary civilization, (5) better individual guidance of students, and (6) better curriculum materials and more effective teaching methods.

In the experiment, 1,475 matched pairs of students were followed from high school through college. The results were convincing: Evaluators found that, compared to those from traditional schools, graduates of the 30 progressive schools earned higher grades; received more academic and nonacademic honors; possessed a higher degree of intellectual curiosity; demonstrated more precise, systematic, and objective thinking; had a clearer idea concerning the meaning of education; were more resourceful; participated more frequently in organized student groups; and took a more active concern in national and world affairs. Unfortunately, the report of the Eight-Year Study, issued in 1942, received little attention amidst the nation's preoccupation with World War II.

Although more students were completing high school by 1940, the graduation rate was still just 50 percent. The average U.S. adult had completed only 8.6 years of schooling. On the eve of World War II, the average American child was expected to complete elementary school and continue on for some secondary school.

After World War II, as Lawrence Cremin explains, the "popularization of schooling combined two elements: the drive to make secondary schooling universal in the United States and the drive to extend the opportunity for higher education to all who wished it and were qualified." The first element was spelled out in a report prepared by the Educational Policies Commission of the NEA and the American Association of School Administrators, titled *Education for ALL American Youth* (1944). It recommended extending compulsory schooling to age 18 and outlined a vastly broadened curriculum for the high school's heterogeneous clientele. This curriculum would include vocational as well as academic instruction keyed to the knowledge and skills young adults would need to function as citizens, workers, and parents.[2]

In the wake of World War II, the Korean War, and the launching of Sputnik, the United States again took stock of where its schools were headed—or perhaps drifting. With each succeeding decade, it became clearer that educational policy, as David Cohen and Michael Garet have written, is not a series of discrete decisions that add up to a coherent and universal course of action. Rather, it is a "grand story: a large and loose set of ideas about how society works, why it goes wrong and how it can be set right."[3] As events revealed, there would be more grand stories to come about the role of schools in society.

The writings of James B. Conant relate the story of the 1950s and early 1960s. While president of Harvard in 1952, Conant advocated the principle of a comprehensive high school with a common core of studies and differentiated programs that would make a special effort to provide gifted students with rigorous study in languages, mathematics, and natural sciences. Conant then called on colleges and universities to help the public schools upgrade secondary school programs. He also recommended expanding the number of junior colleges and their work-experience programs, restraining the number of four-year colleges, reducing their size, and holding all undergraduate programs to high standards. Finally, Conant wanted more public and private scholarships for able students.[4] In short, he outlined a Jeffersonian philosophy that embraced universal elementary education, comprehensive secondary education, and selective higher education.

A few years later the Carnegie Corporation, through the Educational Testing Service, funded a study of the high school that Conant carried out. The findings of this study are reported in *The American High School Today* (1959), which spelled out no less than 21 specific recommendations to improve the nation's secondary schools. The result was to refurbish the meaning of the comprehensive school by tightening the general education of all students, clarifying the nonacademic elective program for those planning to join the work force after graduation, and providing a solid academic curriculum for the college-bound, particularly the academically talented, student.

According to Conant's story, or vision, education has social as well as intellectual goals. The mixing of youngsters from different social backgrounds in schools is essential to creating a cohesive classless society. Coincidentally, it is critical for schools to provide rigorous academic curricula and standards for those who will fulfill technical positions or leadership roles in business, government, and science.[5]

In response to the innovation and radical reforms of the 1960s and 1970s, at least three key reports were promulgated by national committees. In 1973 and 1974, the Panel on Youth of the President's Science Advisory Committee (PSAC) published *Youth: Transition to Adulthood* (1973); the National Commission on the Reform of Secondary Education, sponsored by the Charles F. Kettering Foundation, delivered *The Reform of Secondary Education* (1973); and the National Panel on High School and Adolescent Education, sponsored by the U.S. Office of Education, gave us *The Education of Adolescents* (1974).

In general, all three reports urged secondary schools to become more flexible. High schools, they said, needed to be smaller so students could be treated as individuals; curriculum options needed to be broadened and diversified; students should be able to study in other educative institutions, such as libraries and museums, or participate in supervised work experiences with businesses and government agencies; and compulsory-attendance laws ought to be relaxed so young people who wished to do so could enter the adult world. The national commission even advocated reducing the age when students could legally leave school to 14, so that high schools might shed their custodial function.[6]

The story offered by these 1970s commissions tells us that, as more and more students attend school, they need a wider variety of programs. Young people deserve a range of opportunities to pursue vocational and avocational interests, tailored to their individual needs and backgrounds. In turn, learning should take place in a variety of educational institutions. Schools need to be reconnected to the life of society.

# Schooling after a Century of Democratic Education

By the 1980s, the complaint that the schools were failing was hardly novel. These charges of decline have encompassed many meanings and have served the agendas of diverse groups. "As often as not, it suggests that young people are learning less of what a particular commentator or group of commentators believe they ought to be learning," Cremin remarks. This "ought," he explains, depends on particular conceptions of education and the educated person.[7]

Still, the criticisms of the 1980s differed in several ways from those that had come before. To start, the reports were spirited and pervasive; they were supported variously by business, public and private foundations, education associations, and government, including the White House and state governors. Next, they were fortified by data from studies that compared student achievement across nations. Finally, coming at a time when Americans felt anxious about their place in the world, they fostered strident positions.

School reform in the 1980s is often said to have started with, and even been defined by, the National Commission on Excellence in Education's *A Nation at Risk* report issued in 1983. While this critique captured a prevailing mood of the period, it was neither the first report nor only story.

## The Paideia Proposal: An Educational Manifesto (1982)

Written by Mortimer Adler on behalf of the Paideia Group, published by Macmillan.

> We must end that hypocrisy in our national life. We cannot say out of one side of our mouth that we are for democracy and all its free institutions . . . and out of the other side of our mouth, say that only some of the children—fewer than half—are educable for full citizenship and full human life.[8]

At the beginning of this first major report of the 1980s, Mortimer Adler states that we are on the verge of a new era: "The long-needed educational reform for which this country is at last ready will be a turning point toward that new era." Democracy, he adds, has come into its own for the first time this century, when we have undertaken to give 12 years of schooling to all our children. In turn, universal suffrage and universal schooling are inextricably bound. "The one without the other," Adler writes, "is a perilous delusion."[9]

The democratic promise of equal educational opportunity is an ideal betrayed, however, unless our schools are educationally classless. The key to a democratic education, according to the Paideia Group, is a one-track system with the same objectives and course of study for all students. Unfortunately, the multitrack system of public education in the United States sets different goals for different groups of students and discriminates against those who are diverted to the less demanding tracks.

The course of study offered in *The Paideia Proposal* is 12 years of basic schooling, for students ages 4 to 16. This basic course is required for all students, with one exception; students may choose a second language. In addition to becoming competent in reading, writing, and speaking English, students would acquire a certain facility in a second language, which would be an elective. The Paideia course of study is organized around three modes of learning built on three different teaching styles. These modes or columns, illustrated in Figure 5-1, would extend throughout the years of basic schooling, rising in complexity and difficulty from the first to the twelfth year.

In the first mode of study, the goal is *acquisition of knowledge*. The subject matter includes what Adler calls the "fundamental branches of learning": language, literature, and the fine arts; mathematics and natural sciences; history and the social studies. In turn, the mode of instruction is "didactic," or "teaching by telling." It employs textbooks and other instructional materials, accompanied by laboratory demonstrations.

The goal of the second mode of study is the *development of intellectual skills* in the use of language, primarily English, and competence in dealing with a range of technical devices, including calculators, computers, and scientific instruments. The skills acquired are reading,

FIGURE 5-1   Paideia Course of Study for All

|  | COLUMN ONE | COLUMN TWO | COLUMN THREE |
|---|---|---|---|
| **Goals** | ACQUISITION OF ORGANIZED KNOWLEDGE | DEVELOPMENT OF INTELLECTUAL SKILLS — SKILLS OF LEARNING | ENLARGED UNDERSTANDING OF IDEAS AND VALUES |
|  | by means of | by means of | by means of |
| **Means** | DIDACTIC INSTRUCTION LECTURES AND RESPONSES TEXTBOOKS AND OTHER AIDS | COACHING, EXERCISES AND SUPERVISED PRACTICE | MAIEUTIC OR SOCRATIC QUESTIONING AND ACTIVE PARTICIPATION |
|  | In three areas of subject matter | In the operations of | In the |
| **Areas Operations and Activites** | LANGUAGE, LITERATURE AND THE FINE ARTS  MATHEMATICS AND NATURAL SCIENCE  HISTORY GEOGRAPHY AND SOCIAL STUDIES | READING, WRITING, SPEAKING, AND LISTENING  CALCULATING, PROBLEM-SOLVING, OBSERVING, MEASURING ESTIMATING  EXERCISING CRITICAL JUDGEMENT | DISCUSSION OF BOOKS (NOT TEXTBOOKS) AND OTHER WORKS OF ART AND INVOLVEMENT IN ARTISTIC ACTIVITIES e.g. MUSIC, DRAMA, VISUAL ARTS |

The three columns do not correspond to separate courses, nor is one kind of teaching and learning necessarily confined to any one class.

Reprinted with permission of Macmillan Publishing Company from *The Paideia Proposal: An Educational Manifesto* by Mortimer J. Adler. Copyright © 1982 by the Institute for Philosophical Research.

writing, speaking, listening, observing, measuring, estimating, and calculating. The mode of instruction is coaching to help the learner to do, to organize a sequence of acts in the correct way, and to execute them with skill.

With the third mode of study, the goal is *enlarged understanding of ideas and values* through books (not textbooks) and products of human artistry. The books can be historical, scientific, philosophical, poems, stories, and essays. The products of human artistry include music, visual arts, plays, dance productions, film, and television. The mode of instruction for this study is Socratic questioning, or maieutic teaching, which helps students give birth to ideas.

"The ultimate goal of the educational process," writes Adler, "is to help human beings become educated persons. Schooling is the preparatory state; it forms the habit of learning and provides the means for continuing to learn after all schooling is completed."[10]

## A Nation at Risk: The Imperative for Educational Reform (1983)

A report to the nation and the Secretary of Education, U.S. Department of Education, by the National Commission on Excellence in Education. For sale by the Superintendent of Documents, U.S. Government Printing Office, Washington, D.C. 20402.

> If an unfriendly foreign power had attempted to impose on America the mediocre education performance that exists today, we might well have viewed it as an act of war. As it stands, we have allowed this to happen to ourselves. We have even squandered the gains in student achievement made in the wake of the Sputnik challenge. Moreover, we have dismantled essential support systems which helped make those gains possible. We have, in effect, been committing an act of unthinking, unilateral disarmament.[11]

The National Commission on Excellence in Education was created in 1981 by President Ronald Reagan's first secretary of education, Terrel Bell. The commission included educators, scientists, business people, and government officials, with David P. Gardner, then president of the University of Utah and now president of the University of California, as chairman and Yvonne W. Larsen, immediate past president of the San Diego School Board, as vice-chairwoman. After holding hearings, taking testimony, and visiting schools during 1982, the commission issued its terse, direct, and unequivocal report the following year.

This report, a severe indictment of American education, cited numerous indicators of risk, including the low rankings of American youngsters on various international comparisons of student achievement, high rates of functional illiteracy among high school–aged students, declining scores on the Scholastic Aptitude Test, and the steady decline in science achievement by 17-year-olds. The commission concluded that these declines "are in large part the result of disturbing inadequacies in the way the educational process itself is often conducted."

The report then listed how this decline is illustrated in four telling aspects of the educational process: content (for example, the "curricular smorgasbord" of secondary schools that has become "homogenized, diluted, and diffused"); expectations (for example, lower graduation requirements, reduced amounts of homework, and texts that have been "written down"); time (for example, fewer hours per day and fewer days per year that American students spend in school compared to their foreign counterparts and less time spent studying academic subjects); and teaching (for example, severe shortages of teachers in mathematics, science, and foreign languages, and for gifted and disabled students).

As a remedy, the commission submitted five recommendations:

1. All students seeking a high school diploma should be required to complete during the four years of high school the "new basics"—four years of English, three years of mathematics, three years of science, three years of social studies, and a half year of computer science.
2. Schools, colleges, and universities should adopt more rigorous standards and expectations for their students, and four-year colleges and universities should raise their admission requirements.
3. Schools should devote more time to teaching the new basics by more effectively using the school day, extending the school day, or lengthening the school year.
4. The preparation of teachers should be strengthened, and teaching made a more rewarding and respected profession.
5. Citizens throughout the nation should require educators and elected officials to support these reforms and provide the money necessary to achieve them.[12]

*A Nation at Risk* recognized that education reform must occur in many places beyond schools and called for creating a "learning society." At the heart of the learning society are educational opportunities that extend into homes, workplaces, libraries, art galleries, museums, science centers, and other places where the individual can develop in work and life. Fittingly, the report ends with a message to parents and students, asking parents to raise their expectations and asking students to put forth their best efforts in school.

## High School: A Report on Secondary Education in America (1983)

Written by Ernest L. Boyer for the Carnegie Foundation for the Advancement of Teaching, published by Harper & Row.

And in the debate about public schools equity must be seen not as a chapter of the past but as the unfinished agenda of the future. To expand access without upgrading schools is simply to perpetuate discrimination in a more subtle form. But to push for excellence in ways that ignore the needs of less privileged students is to undermine the future of the nation. Clearly, equity and excellence cannot be divided.[13]

The success of U.S. high schools and our nation's future are irrevocably linked, explains Ernest Boyer in this comprehensive report on secondary education. Schools cannot be society's cure for every social ill, he adds, but "without good schools none of these problems can be solved." Boyer and his research colleagues call for a major reform of our high schools that differs significantly from *A Nation at Risk*. "To blame the schools for the 'rising tide of mediocrity' is to confuse symptoms with the disease. Schools can rise no higher than the communities that support them," Boyer writes. While the overwhelming concern and emphasis of *A Nation at Risk* are on reviving excellence in American schools, *High School* attempts to blend the goal of excellence with that of equity.

Despite the substantial policy differences among the National Commission on Excellence in Education, the Carnegie Foundation, and the Paideia Group, all share a common view of education—that it is essentially the study of the liberal arts. What James Conant a generation ago called general education, Adler terms basic schooling, the national commission labels the new basics, and Boyer calls the integrated core.

Boyer maintains, "A high school to be effective must have a clear and vital mission. Students, teachers, administrators, and parents at the institution should have a shared vision of what, together, they are trying to accomplish." However, school officials seldom ask, What is the purpose of education? The lack of such purpose, Boyer argues, is reflected in the curricular smorgasbord of most schools. This noncoherent curriculum inevitably is the result of schools' attempts to accommodate the diverse, pluralistic student bodies most inherit these days. Given this background, the premise underlying *High School* is that schools can serve all students and find a coherent purpose.

To establish this purpose, the Carnegie report proposes four essential goals to guide all high schools:

1. The high school should help students develop the capacity to think critically and communicate effectively through a mastery of language.
2. It should help all students learn about themselves, the human heritage, and the interdependent world in which they live, through a core curriculum.

3. The high school should prepare all students for work and further education through a program of electives that develop individual aptitudes and interests.
4. The high school should help all students fulfill their social and civic obligations through school and community service.[14]

The first curriculum priority in the Carnegie report is language—the most essential tool for learning. All high schools, the report recommends, must help students develop the capacity to think critically and communicate effectively through the written and spoken word.

The second curriculum priority is a core of common learning. Boyer recommends that required courses in the core curriculum be expanded from one-half to two-thirds of the total units required for graduation. *High School*'s course of study includes literature, history, (U.S. history, Western civilization, non-Western studies), civics, science and the natural world (physical and biological sciences), mathematics, foreign language, the arts, technology, and health.

To augment the core curriculum students would take a one-semester "seminar on work" in which they learn about changes in the economy and job opportunities. Topping off the fourth year of high school, students would undertake a one-semester "senior independent project." This project would culminate in a written report that focuses on a significant contemporary issue.

*High School* also would establish a "new Carnegie unit" in service to the community. This program is designed to enrich students' understanding of the adult world they are entering and impress on them the value of social and civic obligations.[15]

Interestingly, the Carnegie Foundation contends that the Scholastic Aptitude Test (SAT) has outlasted its usefulness and recommends that it be replaced with a new SAAT, Student Achievement and Aptitude Test. The goal of the new assessment program would be to evaluate the academic program of each student and provide advisement to help students make more intelligent decisions about their futures.

Finally, *High School* recommends ways to renew the profession of teaching, clarify the principal's role, provide appropriate learning environments for different kinds of students, and enhance student transition from high school to college.

# A Place Called School: Prospects for the Future (1984)

Written by John Goodlad, published by McGraw-Hill.

American schools are in trouble. In fact, the problems of schooling are of such crippling proportions that many schools may not survive. It is possible that our entire public education system is near collapse. We will continue to have schools, no doubt, but the basis of their support and their relationship to families, communities, and states could be quite different from what we have known.[16]

*A Place Called School* reports the findings of an extensive inquiry titled A Study of Schooling that was headed by John Goodlad. This study was supported by several foundations including Danforth, Ford, International Paper Company, Martha Holding Jennings, Charles F. Kettering, Charles Steward Mott, Rockefeller, and Spenser, as well as Lilly Endowment, Inc., the National Institute of Education, and other organizations. Goodlad conducted this study through the Institute for Development of Educational Activities, Inc.

As Goodlad points out, *A Place Called School* is not a research report so much as "it is a discussion of what appears to be the current state of schooling in our country." The discussion, however, is supported, supplemented, and made real by the use of illustrative data gathered from a small, diverse sample of schools. Juxtaposed with many of Goodlad's disheartening findings is an optimism toward what schools can be. Our nation has not outgrown the need for public schools as some critics imply, yet the schools we need are not the ones we now have, Goodlad explains. However, the current wave of criticism lacks the diagnosis required to reconstruct schools.

What our nation needs, he adds, "is a better understanding of its public schools and the specific problems that beset them." The context of schooling has changed dramatically in the past few decades: "Recordings, radio, and television pervade every resting place, be it home or resort, and accompany us all from birth to death." Consequently, the electronic media and the schools must be viewed side by side as major educating agencies.

Still, the expectations Americans have of their schools are both idealistic and grandiose. Some of these expectations are met by specialized academic and vocational schools, or by special programs for the disabled or the gifted. Given all the educational needs of people growing up in modern society, Goodlad declares, schools must reasonably be expected to play a "relatively distinct and distinguishable role in a configuration of institutions that educate."[17]

At the heart of *A Place Called School* is a detailed taxonomy of the goals for schooling in the United States. These goals are divided into four major categories: academic; vocational; social, civic, and cultural; and personal.

To achieve academic goals, the curriculum would focus on mastery of basic skills (such as reading, writing, and using mathematical concepts) and on intellectual development (including problem-solving, critical and independent thinking to make judgments and decisions, and acquiring a general fund of knowledge).

Vocational goals would emphasize career education and help students select an occupation and develop useful skills, valuable habits (such as pride in good workmanship), and positive attitudes toward work.

The civic, social, and cultural goals would focus on developing interpersonal understandings (such as knowledge of opposing value systems and skill in identifying the concerns of others); citizenship participation (for example, a commitment to the values of liberty and an understanding of the complex interrelationships in modern society); enculturation (including an understanding of one's cultural heritage and the manner in which traditions from the past influence values today); and moral and ethical character (such as the ability to evaluate events, a commitment to truth, and moral integrity).

Personal goals would be designed to enhance students' emotional and physical well-being (through learning skills in coping with social change, effective use of leisure time, physical fitness, and the ability to engage in constructive self-criticism); creativity and aesthetic expression (the ability to tolerate new ideas, consider different ideas, enjoy different forms of creative expression, and communicate through creative work); and self-realization (developing a philosophy of life, self-confidence, and assessment of one's limitations and strengths).

Goodlad identifies these goals and objectives as having emerged over the past 300 years. Given the political structure of education in the United States, one might expect states to have articulated to schools their clear expectations for learning outcomes in these four areas. This has not happened. Thus, the time "has come, past come," he comments, for governors and legislatures to endorse and revise as needed these goals, and for local districts to assure that every student has a balanced program of academic, vocational, civic, social, and personal studies.[18]

## A Nation Prepared: Teachers for the 21st Century (1986)

Carnegie Forum on Education and the Economy, Task Force on Teaching as a Profession, Washington, D.C. The Carnegie Forum is a program of the Carnegie Corporation of New York.

> The 1980s will be remembered for two developments: the beginning of a sweeping reassessment of the basis of the nation's economic strength and an outpouring of concern for the quality of American education. The connection between these two streams of thought is strong and growing.[19]

Although the central thesis of this report concerns the quality and preparation of teachers in U.S. classrooms, it reiterates a theme prevalent in many reports of the decade: The United States' economic competitiveness and thereby the future health of our economy are inexorably tied to the quality of our educational system.

With this premise, the report examines what it considers to be three critical dimensions of the teacher quality issue. First, it explains how the changing nature of the world economy makes it imperative to reverse the American schools' decline in academic performance. Second, the report describes changes in the demographics of the teaching profession that threaten to wipe out earlier gains. Third, it presents a strategy for transforming teaching and restructuring schools.

In order to build a profession of well-educated teachers who can assume new responsibilities and redesign schools, the report calls for sweeping changes in educational policy. This will restore "the nation's cutting edge," the task force states. To achieve these ambitious aims, the authors would:

- Create a National Board for Professional Teacher Standards, with a regional and state membership structure, to establish high standards for teacher competency.
- Restructure schools to provide a professional environment that frees teachers to meet state and local goals and be accountable for student progress.
- Restructure the teaching field and create a category of lead teachers who are capable of taking an active leadership role in redesigning schools and helping colleagues.
- Require bachelor's degrees in the arts and sciences as a prerequisite for the professional study of teaching.
- Develop a new professional curriculum in graduate schools of education leading to a master's in teaching degree based on a systematic knowledge of teaching.

- Mobilize the nation's resources to prepare minority youngsters for careers in teaching.
- Relate incentives for teachers to schoolwide student performance and provide schools with the technology and services essential to teacher productivity.
- Make teacher salaries and career opportunities competitive with those in other professions.

The task force, which was chaired by Lewis Branscomb, chief scientist and vice-president of IBM Corporation, included such notable educators as Albert Shanker, president of the AFT; Mary Hatwood Futrell, past president of the NEA; Bill Honig, California's superintendent of public instruction; John Gardner, a Washington, D.C., consultant; and Fred M. Hechinger, president of the New York Times Company Foundation. They remind readers that the United States' "mass educational system," designed in the early part of the century for a mass-production economy, will not succeed unless it redefines the essential standards of excellence and strives to make quality and equality of opportunity compatible with each other. Futrell, it should be noted, made dissenting comments about several of the document's recommendations.

## James Madison High School: A Curriculum for American Students (1987)

Written by William Bennett, then U.S. Secretary of Education, U.S. Department of Education.

> A teacher was visiting a high school classroom and speaking to a group of average and below average students. They were talking about what their school should teach. The teacher asked these students what they wanted to study and what they wanted to read. One boy in back raised his hand. "We want to read what the smart kids read," he said.[20]

Although he supported the National Commission on Excellence in Education's call for increased course requirements, Bennett urged the schools to go beyond this. "The time any student spends on any subject is no guarantee that he will master it," he argues. The content and quality of high school studies is just as important as their number. To achieve the graduation standards spelled out in *A Nation at Risk*, Bennett offers a course of study, buttressed by high expectations of students.

Like Conant, Adler, and Boyer before him, Bennett recommended a core curriculum that would be applicable to all students, aside from the specialized and vocational programs appropriate for some students.

Under the *James Madison High School* program, students would take from high school a shared body of knowledge and skills, a common language of ideas, and a common moral and intellectual discipline. To accomplish this, many schools need to eliminate the "curricular clutter" that laces their course of studies.

The *James Madison* program would emphasize history, literature, and the humanities. During the high school years, students in the English curriculum would study American, British, and world literature for four years. Social studies would consist of three required years of history, including Western civilization, U.S. history, and principles of American and world democracy. Both the science and mathematics curricula would require three years of study restricted to academic as opposed to applied offerings. All students would be required to take two years of a foreign language.

Bennett dismisses the objections of those who respond that some students, given their different backgrounds and language needs, are not equipped to handle the *James Madison* curriculum. Some students may need remedial help and more time to learn algebra and geometry, or any particular subject, but this is no reason for schools to abandon their responsibility and this quest, he argues. He also cautions that *James Madison High School* should be neither a federal policy nor a "monolithic program to uniformly impose or slavishly follow." We are a nation of local education polices, Bennett adds, and local schools must adopt the plan to local circumstances.[21]

## What Do Our 17-Year-Olds Know? A Report on the First Assessment of History and Literature (1987)

Written by Diane Ravitch and Chester Finn, published by Harper & Row.

> In the battle for public attention and curricular time, the humanities were scarcely contenders. No prestigious body of citizens called on American schools to assess the teaching of history . . . as others had for science. No concerned professors of English banded together to decry their students' ignorance of major works of literature. The representatives of business, labor, government, and education who regularly issue edicts on the need for change in the schools had little to say about history and literature.[22]

*What Do Our 17-Year-Olds Know?* is a report on the first national assessment of history and literature, an outgrowth of a study called the Foundations of Literacy initiated by Diane Ravitch and Chester Finn, then codirectors of the Educational Excellence Network. To carry out this assessment, Ravitch and Finn contacted the National Assessment of Educational Progress (NAEP), which developed and administered it. The assessment was funded by the National Endowment for the Humanities.

Ravitch and Finn focus on literature and history because they believe these two core areas have been shortchanged. Literature has increasingly given way to general language-arts skills across the grade levels. And the social sciences, including economics, sociology, psychology, and global studies, have intruded into history's central place in the curriculum.

The reform movement of the 1980s, they point out, led to many states' passing requirements to strengthen the sciences, mathematics, and basic skills. Although these areas deserve emphasis, little attention has been given to literature and history. It is difficult to make the case that these subjects help keep us abreast of technological developments or strengthen the national economy, they add, but the well-being of a nation does not depend on technology or material wealth alone. An understanding of literature and the humanities is critical to the cohesiveness and morality of a society.

The results of this national assessment testify to our 17-year-olds' lack of knowledge in these areas. The students answered only 54.5 percent of the history questions and 51.8 percent of the literature questions correctly. For example, 65 percent did not know what *1984* or *Lord of the Flies* are about; yet 70 percent could associate Emily Dickinson with the major theme of her work. Three-quarters of the students did not know when Abraham Lincoln was president, and only 32 percent knew during which half-century the Civil War was fought; yet more than 70 percent could identify the Great Depression. What students know best, the authors conclude, comes from popular culture, the historical characters and literary figures who have been represented in movies and television shows. What they know least are the books, ideas, and events taught only in school.

Critics of the national assessment argue that it tests for identification of disconnected names, dates, titles, events, and authors isolated from deeper meanings. Ravitch and Finn counter that knowing facts and content is imperative to grasping ideas and developing generalizations. They blame young people's lack of knowledge on educators who value concepts without regard to underlying and related facts, and who teach skills at the expense of content.

The authors make many recommendations for teachers, educational policymakers, administrators, colleges and universities, the family, and the media to improve the situation. For starters, they recommend teaching more history; enlivening the study of history with narratives, journals, stories, and biographies; and teaching it in the context of social and economic trends and political events. More time should be devoted to literature at every grade level; reading texts should include generous portions of important literary works; and excellent fiction and nonfiction should be a hefty dose of every student's English studies, not just in the gifted, college-bound, and honors classes.[23]

## Coalition for Essential Schools (1984) and Re:Learning (1988)

A school reform organization located at Brown University, Providence, R.I., Theodore R. Sizer, director.

> Most schools are nice places. . . . The academic pressures are limited, and the accommodations to students are substantial. For example, if many members of an English class have jobs after school, the English teacher's expectations for them are adjusted downward. In a word, school is sensitively accommodating, as long as students are punctual, where they are supposed to be, and minimally dutiful about picking things up from the clutch of courses in which they enroll.
>
> This characterization is not pretty, but it is accurate, and it serves to describe the vast majority of American secondary schools. . . . The students are happy taking subjects. The parents are happy, because that's what they did in high school. . . . The adolescents are supervised, safely and constructively most of the time, during the morning and afternoon hours, and they are off the labor market. That is what high school is all about.[24]

American secondary schools above all else, observes Sizer, are comfortable, accommodating, and benign. While this is understandable and perhaps admirable, it is also a fatal weakness. To Sizer, high schools have become vast, impersonal "shopping malls" that offer intellectually complacent students a smorgasbord of courses but fail to teach solid academics.

Sizer heads the Coalition for Essential Schools (CES), a growing network of reform-minded schools that he organized in 1984. In 1988, the coalition teamed up with the Education Commission of the States (ECS) to form the Re:Learning project. As a result of this marriage, "essential schools" are now being developed in cooperation with state educational leaders. States that are fully involved in the Re:Learning approach, with at least five essential schools, are referred to as *participating* states. Other states are at the *networking* stage, preparing to have functioning essential schools.

No two good schools are alike, Sizer explains, nor is a good school exactly the same from one year to the next. "A good school is a special creation of its own faculty—the teachers, counselors, and administrators." The coalition then does not profess to be a model for schools to emulate. Rather, it is a set of principles used to guide the operation of schools, while letting them reflect the goals of their communities and the abilities of their staffs.[25]

Most of the coalition's nine principles are general statements; only two are specific: No teacher in a coalition school is to have responsibility for more than 80 students, and the per-pupil expenditure should not exceed that at comparable traditional high schools by more than 10 percent. All the principles apply to every student, Sizer stresses. The college-bound are not alone in being able to thrive on rigorous academics.

The nine principles that follow bear a striking resemblance to those that guided the Progressive Education Association's Eight-Year Study of experimental schools in the 1930s. In effect, the coalition is attempting to refashion the progressive ideas that emerged earlier in this century, and resurfaced in the informal-school movement of the 1960s, to achieve the rigorous academic goals of the 1990s. Regardless of the era, these principles, when properly executed, meet the tests of both excellence and equity in schools.

1. **Intellectual focus.** The primary purpose of schools is to help students use their minds well. Schools should not be "comprehensive" at the expense of academic rigor.
2. **Less is more.** Each student should master essential skills and areas of knowledge; teachers should teach fewer topics more deeply, guided by the intellectual and creative competencies students need, rather than conventional subjects.
3. **Universal goals.** Academics should be paramount for all students. Although school practices are tailored to meeting the needs of diverse groups of adolescents, everyone deserves an intellectual education.
4. **Personalized learning.** Teachers should have direct responsibility for no more than 80 students each semester. Together with principals, teachers also control course content, curricular materials, pedagogical methods, and schedules.
5. **Student-as-worker.** Rather than serving as a provider of information, teachers should stimulate, coach, and ultimately hold students responsible for their own learning.
6. **Demonstrating competencies.** Students should be passed only after mastering a subject and awarded a diploma after demonstrating the understanding of fundamental skills and knowledge. Projects and writing assignments would replace conventional objective tests to evaluate student work.

7. **School attitude.** School should promote high but "un-anxious" expectations, trust, and decency and encourage parents to collaborate in fostering healthy learning attitudes.
8. **Staff role.** Principals and teachers should share teaching, counseling, and administrative responsibilities. Staff members should view themselves first as general scholars, then as specialists in a particular discipline.
9. **School budget.** The cost of operating the new essential school should be roughly equivalent to, and no more than 10 percent greater than, that of the traditional school. To offset team planning by the staff and competitive salaries, schools would eliminate some of the nonacademic services most offer.

When the nine principles are pursued in combination, schools can realize their synergistic effect. In turn, the sustained support of a cadre of dedicated staff is critical to transforming a comfortable but uninspiring conventional school atmosphere.

## The Forgotten Half: Pathways to Success for America's Youth and Young Families (1988)

Prepared by the William T. Grant Foundation Commission on Work, Family and Citizenship. Copies of the 200-page report can be obtained for $5.00 each postpaid by writing the William T. Grant Foundation Commission on Youth and America's Future, Dept. K, Suite 301, 1001 Connecticut Ave. N.W., Washington, D.C. 20036.

> Educators have become so preoccupied with those who go on to college that they have lost sight of those who do not. And more and more of the noncollege-bound now fall between the cracks when they are in school, drop out, or graduate inadequately prepared for the requirements of the society and the workplace.[26]

The U.S. economy is undergoing a major transformation—from an industrial base to a technological base and from manufacturing to services. The effect on the work force, particularly on those workers with a high school education or less, has been monumental. This report, *The Forgotten Half,* the work of a national panel chaired by Harold Howe II, documents the struggles faced today by the 20 million young people between the ages of 16 and 24 whose formal education ends with high school.

The noncollege-bound are facing tougher times in their search for rewarding careers. While jobs at both the low and high ends of the wage scale are increasing, work opportunities that provide the chance to master new skills and develop careers on the job are decreasing. Data showing that unemployment is relatively low "obscure the radical job market changes of recent years," the commissioners write. Stable employment and well-paying opportunities for young workers in manufacturing, transportation, utilities, and forestry have fallen sharply during the past two decades.

As a result, young workers suffer extraordinarily high unemployment rates, and the economic prospects they face can be disheartening (see Figure 5-2). Between 1973 and 1986, for example, real median income for families headed by a 20- to 24-year-old person fell 26.3 percent, from $20,229 to $14,900. Similarly, the percentage of males (ages 20 to 24) able to support a family of three above the poverty level fell from 58.3 percent to 43.8 percent. In 1986, nearly one out every three families headed by a person under age 25 was poor, triple the rate for all American families, and more than double that of 1967.[27]

"If you recall that the drop in personal income during the Great Depression from 1929 to 1933 was 27 percent, we can better grasp the extent of the 'New Depression' being experienced by America's young families today," write the commissioners.[28]

Young workers, the report makes clear, are not a generation of lazy losers, but rather are scrambling to succeed. Many of them work more than one job at a time, live longer with their parents, delay marriage and family, and seek out training. Still, the earning gap between high-school and college graduates widened significantly after 1973.

FIGURE 5-2    Trends in the Real Median Incomes of Young Families, Headed by Persons 24-Years-Old or Younger; by Type of Family and Race/Ethnic Origin of Family Householder, 1973–1986 (in 1986 Dollars)

| Charactistics of Family Head | 1973 | 1986 | Percent Change 1973–86 |
|---|---|---|---|
| All Families | $20,229 | $14,900 | −26.3 |
| White, non-Hispanic | 21,710 | 17,500 | −19.4 |
| Black, non-Hispanic | 11,997 | 6,400 | −46.7 |
| Hispanic | 14,610 | 11,900 | −18.5 |
| Married Couple | 22,442 | 20,051 | −10.7 |
| Male Head, No Spouse Present | 17,688 | 16,952 | −4.2 |
| Female Head, No Spouse Present | 7,401 | 5,000 | −32.4 |

Source:    The Forgotten Half: Pathways to Success for America's Youth and Young Families (1988).

Taxpayers and private donors contribute more than $10,000 annually to send a student to college, the report adds, and "point with pride to the $124 billion current national investment in higher education." In contrast, "non–college-bound youth who complete high school have been saddled with the thoughtless expectation that they will readily 'find their place' and need not be of further concern to the larger society." For the most part, these young people are left to make it on their own.

This lack of postsecondary programs for the "forgotten half" also is a detriment to the U.S. economy. The key to global economic competitiveness no longer is developing new products, explains MIT economist Lester Thurow. Rather, economic superpowers today are those nations that develop better processes for producing those products. The United States has been at a disadvantage, he adds, because we do not invest enough in developing better processes, and we do not produce workers capable of handling high-tech production. Of all the industrial nations, Thurow says, the United States is the only one that does not have a postsecondary system of apprenticeships or other jobs-skills training.

The panel also argues that blaming schools for the problems of these young people is unwarranted. Even when students work hard, master basic literacy skills, and graduate in good standing, they are likely to have difficulty finding productive careers. At the root of their problem is the changing nature of our economy. Education can help, but it is not a cure-all for the effects of the major restructuring of labor markets.

In response to its analysis, the Grant Commission devotes the bulk of this report to describing four strategies, or "pathways to success," for young people.

First, it recommends that the nation enact policies to *enhance the quality of youth-adult relations*. This would include greater public support to ease the financial burden of raising children and adolescents; expanded and flexible workplace policies on child care, leave, work hours, job sharing, and other family-oriented policies; and greater community support to stengthen relationships between young people, their parents, and other adults. Young people want and need support of adults and stronger families that were commonplace in communities a generation ago.

The second strategy would *expand community supports and opportunities for service to all young people*. Schools and communities are asked to create and revitalize community-based programs that both respond to the developmental needs of youth and promote service activities. These programs should be designed to use young people's opinions and ideas as well as to involve youth in planning and implementing activities that serve them.

Third, the commission explained how the nation can *extend and improve employment and training opportunites* for the forgotten half. This recommendation calls for states and communities to develop local "compacts" or alliances of business, education, and community resources; to provide cooperative education, internships, apprenticeships, and other practical ways to ease the passage from school to work; and to explore incentives for businesses to expand employment and training opportunities.

Finally, the commission calls for *providing youth with a fair chance through education and training policies* to acquire rewarding jobs. This would be achieved by legislating a Fair Chance: Youth Opportunities Demonstration Act designed to broaden access to post–high school education and training for youth who can profit from further study.

> The Challenge before us all is seeing the forgotten half in a new light, one that recognizes their strengths, respects their diversity, and challenges their talents. Without such a vision, we run the risk of pitting one-half of our youth against the other.[29]

# Turning Points: Preparing American Youth for the 21st Century (1989)

The Report of the Task Force on Education of Young Adolescents, the Carnegie Council on Adolescent Development. Copies of this report can be obtained for $9.95 from the Carnegie Council on Adolescent Development, 11 Dupont Circle, N.W., Washington, D.C. 20036. Phone: (202) 265-9080.

> Young adolescents today make fateful choices, fateful for them and for our nation. The period of life from ages 10 to 15 represents for many young people their last best chance to choose a path toward productive and fulfilling lives.[30]

In *Turning Points,* the Carnegie Council on Adolescent Development turns its attention to restructuring the nation's middle-grade schools. For a growing number of 10- to 15-year-olds, even those from affluent communities, early adolescence is a turning point toward a diminished future. A substantial number will grow into adults who have low expectations, are alienated from other people, have little hope of joining the ranks of achievers and leaders in society, and are likely to represent a large share of the unhealthy, the addicted, the criminal, the violent, and the chronically poor.

Young adolescents face risks in today's postindustrial society that were nearly unheard of a generation or two ago. The erosion of the sense of community that once existed in urban neighborhoods and rural towns has added to the struggle young people face.

Middle-grade schools, the report explains, have been virtually ignored in the discussion of educational reform in the past decade. Schools alone, however, cannot improve the prospects of many youths; it will take a cooperative effort of schools and community agencies. The task force that prepared the report unveiled eight essential principles required to reshape education for young adolescents:

1. **Creating a community for learning.** Enormous middle-grade schools, containing as many as 2,000 students, would be restructured into smaller learning environments on a "human scale" to help teachers meet the intellectual and emotional needs of students. Teachers and students would form teams so that teachers would have the opportunity to work with students as individuals, and students could get to know each other well. Each student should have an adult advisor to whom he or she can talk about academic matters and personal problems.

2. **Teaching a core of common knowledge.** Every student would complete a curriculum that integrates subjects across disciplines, with emphasis on teaching students to learn as well as to test successfully. With this, young adolescents would learn to think critically, develop healthful life-styles, and become active citizens.

3. **Ensuring success for all students.** In addition to ensuring that all students successfully complete a core instructional program, middle-grade schools would offer each student the opportunity to gain confidence and personal satisfaction from excelling in some aspect of the total school curriculum. For many young people mastering the core academic program will provide this opportunity. For others the chance to achieve excellence may lie in music, athletics, drama, or outside the schoolhouse through youth service or other community-based activities.

4. **Empowering teachers and administrators.** Teachers would have greater authority to make decisions and would be responsible for the consequences of those decisions. Each middle school would establish a governing committee that would include students.

5. **Preparing teachers for the middle grades.** Teachers in the middle-grade schools must be particularly suited for working with young adolescents, and prospective teachers would receive special training and certification for this age level. In particular, teachers would learn to work as members of teams and share their expertise with others on the team.

6. **Improving academic performance through health and fitness.** Middle-grade schools must provide sufficient services for mental and physical health. Schools should be able to identify health problems and provide treatment or referral to outside agencies.

7. **Involving parents in the student's education.** Families and schools must become active allies in the education of young adolescents. Parents would play meaningful roles in school governance, be kept informed on school operations, and be encouraged to support the instruction offered.

8. **Creating partners with communities.** Schools would build bridges to community organizations and businesses. This includes placing students in youth services, working with organizations that can augment the school curriculum, and ensuring student access to social services.[31]

## National Goals for Education (1990)

A Report from an Education Summit held by the White House and the National Governors Association, September 1989, in Charlottesville, Virginia.

> All of our people, not just a few, must be able to use their minds well, to think for a living, and to understand the world around them. They will need to communicate complex ideas, analyze and solve problems, and think and reason abstractly. They will need a deep understanding of a wide range of subjects in order to bring appropriate knowledge and judgment to situations they confront.[32]

At the Education Summit in September 1989, the President and the governors declared that the time had come to establish clear national performance goals that will make the United States internationally competitive. U.S. educational performance, the political leaders said, must be second to none in the twenty-first century. Education is at the heart of our economic strength and security, our creativity in the arts and letters, our invention in the sciences, and the perpetuation of our cultural values. White House officials remarked, "Education is the key to America's international competitiveness."

To this end, the White House and the governors established six national goals to be accomplished during this final decade of the twentieth century. By the year 2000, they declared,

**Goal 1. All children in the United States of America will start school ready to learn.** All disadvantaged and disabled children will have access to high-quality preschool programs; every parent will devote time each day to help his or her preschool child learn; and children will receive the nutrition and health care needed to arrive at school with healthy minds and bodies.

**Goal 2. The high school graduation rate will increase to at least 90 percent.** The nation must dramatically reduce its dropout rate, and the gap in graduation rates between minority and nonminority students will be eliminated.

**Goal 3. American students will leave grades four, eight, and twelve having demonstrated competency over a challenging curriculum that will enable them to be responsible citizens and compete in the twenty-first century.** The academic performance of elementary and secondary students will increase significantly, and the achievement of minority students will more closely reflect the student population as a whole. Students' ability to reason, solve problems, write, and communicate effectively will increase substantially. All students will engage in community service and citizenship activities; more students will become competent in a second language; and all students will be knowledgeable about the diverse cultural heritage of this nation and about the world community.

**Goal 4. U.S. students will be first in the world in science and mathematics achievement.** Mathematics and science education will be strengthened throughout the grades; the number of qualified math and science teachers will increase by 50 percent; and the number of college students completing degrees in mathematics, science, and engineering will increase significantly.

**Goal 5. Every adult American will be literate and will possess the knowledge and skills necessary to compete in a global economy and exercise the rights and responsi-**

**bilities of citizenship.** All workers will have the opportunity to acquire the knowledge and skills needed for positions in our increasingly technological workplace; the number of training programs for part-time and mid-career students will increase substantially; and the proportion of qualified students who complete degree programs and can demonstrate an advanced ability to think critically and communicate effectively will increase substantially.

**Goal 6. Every school in the United States will be free of drugs and violence and will offer a disciplined environment conducive to learning.** Every school will implement an effective drug and alcohol policy. Parents, businesses, and community organizations will work to ensure that schools are safe for all children, and every school district will develop a comprehensive drug and alcohol prevention-education program for grades one through twelve.

The report ends with recommendations to restructure education within both the schools and the communities. To start, federal and state governments should cooperate to provide programs that will help parents play a constructive role in the early education of their children and that provide for preschool learning. Next, the public school system must be fundamentally restructured to ensure that all students are engaged in rigorous programs of instruction that meet higher standards. Then, in the after-school years, our multilayered system of vocational and technical schools, community colleges, and specific training programs must be restructured to give all adults access to flexible and comprehensive programs that meet their needs and lead to productive positions in our economic society.

In April 1991 the Bush Administration followed with *America 2000: An Educational Strategy,* its plan to achieve the six national goals. The plan is built on four strategies:

1. To improve existing schools through new accountability measures. This will include developing New World Standards and a nationwide examination system for each of five core subjects.
2. To create a "new generation of schools." Research and development teams, funded by a new nonprofit development corporation, will help communities across the land design one of the first of the more than 535 New American Schools.

3. To foster continuing education for adults already in the work-force. Business and labor are asked to help government establish job-related skill standards, and adult Americans are encouraged to "go back to school" to learn more family, job, and citizenship skills.
4. To challenge Americans to cultivate communities where children can learn. The President is "challenging every city, town, and neighborhood in the nation to become an America 2000 Community" by adopting the six national goals, drafting a strategy to reach the goals, developing a report card to measure its progress, and demonstrating a readiness to support an experimental school.

## Study of the Education of Educators (1990)

A study on teacher education conducted by the Center for Education Renewal, University of Washington, Seattle, John I. Goodlad, director.

> As my colleagues and I delved into the shamefully neglected past and present of the business of seeing to it that the nation's classrooms are staffed with sensitive, well-prepared teachers, anger rose within us. We needed no carefully crafted statements of belief regarding what is right and just to stir our passions either: persistent patterns arising out of the data were sufficient. The history of teacher education—whether we examine the long-standing indifference of the larger society or that of all those individuals who should be making it work—is a sorry one for which we should all be ashamed. As James Conant was heard to say during a discussion with his research team about the neglect on both these fronts: "A plague on both their houses."[33]

Central to the message of this study is the conclusion that teacher education and schooling go hand-in-hand. If we expect reform to occur in one arena, it also must take place in the other. This connection has been conspicuously overlooked in reform efforts past and present.

Goodlad and his colleagues propose that schooling and teacher education be productively linked through a cluster of "reasonable expectations" for those who are to be stewards of schooling in a democratic society.

First, teachers must understand the central importance of citizenship to a constitutional government and possess a "foundation knowledge about the nation's government and its expectations for citizens." Second, teachers must have the "intellectual tools to participate broadly in the human conversation and to introduce young people to it." Third, "teachers must possess the pedagogical knowledge and skills

necessary to arrange optimal conditions for educating the young."
Fourth, "teachers must thoroughly understand the commonplaces of
schooling (goals, clients, organization, curriculum, instruction, and
evaluation), promising alternatives, the nature of healthy schools,
and how to sustain renewal."[34]

These expectations underscore the moral nature of teaching, working with all students, and bringing about change in schools.

During the study, Goodlad and his colleagues developed conditions they deemed necessary to realize the overarching expectations.
They arrived at 19 "essential suppositions" or "postulates" to guide
their investigation and shape their evaluation of it. These postulates
offer specific, though not unfamiliar, goals to help institutions reformu-
late teacher-education programs. Ultimately, the aim of effective programs, beyond nurturing competence in the classroom, is to impart in
teachers a sense of moral commitment and vision that they can take to
teaching and renewing schools.

Teacher-education programs in colleges and universities, the
researchers found, suffer from debilitating conditions including
low prestige and low status, unclear mission and identity, ambiguity
toward teaching, and an ill-defined student body. These shortcomings prohibit these programs from pursuing this set of expectations
and sustaining "vigorous, coherent, and self-renewing programs of
teacher education."

At the heart of the recommendations from this study is the creation
of a "center of pedagogy," devoted exclusively to the preparation of
educators for the schools and to the advancement of pedagogy. These
proposed centers, Goodlad points out, are not necessarily "coterminous
with schools of education." Institutions of higher education might form
the centers in a variety of ways. Whatever the arrangement, the centers
should have a clearly defined mission, faculty, student body, and curriculum. Likewise, centers are encouraged to develop strong, collabora-
tive relations with schools to provide an infrastructure in which these
partners can serve as professional development schools.[35]

## America's Choice: High Skills or Low Wages! (1990)

A report prepared by the National Center on Education and the
Economy's Commission on the Skills of the American Workforce,
Chair, Ira C. Magaziner, President, SJS, Inc. Copies of the report
can be obtained for $18.00 each ($15.00 for 10 or more) from the
National Center on Education and the Economy, P.O. Box 10670,
Rochester, New York 14610.

> More than any other country in the world, the United States believes that natural ability, rather than effort, explains achievement. The tragedy is that we communicate to millions of students every year, especially low-income and minority students, that we do not believe that they have what it takes to learn. They then live up to our expectations, despite the evidence that they can meet very high performance standards under the right conditions.[36]

Since 1973, the productivity of the U.S. work force has increased by a dismal 1 percent each year. From 1960 to 1973, U.S. productivity averaged nearly three times this rate or 2.9 percent annually. For much of the twentieth century, U.S. economic expansion lead the world. As a result the United States became a premier industrial power. Over the past two decades, however, this position has been eroding.

Today, Japan's annual productivity rate is over 3 percent, and several other nations are not far behind. Even Great Britain, whose economic vitality slipped sharply this century, increases its productivity about 2 percent each year. From year to year such differences appear insignificant, but translated over several decades, the results can be astounding. The bottom line is that if this trend continues, the United States will soon become a second-rate economic power, explains economist Alan Blinder. The consequences of this transformation—to business, families, and today's children—are grim.

*America's Choice: High Skills or Low Wages!* examines the reasons behind sagging productivity and economic growth, then offers five recommendations for reversing this trend.

1. The commission recommends establishing a **new educational performance standard to be met by all 16-year-olds.** This standard would be "established nationally and benchmarked to the highest in the world." Students passing the series of performance-based assessments would be awarded a Certificate of Initial Mastery. Possession of this certificate would qualify the student to choose among going to work, entering a college preparatory program, or studying for a Technical and Professional Certificate.
2. The states should assure that virtually all students achieve the Certificate of Initial Mastery. Through new Local Employment and Training Boards, states, with federal assistance, would establish **alternative learning environments, or Youth Centers, to help dropouts reach the mastery standard.** Once the Youth Centers are created, young people should not be permitted to work before the age of 18.

3. **A comprehensive system of Technical and Professional Certificates and associate's degrees should be created** for the majority of students and adult workers who do not pursue a baccalaureate degree. In these two- to four-year work and study programs, students who do not go on to college can master complex skills for the workplace.

4. All employers would be given **incentives and assistance to invest in the further education and training of their workers** and to develop more productive ways of organizing the workplace. The Commission proposes that all employers invest at least 1 percent of their payroll in this employee development.

5. A system of **Employment and Training Boards would be established** by Federal and state governments, together with local leadership, to organize and oversee the new school-to-work transition and training systems. The function of these boards would include managing the Youth Centers and a labor market information system while administering the Certificate of Initial Mastery and Technical and Professional Certificates awards.

"America," the commissioners point out, "may have the worst school-to-work transition system of any advanced industrial country. Students who know few adults to help get their first job are left to sink or swim."[37]

During the 1980s, the United States enjoyed one of its longest economic expansions in history. As the authors of this report explain, the expansion has been built largely on a rapidly growing workforce, fed by the baby boom reaching working age and more women joining the work force. Work force growth, however, will slow dramatically during the 1990s as our economy is no longer buoyed by adding new workers. America's economic growth and standard of living in the future will have to be driven by a substantial improvement in work force skills and productivity.

Americans are unwittingly making a choice. It is a choice that most of us would probably not make were we aware of its consequences. Yet every day, that choice is becoming more difficult to reverse. It is a choice that undermines the American dream of economic opportunity for all. It is a choice that will lead to an America where 30 percent of our people may do well—at least for awhile—but the other 70 percent will see their dreams slip away.[38]

# Summary

One theme that appears in many of the reports on school reform during the past decade is that schools once again need to reestablish a core curriculum as their central purpose. To do so requires shedding some of the nonessential vocational, social, and extracurricular programs and services they have somewhat imperceptibly but inexorably acquired over the past few decades.

"If there is a crisis in education," concludes Lawrence Cremin, "it is not the crisis of putative mediocrity and decline charged by recent reports but rather the crisis inherent in balancing this tremendous variety of demands Americans have made on their schools."[39]

### Notes

1. Lys d'Aimee, "The Menace of Present Educational Methods," *Gunton's Magazine* no. 19 (September 1900): 236.

2. Lawrence A. Cremin, *Popular Education and Its Discontents* (New York: Harper & Row, 1990), 14–15.

3. David K. Cohen and Michael S. Garet, "Reforming Educational Policy with Applied Social Research," *Harvard Educational Review* 45 (February 1975): 21.

4. James Bryant Conant, *Education and Liberty: The Role of Schools in Modern Democracy* (Cambridge, MA: Harvard University Press, 1953), 57–58.

5. Cremin, *Popular Education and Its Discontents*, 22–25.

6. Panel on Youth of the President's Science Advisory Committee, *Youth: Transition to Adulthood* (Washington, D.C.: Government Printing Office, 1973); National Commission on the Reform of Secondary Education, *The Reform of Secondary Education: A Report to the Public and the Profession* (New York: McGraw-Hill, 1973); and National Panel on High School and Adolescent Education, *The Education of Adolescents* (Washington, D.C.: U.S. Office of Education, 1974).

7. Cremin, *Popular Education and Its Discontents*, 7.

8. Mortimer J. Adler, *The Paideia Proposal: An Educational Manifesto* (New York: Macmillan, 1982), 7.

9. Ibid., 3.

10. Ibid., 10.

11. National Commission on Excellence in Education, *A Nation at Risk: The Imperative for Educational Reform* (Washington, D.C.: U.S. Government Printing Office, 1983), 5.

12. Ibid., 23–33.

13. Ernest L. Boyer, The Carnegie Foundation for the Advancement of Teaching, *High School: A Report on Secondary Education in America* (New York: Harper & Row, 1983), 6.

14. Ibid., 66–67.

15. Ibid., 85–93, 94–117, 202–215.

16. John I. Goodlad, *A Place Called School: Prospects for the Future* (New York: McGraw-Hill, 1984), 1.

17. Ibid., 33–35.

18. Ibid., 46–60.

19. The Carnegie Task Force on Teaching as a Profession, *A Nation Prepared: Teachers for the 21st Century* (New York: Carnegie Forum on Education and the Economy, 1986), 11.

20. William J. Bennett, *James Madison High School: A Curriculum for American Studies* (Washington, D.C.: U.S. Department of Education, 1987), 7.

21. Ibid., 2–8.

22. Diane Ravitch and Chester E. Finn, Jr., *What Do Our 17-Year-Olds Know? A Report on the First National Assessment of History and Literature* (New York: Harper & Row, 1987), 6.

23. Ibid., 200–247.

24. Theodore R. Sizer, *Horace's Compromise: The Dilemma of the American High School* (Boston: Houghton Mifflin, 1985), 82–83.

25. Theodore R. Sizer, "Diverse Practice, Shared Ideas: The Essential School," in *Organizing for Learning: Toward the 21st Century* (Reston, VA: The National Association of Secondary School Principals, 1989), 1.

26. The William T. Grant Foundation Commission on Work, Family and Citizenship, *The Forgotten Half: Pathways to Success for America's Youth and Young Families* (Washington, D.C.: Youth and America's Future, The William T. Grant Foundation Commission on Work, Family and Citizenship, 1988), 3.

27. Ibid., 2.

28. Ibid., 16.

29. Ibid., 10.

30. *Turning Points: Preparing American Youth for the 21st Century* (Washington, D.C.: Carnegie Council on Adolescent Development, 1989), 20.

31. Ibid., 36–70.

32. From the text of the goals statement adopted by the National Governors Association, Washington, D.C., February 1990.

33. John I. Goodlad, "Better Teachers for Our Nation's Schools," *Phi Delta Kappan* 72, no. 3 (November 1990): 190–191.

34. Ibid., 185–186.

35. Ibid., 192–193.

36. *America's Choice: High Skills or Low Wages* (Rochester: NY: National Center on Education and Economy), 3–4.

37. Ibid., 4.

38. Ibid., 5.

39. Cremin, *Popular Education and Its Discontents*, 43.

# 6

## Facts and Data

THE LIST OF SCHOOL DISCIPLINE PROBLEMS in the 1950s was headed by such behaviors such as talking, chewing gum, making noise, and running in hallways. By the 1980s the nature of student problems had changed dramatically: Drug and alcohol abuse, pregnancy, suicide, rape, robbery, and assault are commonplace today in many schools.

Americans over the decades have taken a concerned interest in the problems and progress of their schools, particularly as secondary school enrollments have increased. In recent years, however, the nation's concern with public education issues has intensified. These issues include declining test scores, unqualified and discontented teachers, less demanding curricula, and insufficient operating funds, in addition to disruptive student behavior. Although studies and reports on schools have a rich history in the United States, the decade of the 1980s witnessed an unprecedented involvement of foundations, businesses, and government at all levels in education. The result has been the most serious commitment to reform since the transformation of American schools at the turn of the century.

Many of the issues and problems of our schools are illustrated in this chapter through a series of figures. These indicators are presented in six sections: school population, behavioral problems, student achievement, school curriculum, the teaching profession, and financial support.[1]

# School Population

Elementary school enrollment, as Figure 6-1 shows, declined sharply during the 1970s, then leveled out in the early 1980s. In 1986 enrollment in the nation's public elementary schools turned up, a trend that promises to continue into the 1990s. Public high school enrollments rose in the early to mid-1970s, then began to decline. This fall should continue until 1991; then, following the lead of elementary school enrollments, the number will rise for the remainder of the decade. (See Figure 6-2.)

Despite fluctuations in overall school enrollment, the number of minority students enrolled in public schools steadily increases (Figure 6-3). Hispanic enrollment grew from 2.8 million in 1976 to more than 4 million ten years later, up 44 percent. And these figures will continue to climb (Figure 6-4). Over the same period, Asian-American enrollment more than doubled from 535,000 to more than 1,000,000. The percentage of white enrollment, in turn, decreased. In the mid-1970s, white students accounted for 76 percent of public school enrollment; by 1986 this figure was down to 70 percent, and declining.

The Education for All Handicapped Children Act of 1975 has led to an increase in the number of special-education students since it was implemented on September 1, 1978 (Figure 6-5). From 1976 to 1988, the number of special-education students rose from 3.7 million to 4.4 million, or from 8 to 11 percent of total public school enrollment. This happened primarily because of the growing number of students classified as learning-disabled. During this same period, the number of students classified as mentally retarded declined.

# Behavioral Problems

The Gallup Organization's poll of the public's attitude toward public schools each year asks people to identify the biggest problems their schools face. "Lack of discipline" consistently headed this list until 1986 when "use of drugs" took over the top spot. Every year since then more people have mentioned the drug problem, and discipline has slid deeper into second place (Figure 6-6).

Somewhat paradoxically, when public schoolteachers were surveyed by the U.S. Department of Education in 1987, they said there was more disruptive behavior in schools than five years earlier. As Figure 6-7 illustrates, 19 percent of the teachers surveyed indicated that their schools are "much more" disruptive, and another 25 percent said "somewhat more" disruptive. In fact, teachers depart sharply from the public in their view of the schools' most serious problems (Figure 6-8).

In turn, studies by the National Institute on Drug Abuse show that high school seniors' use of alcohol and other, illegal drugs actually decreased during the 1980s (Figure 6-9). For example, the share of students who had used cocaine in the past year declined from its high of 13 percent in 1985 to 8 percent three years later. Still, high schools students' consumption of sedatives, hallucinogens, and stimulants is widespread. By the time they are seniors, more than one-half of the students will have tried an illicit drug.

As Stanley Elam remarked in *Phi Delta Kappan,* educators can perhaps take some comfort in the Gallup finding that people blame society for the problems confronting the nation's schools (Figure 6-10). Even families whose children do not attend public school say its problems are embedded in the fabric of society.

# School Performance and Student Achievement

In an attempt to find out if people believe that the current wave of school reform is succeeding, Gallup interviewers asked whether or not schools were improving. The results are not encouraging (Figure 6-11). In 1988, 29 percent of the sample said the schools were indeed improving; two years later only 22 percent were as optimistic.

When asked to grade the schools, however, 41 percent of those interviewed in 1990 would give the public schools in their community an A or a B. This is 6 percentage points higher than ten years earlier and 10 points higher than in 1983, just after *A Nation at Risk* was released by the National Commission on Excellence in Education.

The grade given local schools by those closest to them, parents of children currently attending, is striking and even more encouraging: 72 percent say the school their child attends deserves an A or a B. Nevertheless, when people were asked to rate the nation's schools as a whole, they apparently demonstrated the strong influence of the mass media. Only 21 percent thought our public schools deserved an A or a B, and nearly one-half gave them a mediocre C. (See Figure 6-12.)

Turning to specific indicators of student achievement, the average reading proficiency is lower for black and Hispanic students than for white students across grade levels (Figure 6-13). Students at all grade levels, however, had difficulty elaborating on basic understandings and trying to defend their judgments and interpretations of what they had read.

Over the past 20 years, mathematics competency has remained relatively stable. As Figure 6-14 reveals, the proficiency of 17-year-olds has increased slightly since 1982, while 9- and 13-year-olds improved between 1978 and 1986. Even with these gains, barely one-half of the nation's high school seniors are capable of performing moderately complex mathematical procedures.

Students' science understanding is less promising. While American students show slight overall gains in recent years, their proficiency in science has slipped since the 1970s (Figure 6-15). In comparisons with students in five other countries, the showing of American students is dismal. U.S. students scored in the lowest group in mathematics proficiency and performed well below the mean in science. (See Figure 6-16.)

Finally, school dropouts have emerged as a major issue in recent years, despite indicators that the proportion of students completing high school has increased. Nationally, nearly one out of every four 18- and 19-year-olds has not graduated, but many in this group complete their high school education in their early twenties. As Figure 6-17 also shows, blacks ages 20–24 are now almost as likely as whites to have completed high school.

Throughout the twentieth century, the percentage and total number of students dropping out of school have steadily declined. Although this downward trend has flattened somewhat since the advent of "universal secondary schooling," dropout rates continue to decrease (Figure 6-18). According to the William T. Grant Foundation's report on *Youth and America's Future*, the high school dropout rate was reduced from 18 percent in 1973 to 15 percent a decade later. This improvement was due almost entirely to young black men staying in school.

As Albert Shanker points out, the underlying problem is that a generation or more ago when kids dropped out of school they had somewhere to "drop in"—namely, jobs and community activities. Aside from unskilled work in fast-food restaurants, supermarkets, and retail malls, there are few places in our economic society for the young person who has not completed high school. And as the Grant Foundation's report found, the employment situation is not much better for those high school graduates not going on to college.[2] In addition to this holding function, business leaders see that the work force of tomorrow will need more training and advanced skills than in the past. And these workers will come increasingly from minority groups.

# School Curriculum

When *Phi Delta Kappan* and the Gallup Organization polled the public during the past decade on what subjects high school students should be required to take, the picture was clear. For those students going on to college, five subjects stood out as the core: mathematics, English, history/U.S. government, science, and computer training. More than half of those responding also would require geography, career education, business education, foreign language, and health education. As Figure 6-19 also reveals, people believe that science and foreign languages are not as important for noncollege-bound students. Vocational training would replace science as a core course in their curriculum.

Beyond offering the core academic program, people want their public schools to do much more, as Figure 6-20 shows. More than one-half of those polled would require schools to teach about drug abuse, alcohol abuse, AIDS, sex, driving, character education, environmental issues, and teen pregnancy. It appears that if the school curriculum were subject to a vote, education on drugs, alcohol, and AIDS would be among core requirements. As the figures for drug- and alcohol-abuse education during the past decade suggest, these demands on schools are increasing.

In *A Nation at Risk* (1983), the National Commission on Excellence in Education recommended that high schools require all students to take the "new basics:" four credits in English; three each in science, social studies, and mathematics; two in foreign languages; and one semester in computer science. Figure 6-21 illustrates progress in the proportion of students taking the "new basics" during the five-year period from 1982 to 1987.[3] While the increases for all ethnic groups are substantial, most students still do not meet the recommendations of this basic curriculum. Note that Asian-American students as a group far outdistance their fellow students.

Some states have responded to the push for educational excellence during the past decade by increasing the course credits in the "new basics" required for graduation. Still, as Figure 6-22 shows, many have not set requirements that meet the commission's standards. While the picture in English is relatively bright (two-thirds of states require the recommended four credits), the other core subjects lag, particularly mathematics and science. Most states require just two credits in each subject, one short of that recommended. These figures, however, understate the actual requirements for individual schools and students. Many states, particularly those in the Northeast and the Midwest, let local school districts set the standards for their schools.

# The Teaching Profession

Public opinion toward teachers' pay is ambivalent. On one hand, as Figure 6-23 shows, 50 percent of the public feels that salaries are too low, and only 5 percent say they are too high. This sentiment for greater teacher compensation in 1990 is at an all-time high and nearly twice as strong as in 1981. A majority also say that higher salaries will improve the quality of schooling (51 percent), as will better working conditions (62 percent). Still, teachers frequently hear that their pay is appropriate for their nine- or ten-month contracts and 180-day school year.

These Gallup findings are intriguing in light of reality. Teachers' salaries, in constant (inflation-adjusted) dollars, steadily rose during the 1980s—a period during which the public felt they deserved more money (Figure 6-24). In 1981, the average annual salary for all teachers was $23,595, in constant 1987–1988 dollars. By 1988, the average salary was up to $28,044 and rising.[4] In contrast, teachers' salaries had declined during much of the 1970s: In 1973 teachers were earning $27,532 (in 1987–1988 dollars); by 1980, this figure had dipped to $23,595. It may be that public perceptions of the educational environment are about a decade behind social reality.

In other ways, the teacher's lot has improved in recent years. As seen in Figure 6-25, class sizes in both elementary and secondary schools have been declining. A generation ago in 1959–1960, the pupil/teacher ratio was 26 students (28.7 in elementary school and 21.5 in secondary school) per teacher. In 1987–1988, this ratio was down to 17.6 (19.5 and 15 3 for elementary and secondary classrooms, respectively).

No doubt, much of the decline in class size can be attributed to the substantial increase in resources devoted to the learning disabled student during the 1980s. In a recent study, the Sandia National Laboratories found that most of the increase in public school spending over the past 20 years has been for special education.[5]

# Financial Support

School districts in the United States seldom seem to have enough money to build needed facilities, repair those built a generation or more ago, offer teachers opportunities for professional growth, and fund their many programs. School finance is a modern American paradox: While most schools are frugal and efficient, and revenues are increasing, schooling remains underfunded. Still, the hearts, and the pocketbooks, of most Americans appear to be in sympathy with school costs.

As Figure 6-26 shows, nearly two-thirds (64 percent) of those polled by Gallup would be "willing to pay more taxes to help raise the standards of education in the United States." In fact, Americans have been spending more to educate the young in schools (Figure 6-27). Between 1950 and 1987 expenditures per pupil in constant dollars almost quadrupled, from $982 to $3,977.

Furthermore, when public school revenue per pupil is considered in relationship to per capita income (citizens' ability to pay), Americans have been loosening their purse strings. This national index, shown in Figure 6-28, has risen 64 percent since 1940. In that year the index stood at 16.5, and by 1987 it had risen to 27.3.[6] Note that both expenditures per pupil and the national index suffered in the 1981 and 1982 school years, a recessionary period. The index then fell one point, but has risen two points since 1982. Yet, as a percentage of gross national product (GNP), funds for public schools are lower today than in 1970 (Figure 6-29).

Finally, as Figure 6-30 shows, the cost of public schooling is being assumed more and more by state governments. As courts and legislatures continue to address the inequality of revenue among school districts, the state's role in school finance also will likely grow. In the past 20 years, the state share of total school revenue rose from about 40 percent to roughly 50 percent, while the local share decreased from about 52 percent to about 44 percent. During this period, the federal government's share of expenditures for the nation's public elementary and secondary schools also declined from approximately 8 percent to about 6 percent. Most of this decline occurred during the 1980s.

It is no mystery why spending for schooling in the United States, however viewed and measured, has increased over the years. Throughout the twentieth century, and particularly during the first 50 to 60 years, more and more of the nation's children attended school for more years. Then, during the past 30 years, schools have taken on increasingly more of society's educative chores. In the words of economists, education has been a growth industry.

## Notes

1. Many of the facts, statistics, and other data cited in this chapter have been gathered by the National Center for Educational Statistics (NCES). The center publishes the information it collects and analyzes in several volumes. Indicators of trends and developments are contained in *The Conditions of Education* (two volumes—one address-

ing elementary and secondary schooling and the other postsecondary schooling) and *1989 Education Indicators*. Each volume includes a series of illustrative tables and charts. By contrast, the *Digest of Education Statistics* contains a large number of detailed statistical tables, plus figures and appendices. The sources, both of which are updated and published annually, complement each other and contain a wealth of data on the schooling environment.

2. See the discussion in Chapter 5 on *The Forgotten Half: Pathways to Success for America's Youth and Young Families,* prepared by the William T. Grant Foundation on Work, Family and Citizenship.

3. The "new basics" in Figure 6–19 include those credits recommended in mathematics, English, science, and social studies by the National Commission on Excellence in Education.

4. Historically, elementary schoolteachers' yearly salaries have lagged behind their secondary school counterparts by at least $1,000. In 1988, for example, secondary teachers averaged $28,895, while elementary teachers averaged $27,423.

5. C. C. Carson, R. M. Huelskamp, and T. D. Woodall, *Perspectives on Education in America,* an unpublished paper (Albuquerque, NM: Sandia National Laboratories, Systems Analysis Department, May 10, 1991), p. 4.

6. The national index is a refinement on using the percent of gross national product (GNP) devoted to schooling as an indicator of fiscal effort. Four factors make up the index: number of pupils enrolled in public schools, public school revenues, total personal income, and total population.

# Figures

FIGURE 6-1    Trends in School Enrollment: 1970–1986

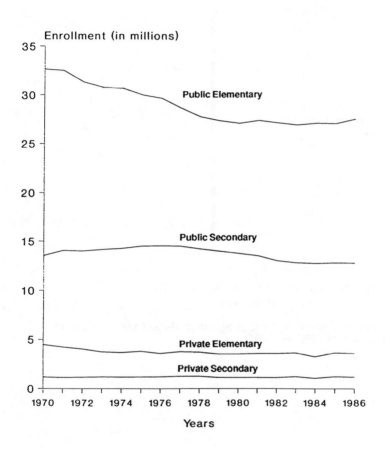

Source:    U. S. Department of Commerce, Bureau of the Census. Current
           Population Reports.

FIGURE 6-2   Projected Trends in Public School Enrollment to 1997

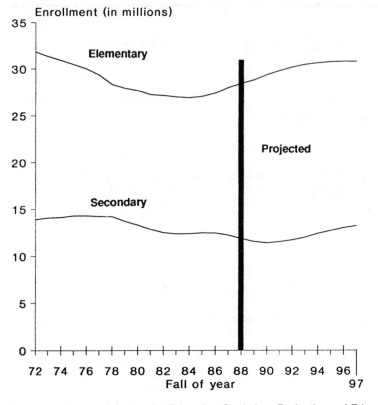

Enrollment (in millions)

Fall of year

Source:   National Center for Education Statistics. *Projections of Education Statistics to 1997–98.* 1988.

FIGURE 6-3    Enrollment in Public Elementary and Secondary
Schools, by Race and Ethnicity: Fall 1976, 1984,
1986

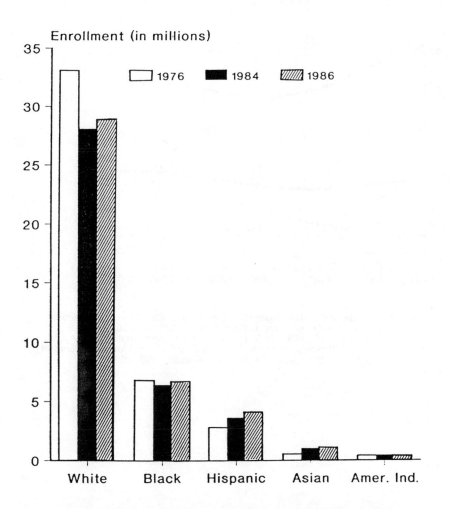

Sources:    U.S. Department of Education, Office for Civil Rights. *Directory
of Elementary and Secondary School Districts and Schools in
Selected Districts: 1976–77,* as well as 1984 and 1986 Elementary
and Secondary School Civil Rights Survey.

FIGURE 6-4    Population Projection for Youth: Ages 15–24

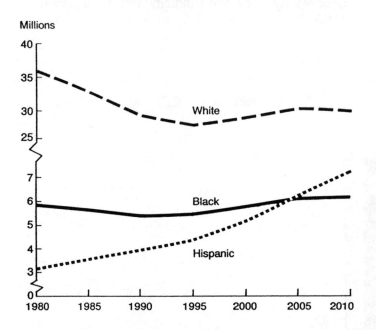

Sources:    U.S. Department of Commerce, Bureau of the Census. *Projections of the Population of the United States: 1988 to 2080,* Series P-25, Number 1018. 1989. U.S. Department of Commerce, Bureau of the Census. *Projections of the Spanish Origin Population of the United States: 1983 to 2080,* Series P-25, Number 995. 1986.

FIGURE 6-5     Special-Education Enrollment in Federally Supported
Programs

**Percent of learning disabled, speech impaired,
and mentally retarded as a percent of the
total number served by the Education for All
Handicapped Children Act: 1977–1988**

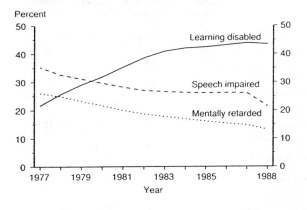

**Percent of total enrollment enrolled in federally
supported programs for the handicapped:
1977–1988**

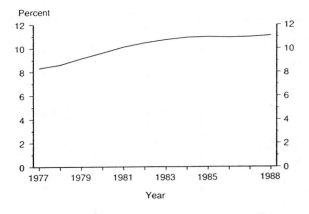

Source:     U.S. Department of Education, Office of Special Education and
Rehabilitative Services. *Annual Report to Congress on the
Implementation of the Handicapped Act.* Various years.

FIGURE 6-6    Biggest Problems Facing Local Public Schools

**What do you think are the biggest problems with which the public schools in this community must deal?**

|  | National Totals % | No Children In School % | Public School Parents % | Nonpublic School Parents % |
|---|---|---|---|---|
| Use of drugs | 38 | 40 | 34 | 39 |
| Lack of discipline | 19 | 19 | 17 | 25 |
| Lack of proper financial support | 13 | 18 | 17 | 21 |
| Poor curriculum/poor standards | 8 | 9 | 7 | 6 |
| Large schools/ overcrowding | 7 | 6 | 10 | 16 |
| Difficulty getting good teachers | 7 | 6 | 10 | 10 |
| Pupils' lack of interest/ truancy | 6 | 7 | 3 | 3 |
| Low teacher pay | 6 | 5 | 6 | 8 |
| Crime/vandalism | 5 | 7 | 4 | 1 |
| Integration/busing | 5 | 5 | 4 | 6 |
| Parents' lack of interest | 4 | 5 | 3 | 3 |
| Drinking/alcoholism | 4 | 4 | 4 | 3 |
| Teachers' lack of interest | 4 | 3 | 5 | 5 |
| Moral standards | 3 | 4 | 2 | 1 |
| Lack of respect for teachers/other students | 3 | 3 | 3 | 4 |
| Lack of needed teachers | 3 | 3 | 3 | 1 |
| Lack of family structure | 3 | 3 | 3 | 2 |
| Lack of proper facilities | 2 | 1 | 2 | 4 |
| Parents' involvement in school activities | 2 | 2 | 2 | 2 |
| Mismanagement of funds/ programs | 2 | 1 | 2 | 1 |
| Problems with administration | 2 | 2 | 3 | 3 |
| Communication problems | 2 | 2 | 2 | 2 |
| Fighting | 2 | 2 | 2 | * |
| Lack of after-school programs | 1 | 1 | 2 | 2 |
| Transportation | 1 | 1 | 1 | 2 |
| Taxes are too high | 1 | 1 | 1 | 1 |
| Too much emphasis on sports | 1 | 1 | 1 | * |
| School board politics | 1 | 1 | 2 | * |
| Non-English-speaking students | 1 | 1 | * | * |
| Peer pressure | 1 | 1 | * | * |
| There are no problems | 1 | 1 | 2 | 3 |
| Miscellaneous | 5 | 4 | 6 | 6 |
| Don't know | 6 | 7 | 2 | 5 |

*Less than one-half of 1%.
(Figures add to more than 100% because of multiple answers.)

Source:    Elam, Stanley M. "The 22nd Annual Gallup Poll of the Public's Attitudes toward the Public Schools." *Phi Delta Kappan* (September 1990).

FIGURE 6-7    Changes in Disruptive Behavior as Reported by
Teachers: School Year Ending 1987

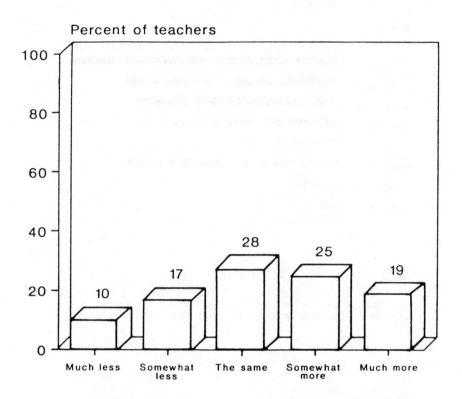

Percent of teachers

Source:    National Center for Education Statistics. "Public School Teacher
Perspectives on School Discipline." *OREI Bulletin,* 1987.

FIGURE 6-8    Problems in the Schools Considered Most Serious
by Teachers and the U.S. Public: 1988–1989

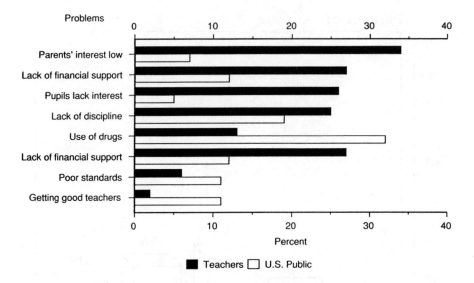

Source:    "The Second Gallup/Phi Delta Kappan Poll of Teachers' Attitudes
toward the Public Schools." *Phi Delta Kappan* (June 1989).

FIGURE 6-9    Student Drug and Alcohol Use: 1975–1989

Percent of high school seniors who have
ever used illegal drugs, cocaine, or alcohol

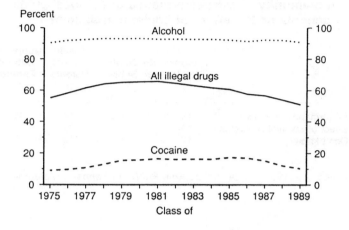

Percent of high school seniors who have used
illegal drugs, cocaine, or alcohol within the past
30 days

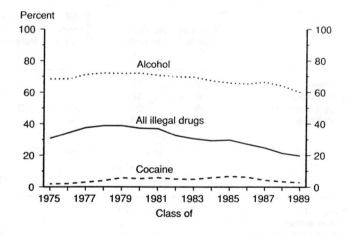

Source:    U.S. Department of Health and Human Services, Alcohol, Drug Abuse,
and Mental Health Administration, National Institute on Drug Abuse.
*Drug Use among American High School Students, College Students,
and Other Young Adults.* 1989.

FIGURE 6-10  Who's To Blame: Schools or Society

**In your opinion, which is more at fault for the problems currently facing public education in this community — the performance of the local public schools or the effect of societal problems?**

|  | National Totals % | No Children In School % | Public School Parents % | Nonpublic School Parents % |
|---|---|---|---|---|
| Performance of schools | 16 | 14 | 18 | 26 |
| Effect of societal problems | 73 | 73 | 75 | 63 |
| Don't know | 11 | 13 | 7 | 11 |

Source:    1990 Annual Gallup Poll. *Phi Delta Kappan* (September 1990).

FIGURE 6-11  Have Schools Improved?

**Would you say that the public schools in this community have improved from, say, five years ago, gotten worse, or stayed about the same?**

|  | National Totals % | No Children In School % | Public School Parents % | Nonpublic School Parents % |
|---|---|---|---|---|
| Improved | 22 | 20 | 29 | 18 |
| Gotten worse | 30 | 30 | 27 | 37 |
| Stayed about the same | 36 | 36 | 36 | 39 |
| Don't know | 12 | 14 | 8 | 6 |

|  | National Totals | |
|---|---|---|
|  | 1990 % | 1988 % |
| Improved | 22 | 29 |
| Gotten worse | 30 | 19 |
| Stayed about the same | 36 | 37 |
| Don't know | 12 | 15 |

Source:    The 1990 Annual Gallup Poll. *Phi Delta Kappan* (September 1990).

FIGURE 6-12 Rating the Public Schools

What grade would you give the public schools in your community?

| | National Totals % | No Children In School % | Public School Parents % | Nonpublic School Parents % |
|---|---|---|---|---|
| A & B | 41 | 39 | 48 | 32 |
| A | 8 | 7 | 12 | 6 |
| B | 33 | 32 | 36 | 26 |
| C | 34 | 34 | 36 | 37 |
| D | 12 | 12 | 9 | 18 |
| FAIL | 5 | 5 | 4 | 6 |
| Don't know | 8 | 10 | 3 | 7 |

Using the A, B, C, D, and FAIL scale again, what grade would you give the school your oldest child attends?

| | National Totals % | No Children In School % | Public School Parents % | Nonpublic School Parents % |
|---|---|---|---|---|
| A & B | 21 | 20 | 23 | 18 |
| A | 2 | 2 | 2 | 1 |
| B | 19 | 18 | 21 | 17 |
| C | 49 | 49 | 51 | 50 |
| D | 16 | 16 | 14 | 24 |
| FAIL | 4 | 4 | 4 | 5 |
| Don't know | 10 | 11 | 8 | 3 |

What grade would you give the public schools nationally?

| | 1990 % | 1989 % | 1988 % | 1987 % | 1986 % | 1985 % |
|---|---|---|---|---|---|---|
| A & B | 72 | 71 | 70 | 69 | 65 | 71 |
| A | 27 | 25 | 22 | 28 | 28 | 23 |
| B | 45 | 46 | 48 | 41 | 37 | 48 |
| C | 19 | 19 | 22 | 20 | 26 | 19 |
| D | 5 | 5 | 3 | 5 | 4 | 5 |
| FAIL | 2 | 1 | 2 | 2 | 2 | 2 |
| Don't know | 2 | 4 | 3 | 4 | 3 | 3 |

Source: The 1990 Annual Gallup Poll. *Phi Delta Kappan* (September 1990).

## FIGURE 6-13  Average Reading Proficiency: 1986

**Note: The reading proficiency scale ranges from 0 to 100. The average
scores by grade were 38.1 for grade 3, 48.9 for grade 7, and 56.1 for grade 11.**

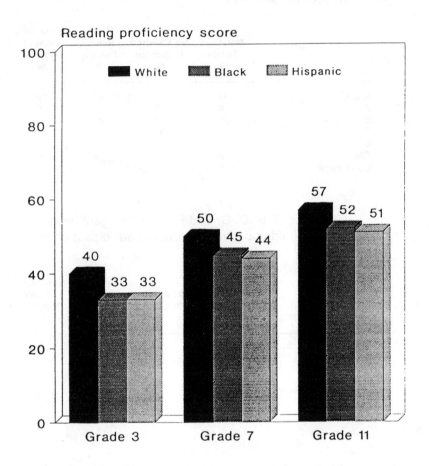

Reading proficiency score

Source:      National Assessment of Educational Progress. 1988.

# FIGURE 6-14   Trends in Average Mathematics Proficiency

Mathematics proficiency scale

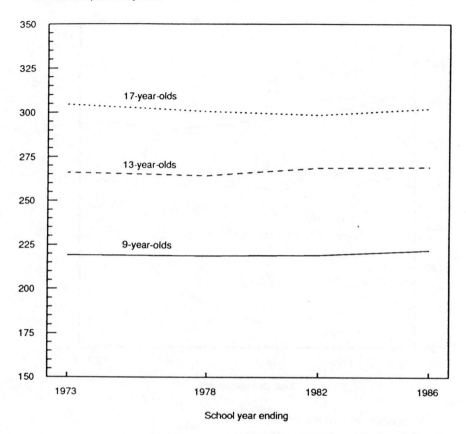

School year ending

NOTE: Mathematics Proficiency Scale
    Level 150＝Simple arithmetic facts
    Level 200＝Beginning skills and understanding
    Level 250＝Basic operations and beginning problem solving
    Level 300＝Moderately complex procedures and reasoning
    Level 350＝Multistep problem solving and algebra.

Source:    National Assessment of Educational Progress. *The Mathematics Report Card: Are We Measuring Up?* 1988.

## FIGURE 6-15  Trends in Average Science Proficiency

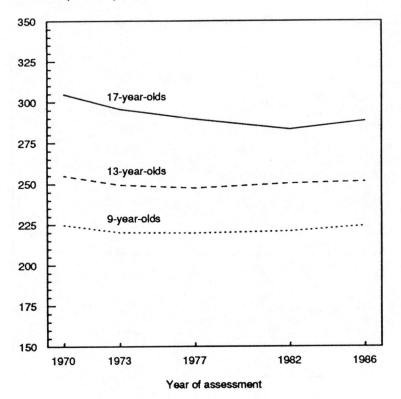

Science proficiency scale

Year of assessment

NOTE: Science Proficiency Scale
  Level 150=Knows everyday science facts
  Level 200=Understands simple scientific principles
  Level 250=Applies basic scientific information
  Level 300=Analyzes scientific procedures and data
  Level 350—Integrates specialized scientific information.

Source:     National Assessment of Educational Progress. *The Science Report Card, Elements of Risk and Recovery.* 1988.

FIGURE 6-16   Average Proficiency of 13-Year-Old Students in
Six Countries: 1988

Mathematics

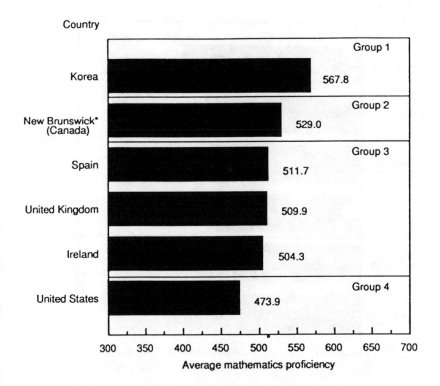

Skills characteristic of different levels on the mathematics scale:
Level 300=Simple addition and subtraction
Level 400=Basic operations to solve simple problems
Level 500=Intermediate level skills to solve two-step problems
Level 600=Measurement and geometry concepts to solve more complex problems
Level 700=More advanced mathematical concepts.

## FIGURE 6-16  *(continued)*

### Science

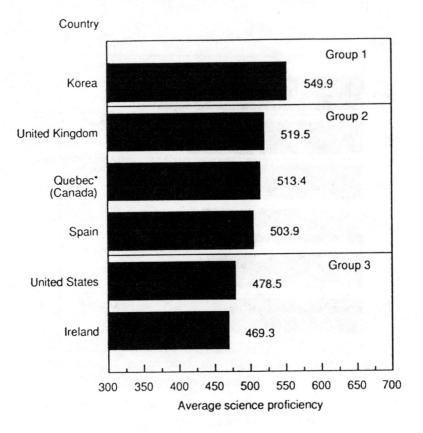

Country

Skills characteristic of different levels of proficiency on the science scales:
Level 300 = Knows everyday science facts
Level 400 = Understands and applies simple scientific principles
Level 500 = Uses scientific procedures and analyzes scientific data
Level 600 = Understands and applies scientific knowledge and principles
Level 700 = Integrates scientific information and experimental evidence.

Source:      National Assessment of Educational Progress. *A World of Differences, An International Assessment of Mathematics and Science.* 1989.

## FIGURE 6-17  Trends in High School Completion Rates: 1974–1986

| Year | Age: 18–19 | | | Age: 20–24 | | |
|------|-------|-------|----------|-------|-------|----------|
| | White | Black | Hispanic | White | Black | Hispanic |
| | Percent of age group | | | Percent of age group | | |
| 1974 | 76 | 56 | 49 | 86 | 73 | 59 |
| 1980 | 76 | 59 | 46 | 85 | 74 | 57 |
| 1986 | 77 | 65 | 55 | 85 | 81 | 62 |

Source:    U.S. Department of Commerce, Bureau of the Census. "School Enrollment—Social and Economic Characteristics of Students," October [various years]. Current Population Reports. Series P–20, and unpublished tabulations.

## FIGURE 6-18  Years of Schooling Completed by Persons 25–29 Years of Age

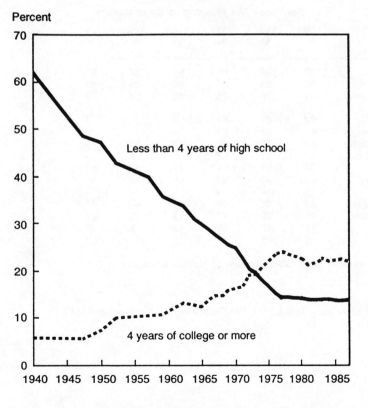

Source:    U.S. Department of Commerce, Bureau of the Census.

## FIGURE 6-19  Required Core Courses

### For Those Planning to Go to College

| | 1990 % | 1987 % | 1985 % | 1984 % | 1983 % | 1981 % |
|---|---|---|---|---|---|---|
| Mathematics | 96 | 94 | 91 | 96 | 92 | 94 |
| English | 92 | 91 | 88 | 94 | 88 | 91 |
| History/U.S. government | 84 | 84 | 76 | 84 | 78 | 83 |
| Science | 81 | 83 | 76 | 84 | 76 | 76 |
| Computer training | 75 | 72 | 71 | – | – | – |
| Geography | 63 | – | – | – | – | – |
| Career education | 62 | 63 | 57 | – | – | – |
| Business education | 59 | 59 | 59 | 68 | 55 | 60 |
| Foreign language | 56 | 56 | 53 | 57 | 50 | 54 |
| Health education | 53 | 54 | 48 | 52 | 43 | 47 |
| Physical education | 40 | 45 | 40 | 43 | 41 | 44 |
| Vocational training | 29 | 31 | 27 | 37 | 32 | 34 |
| Art | 24 | 23 | 23 | 24 | 19 | 28 |
| Music | 22 | 23 | 24 | 22 | 18 | 26 |

(Figures add to more than 100% because of multiple answers.)

### For Those *Not* Planning to Go to College

| | 1990 % | 1987 % | 1985 % | 1984 % | 1983 % | 1981 % |
|---|---|---|---|---|---|---|
| Mathematics | 90 | 88 | 85 | 92 | 87 | 91 |
| English | 86 | 85 | 81 | 90 | 83 | 89 |
| Vocational training | 74 | 78 | 75 | 83 | 74 | 64 |
| History/U.S. government | 67 | 69 | 61 | 71 | 63 | 71 |
| Computer training | 63 | 61 | 57 | – | – | – |
| Business education | 63 | 65 | 60 | 76 | 65 | 75 |
| Career education | 60 | 61 | 57 | – | – | – |
| Science | 58 | 57 | 51 | 61 | 53 | 58 |
| Health education | 50 | 49 | 43 | 50 | 42 | 46 |
| Geography | 48 | – | – | – | – | – |
| Physical education | 38 | 41 | 40 | 44 | 40 | 43 |
| Foreign language | 25 | 20 | 17 | 19 | 19 | 21 |
| Art | 17 | 17 | 15 | 18 | 16 | 20 |
| Music | 16 | 15 | 15 | 18 | 16 | 20 |

(Figures add to more than 100% because of multiple answers.)

Source:     1990 Annual Gallup Poll. *Phi Delta Kappan* (September 1990).

## FIGURE 6-20   Beyond the Academic Core

| | National Totals % | Public School Parents % | No Children In School % |
|---|---|---|---|
| **Would Require** | | | |
| Drug abuse education | 90 | 92 | 89 |
| Alcohol abuse education | 84 | 86 | 82 |
| AIDS education | 77 | 77 | 77 |
| Sex education | 72 | 74 | 71 |
| Environmental issues and problems | 66 | 65 | 66 |
| Teen pregnancy | 64 | 64 | 65 |
| Driver education | 59 | 62 | 59 |
| Character education | 57 | 56 | 57 |
| Parenting/parent training | 46 | 48 | 45 |
| Dangers of nuclear waste | 30 | 29 | 31 |
| Dangers of nuclear war | 28 | 28 | 28 |
| Communism/socialism | 24 | 23 | 25 |

(Figures add to more than 100% because of multiple answers.)

| | National Totals | | |
|---|---|---|---|
| | 1990 % | 1984 % | 1983 % |
| **Would Require** | | | |
| Drug abuse education | 90 | 82 | 81 |
| Alcohol abuse education | 84 | 79 | 76 |
| AIDS education | 77 | – | – |
| Sex education | 72 | – | – |
| Environmental issues and problems | 66 | – | – |
| Teen pregnancy | 64 | – | – |
| Driver education | 59 | 73 | 72 |
| Character education | 57 | – | – |
| Parenting/parent training | 46 | 55 | 58 |
| Dangers of nuclear waste | 30 | 61 | 56 |
| Dangers of nuclear war | 28 | 51 | 46 |
| Communism/socialism | 24 | 57 | 51 |

(Figures add to more than 100% because of multiple answers.)

Source:   1990 Annual Gallup Poll. *Phi Delta Kappan* (September 1990).

FIGURE 6-21   Percentage of High School Graduates Who
Earned Credits in the New Basics: 1982–1987

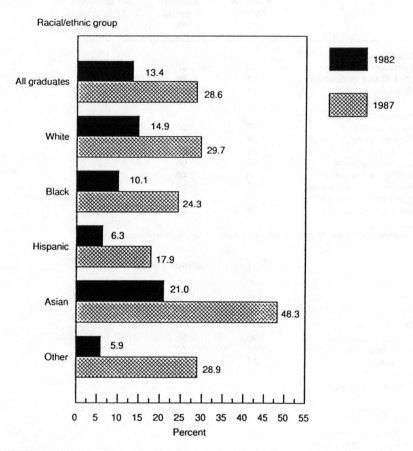

NOTE: Recommended credits in "new basics" include 4 credits of English plus 3 each of social studies,
mathematics, and science.


Source:      U.S.Department of Education, National Center for Education Statistics.
             *High School Transcript Study.* 1987.

## FIGURE 6-22  Number of Courses Required by States for High School Graduation: 1988

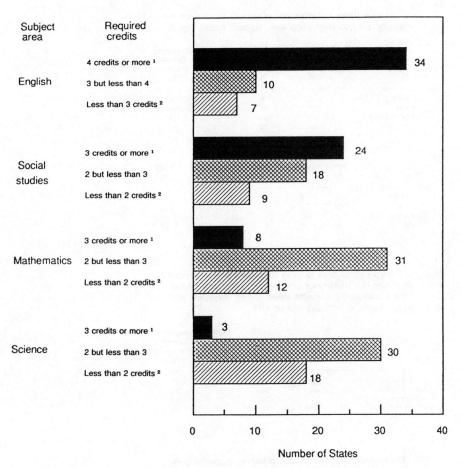

¹ Number of credits recommended by the National Commission on Excellence in Education.

² Includes those States with no requirements in the subject.

Source:     Council of Chief State School Officers. *1988 Policies and Practices Questionnaire.*

## FIGURE 6-23  Teachers' Salaries and Working Conditions

**Do you think salaries for teachers in this community are too high, too low, or just about right?**

|  | National Totals % | No Children In School % | Public School Parents % | Nonpublic School Parents % |
|---|---|---|---|---|
| Too high | 5 | 5 | 3 | 1 |
| Too low | 50 | 49 | 54 | 54 |
| Just about right | 31 | 31 | 32 | 34 |
| No opinion | 14 | 15 | 11 | 11 |

|  | National Totals | | | | | |
|---|---|---|---|---|---|---|
|  | 1990 % | 1985 % | 1984 % | 1983 % | 1981 % | 1969 % |
| Too high | 5 | 6 | 7 | 8 | 10 | 2 |
| Too low | 50 | 33 | 37 | 35 | 29 | 33 |
| Just about right | 31 | 43 | 41 | 31 | 41 | 43 |
| No opinion | 14 | 18 | 15 | 26 | 20 | 22 |

**Do you think that raising teacher salaries would improve the quality of education in the schools in this community a great deal, a fair amount, not very much, or almost not at all?**

|  | National Totals % | No Children In School % | Public School Parents % | Nonpublic School Parents % |
|---|---|---|---|---|
| A great deal | 16 | 14 | 18 | 21 |
| A fair amount | 35 | 36 | 35 | 33 |
| Not very much | 28 | 28 | 28 | 23 |
| Almost not at all | 17 | 17 | 17 | 18 |
| Don't know | 4 | 5 | 2 | 5 |

**Do you think that providing better working conditions for teachers would improve the quality of education in the public schools in this community a great deal, a fair amount, not very much, or almost not at all?**

|  | National Totals % | No Children In School % | Public School Parents % | Nonpublic School Parents % |
|---|---|---|---|---|
| A great deal | 25 | 24 | 29 | 31 |
| A fair amount | 37 | 38 | 34 | 36 |
| Not very much | 21 | 21 | 20 | 19 |
| Almost not at all | 12 | 11 | 14 | 12 |
| Don't know | 5 | 6 | 3 | 2 |

Source:     1990 Annual Gallup Poll. *Phi Delta Kappan.*

FIGURE 6-24  Trends in average annual salary of public
schoolteachers in constant 1989 dollars:
Selected school years ending 1960–1988

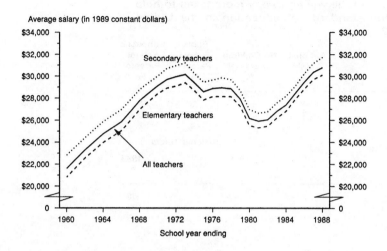

Average salary (in 1989 constant dollars)

Source:        National Education Association. *Estimates of School Statistics.*
Copyright 1988 by the National Education Association. All rights
reserved.

FIGURE 6-25  Pupil/Teacher Ratios in Public Schools

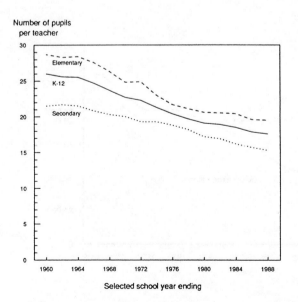

Number of pupils
per teacher

Sources:      National Center for Education Statistics. *Statistics of Elementary
and Secondary Day School.* Various years. Common Core of Data
survey. Various years.

### FIGURE 6-26   Public Attitudes toward Financial Support for Public Schools: 1983–1986

**Would you be willing to pay more taxes to help raise the standards of education in the United States?**

|  | National Totals % | No Children In School % | Public School Parents % | Nonpublic School Parents % |
|---|---|---|---|---|
| Yes | 64 | 61 | 73 | 68 |
| No | 29 | 31 | 23 | 30 |
| Don't know | 7 | 8 | 4 | 2 |

|  | National Totals | |
|---|---|---|
|  | 1988 % | 1983 % |
| Yes | 64 | 58 |
| No | 29 | 33 |
| Don't know | 7 | 9 |

Source:   20th Annual Gallup Poll. *Phi Delta Kappan* (September 1988)

### FIGURE 6-27   Current Expenditures per Pupil in Public Schools: 1950–1987

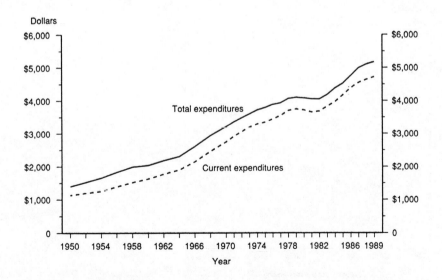

Source:   National Center for Education Statistics. *Statistics of State School Systems and Revenues and Expenditures for Public Elementary and Secondary Education.*

FIGURE 6-28   The National Index of Public School Revenues per
Pupil in Relation to Per Capita Income: 1940–1988

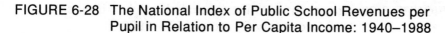

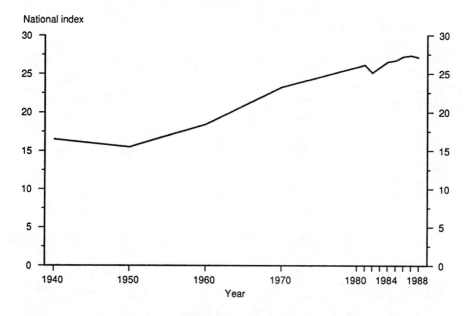

Source:      U.S. Department of Education, National Center for Education Statistics.
*Digest of Educational Statistics.* 1989.

FIGURE 6-29   Public School Revenues as a Percent of GNP:
1970–1987

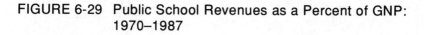

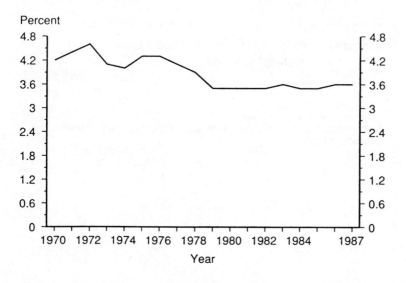

Source:      U.S. Department of Education, National Center for Education Statistics.
*Digest of Education Statistics.* 1989.

## FIGURE 6-30  Trends in Revenue Sources for Public Elementary and Secondary Schools: 1970–1988

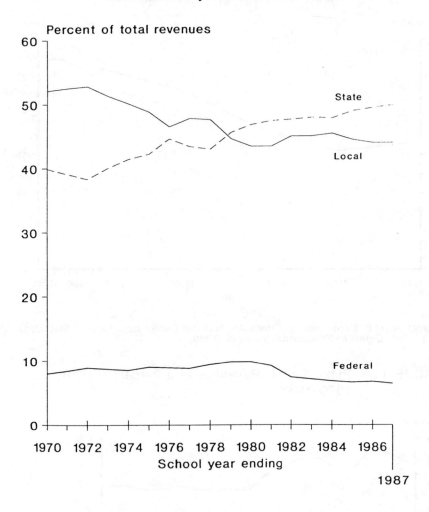

Source:    National Center for Education Statistics. *Digest of Educational Statistics.* 1988.

# 7

# Education Associations, Organizations, and Agencies

THIS IS A SELECTIVE LIST of national organizations, associations, and government agencies that are doing significant work in education. They serve various purposes: Some are the professional organizations for practitioners in a particular educational specialty. In this capacity, they generally hold national conferences in which members participate in workshops and share ideas, and publish professional journals and newsletters. Information on many of these publications is included in Chapter 9.

Other organizations are devoted to carrying out research, evaluations, curriculum development, training, and other functions related to educational institutions. A few organizations serve as clearinghouses for instructional materials, research findings, and information on specific areas of education.

## National Associations and Councils

**American Alliance for Health,
Physical Education, Recreation,
and Dance (AAHPERD)**

1900 Association Drive
Reston, VA 22091
(703) 476-3400
*Charles H. Hartman, Executive Vice-President*

The purpose of this organization is to encourage cooperation among those in the fields of health, physical education, recreation, and dance and to increase the public awareness of these fields. AAHPERD also supports and disseminates research related to these fields.

PUBLICATIONS: *Journal of Physical Education, Recreation and Dance* (9 issues per year), *Health Education* (6 issues per year), *Research Quarterly for Exercise and Sport* (4 issues per year), *Update* (monthly).

### American Association for Adult and Continuing Education (AAACE)
1201 16th Street, NW
Suite 230
Washington, DC 20036
(202) 822-7866
*Judith A. Koloski, Executive Director*

AAACE was established in 1982 to promote education as lifelong learning. It works with national, state, and local governments to help set up educational programs.

PUBLICATIONS: *Lifelong Learning: An Omnibus of Practice and Research* (monthly), *Adult Education Quarterly, AAACE Newsletter.*

### American Association for Counseling and Development (AACD)
5999 Stevenson Avenue
Alexandria, VA 22304
(703) 823-9800
*Theodore Remley, Executive Director*

AACD works to improve counseling, guidance, and personnel services by enhancing professional skills through research and training programs and by advancing standards of conduct. It hosts an annual conference and conducts a variety of professional development institutes.

PUBLICATIONS: *Journal of Counseling and Development* (10 issues per year), *Guidepost* (18 issues per year).

### American Association for Higher Education (AAHE)
One Dupont Circle, NW
Suite 600
Washington, DC 20036
(202) 293-6440
*Russell Edgerton, President*

This association provides a forum for administrators, policymakers, and teachers to discuss critical issues that face the nation's colleges and universities.

PUBLICATIONS: *Change: The Magazine of Higher Education* (bimonthly), *AAHE Bulletin* (monthly, September–June).

## American Association of Colleges for Teacher Education (AACTE)
One Dupont Circle, NW
Suite 610
Washington, DC 20036
(202) 293-2450
*David G. Imig, Executive Director*

This association works to uphold standards and improve the training and development of teachers and other professionals in schools. Its members are colleges with accredited teacher-education programs, and it sponsors professional development conferences and workshops.

PUBLICATIONS: *Journal of Teacher Education* (bimonthly).

## American Association of Community and Junior Colleges (AACJC)
One Dupont Circle, NW
Suite 410
Washington, DC 20036
(202) 293-7050
*Dale Parnell, President and Chief Executive Officer*

The primary purpose of this organization is to promote the development and welfare of two-year colleges. It monitors and lobbies government bodies and provides various services for community, technical, and junior colleges.

PUBLICATIONS: *Community, Technical, and Junior College Journal* (bimonthly).

## American Association of School Administrators (AASA)
1801 N. Moore Street
Arlington, VA 22209
(703) 528-0700
*Richard D. Miller, Executive Director*

AASA is the professional organization for school administrators (particularly superintendents), college administrators, and professors of educational administration. It provides a number of services for school administrators, including conducting studies and surveys on educational issues.

PUBLICATIONS: AASA's major journal is *The School Administrator,* published monthly.

## American Association of State Colleges and Universities (AASCU)

One Dupont Circle, NW
Suite 700
Washington, DC 20036
(202) 293-7070
*Allan W. Ostar, President*

This association for state-supported colleges and universities represents the interests of these schools before legislatures. It assists with state and national governmental relations, public policy issues, community development concerns, public service, and international programs.

PUBLICATIONS: *Proceedings* and *AASCU*, both annual.

## American Council on Education (ACE)

One Dupont Circle, NW
Washington, DC 20036
(202) 939-9300
*Robert H. Atwell, President*

The American Council on Education is the principal organizing agency for all accredited institutions of higher education. It promotes higher education before Congress, monitors Supreme Court and federal court decisions, and assists colleges and universities on management issues. It also promotes adult education and administers the GED high school equivalency exam on a national basis.

PUBLICATIONS: *Educational Record: The Magazine of Higher Education* (quarterly), *Higher Education and National Affairs* (biweekly).

## American Educational Research Association (AERA)

1230 17th Street, NW
Washington, DC 20036
(202) 223-9485
*William J. Russell, Executive Officer*

AERA is the major professional organization of educators involved in educational research. Its primary purpose is to improve school learning and supervision practices through promoting research, helping interpret the practical implications of this research, and disseminating the results. AERA hosts a major annual conference for school and university educators.

PUBLICATIONS: *Educational Researcher* (10 issues per year), *Review of Educational Research* (quarterly), *American Educational Research Journal* (quarterly), *Educational Evaluation and Policy Analysis* (quarterly), *Journal of Educational Statistics* (quarterly).

## American School Counselor Association (ASCA)
5999 Stevenson Avenue
Alexandria, VA 22304
(713) 823-9800
*Beverly O'Bryant, President*

This professional organization of school counselors, founded in 1953, is a division of AACD (American Association for Counseling and Development). Its purpose is to promote the rights and welfare of children and to improve professional standards in school counseling.

PUBLICATIONS: *The School Counselor* (5 issues per year), *Elementary School Guidance and Counseling* (quarterly).

## American Vocation Association (AVA)
1410 King Street
Alexandria, VA 22314
(703) 683-3111
*Kermeta "Kay" Clayton, President*

The aim of AVA is to promote and improve vocational education in high school, postsecondary, and adult education. It works closely with the Office of Vocational Rehabilitation in the Department of Health and Human Services. Its several divisions include industrial arts, distributive education, agriculture, and home economics.

PUBLICATIONS: *Vocational Education Journal* (monthly), *Vocational Education Weekly.*

## Association for Childhood Education International (ACEI)
11141 Georgia Avenue
Suite 200
Wheaton, MD 20902
(301) 942-2443
*Gilson Brown, Executive Director*

The ACEI is an advocate for human rights and educational practices that are sensitive to the needs of children from infancy through adolescence. It hosts regional conferences, conducts workshops, and works with government agencies.

PUBLICATIONS: *Childhood Education* (5 issues per year), *ACEI Exchange* (monthly), *Journal of Research and Childhood Education* (biannual).

## Association for Supervision and Curriculum Development (ASCD)
125 North West Street
Alexandria, VA 22314
(703) 549-9110
*Gordon Cawelti, Executive Director*

The purpose of ASCD is to support educators as they develop, evaluate, and improve curricula. To this end, it sponsors curriculum institutes, publishes books and pamphlets on curriculum issues, produces audio and videotapes, and hosts an annual conference. Its membership includes curriculum supervisors as well as teachers, principals, superintendents, and others interested in curriculum development.

PUBLICATIONS: *Educational Leadership* (8 times per year), *Journal of Curriculum Supervision* (quarterly).

## Association of American Colleges (AAC)
1818 R Street, NW
Washington, DC 20009
(202) 387-3760
*John W. Chandler, President*

The Association of American Colleges is a voice for liberal arts programs in the nation's colleges and universities. It works to improve undergraduate curricula and to integrate professional programs with the liberal arts. It also helps campuses provide supportive environments in which minority students can succeed.

PUBLICATIONS: *Liberal Education* (5 issues per year), *On Campus with Women* (quarterly).

## Council for Exceptional Children (CEC)
1920 Association Drive
Reston, VA 22091
(703) 620-3660
*Jeptha Greer, Executive Director*

The Council for Exceptional Children promotes the educational rights and interests of both disabled and gifted children. It sponsors conferences and workshops and provides information pertinent to the education of exceptional children for teachers, administrators, and parents.

PUBLICATIONS: *Exceptional Children* (bimonthly), *Teaching Exceptional Children* (quarterly), *Exceptional Child Education Resources* (quarterly).

## International Reading Association (IRA)
P.O. Box 8139
800 Barksdale Road
Newark, DE 19714
(302) 731-1600
*Ronald W. Mitchell, Executive Director*

IRA is an association of classroom teachers, reading specialists, teacher educators, researchers, and others interested in improving reading effectiveness at all levels of schooling. It also promotes lifetime reading habits in the general population. To accomplish this, IRA maintains a clearinghouse for information related to reading and the teaching of reading, and it publishes a range of materials on reading.

PUBLICATIONS: *The Reading Teacher* (9 issues per year), *Journal of Reading* (8 issues per year), *Reading Research Quarterly, Lectura y Vida* (Spanish quarterly).

### International Society for Technology in Education
University of Oregon
1787 Agate Street
Eugene, OR 97403
(503) 686-4414
*David G. Moursund, Chief Executive Officer*

This international organization works to promote the use of computer technology in the classroom, to maintain the integrity of software program use, and to improve classroom instruction through computers.

PUBLICATIONS: Its major publication is *The Computing Teacher* (8 issues per year).

### Modern Language Association
### of America (MLA)
10 Astor Place
New York, NY 10003
(212) 475-9500
*Phyllis Franklin, Executive Director*

MLA promotes the study of English and modern foreign languages, literature, and the humanities. It does this by advocating the humanities and the study of languages and literature before Congress and governmental agencies, publishing books, and providing other professional services for its members. This membership is primarily made up of secondary schoolteachers and college professors.

PUBLICATIONS: *PMLA* (6 issues per year), *ADFL Journal* (3 issues per year), *ADE Journal* (3 issues per year).

### Music Teachers National Association (MTNA)
2113 Carew Tower
Cincinnati, OH 45202
(513) 421-1420
*Robert J. Elias, Executive Director*

MTNA is the professional organization for music teachers at all levels of schooling. Its goals are to improve the quality of music teaching and to raise the level of music performance among students. To accomplish this, MTNA has developed a national course of study and sponsors music competitions at the local, state, and national levels.

PUBLICATIONS: *The American Music Teacher* (bimonthly), *Directory of Nationally Certified Teachers* (annual).

## National Art Education Association (NAEA)
1916 Association Drive
Reston, VA 22091
(703) 860-8000
*Thomas A. Hatfield, Executive Director*

NAEA is the professional organization for art teachers; its goal is to promote high standards in teaching the visual arts. It maintains a clearinghouse of information on teaching art, conducts workshops for teachers, and sponsors a national honor society for high school students.

PUBLICATIONS: *Art Education* (bimonthly), *NAEA News* (bimonthly), *Studies in Art Education* (quarterly).

## National Association for Bilingual Education (NABE)
Union Center Plaza
810 First Street
Third Floor
Washington, DC 20002
(202) 898-1829
*James Lyons, Executive Director*

The purpose of NABE, which was founded in 1975, is to promote the public understanding of bilingual education and its effective implementation in schools. It works to improve instructional practices, clarify language policies, and promote research.

PUBLICATIONS: NABE's major publication is *NABE Journal,* a quarterly that focuses on instructional planning, language policies, and research findings.

## National Association for the Education of Young Children (NAEYC)
1834 Connecticut Avenue, NW
Washington, DC 20009
(202) 232-8777
*Marilyn M. Smith, Executive Director*

This organization of professionals and laypersons promotes awareness of the rights and special needs of preschool, kindergarten, and primary school children and seeks to improve the education of these children. It hosts training conferences and workshops and provides guidelines on early childhood education for two-year and four-year college-preparatory programs.

PUBLICATIONS: *Young Children* (bimonthly), *Early Childhood Research Quarterly.*

**National Association for Gifted Children (NAGC)**
4175 Lovell Road
Suite 140
Circle Pines, MN 55014
(612) 784-3475
*Joyce E. Juntune, Executive Director*

NAGC is a public advocate for the needs of gifted learners, which works to improve learning environments and instructional programs for these students. It conducts training institutes for teachers and parents and negotiates for national legislation that affects gifted children.

PUBLICATIONS: *Gifted Child Quarterly.*

**National Association of Elementary School Principals (NAESP)**
1615 Duke Street
Alexandria, VA 22314
(703) 684-3345
*Samuel G. Sava, Executive Director*

The goal of this professional organization for elementary and middle-school principals is to promote academic and leadership qualities. It sponsors programs designed to teach principals about new curricula and technology, to clarify educational issues and trends, and to inform them of new educational research developments.

PUBLICATIONS: *Principal* (5 issues per year), *Communicator* (10 issues per year), *Report to Parents* (6 issues per year), *Here's How* (6 issues per year).

**National Association of Independent Colleges and
Universities (NAICU)**
122 C Street, NW
Suite 750
Washington, DC 20001
(202) 383-5950
*John D. Phillips, Chief Executive Officer*

This association advocates for independent colleges and universities in federal government legislative matters, and it provides a forum for these institutions to exchange ideas on academic and administrative issues.

PUBLICATIONS: *The Week in Review* (weekly), *The Voice of Independents* (quarterly).

**National Association of Independent Schools (NAIS)**
18 Tremont Street
Boston, MA 02108
(617) 723-6900
*John C. Esty, Jr., President*

NAIS assists independent elementary and secondary schools to strengthen their programs and more effectively serve their students and families. Its services for these schools in the United States and abroad include fund-raising, admissions, financial aid, public relations, and management information.

PUBLICATIONS: Its major publication is *Independent School* (quarterly).

### National Association of Secondary School Principals (NASSP)
1904 Association Drive
Reston, VA 22091
(703) 860-0200
*Scott D. Thomson, Executive Director*

NASSP conducts activities and events to enhance the effectiveness of middle-grade and high school principals. It defines professional standards, conducts research, and provides in-service training, public relations support, legal counsel, and other services for principals.

PUBLICATIONS: *NASSP Bulletin* (9 issues per year), *NASSP Newsletter* (9 issues per year), *Curriculum Report* (5 issues per year), *Practitioner* (quarterly), *Legal Memorandum* (quarterly), *School Technology News* (6 issues per year), *School in the Middle* (5 issues per year).

### National Association of State Boards of Education (NASBE)
701 North Fairfax Street
Suite 340
Alexandria, VA 22314
(703) 684-4000
*Gene Wilhoit, Executive Director*

The purpose of NASBE is to improve the policymaking skills and leadership abilities of state boards of education. It holds national and regional conferences, trains board members, and helps to select and evaluate state school officers.

PUBLICATIONS: *State Board Connection* (10 issues per year).

### National Association of State Universities and Land-Grant Colleges (NASULGC)
One Dupont Circle, NW
Suite 710
Washington, DC 20036
(202) 778-0818
*Robert L. Clodius, President*

This association represents major public universities, particularly the 72 land-grant schools. It promotes federal and state legislation to assist these schools and works to improve their organization, curricula, and programs for special-needs students.

PUBLICATIONS: In addition to producing several annual publications, NASULGC publishes *The Green Sheet* (20 times a year).

## National Congress of Parents and Teachers (National PTA)
700 North Rush Street
Chicago, IL 60611
(312) 787-0977
*Robert N. Woerner, Executive Director*

The National PTA serves its constituents of teachers and parents by helping them improve the welfare and education of children and youth in home, school, and the community. It sponsors several programs including Parent Involvement in Strengthening Public Education, Keeping Children Safe and Healthy, Parent Education, and Promoting the Cultural Arts.

PUBLICATIONS: Its major publication is *PTA Magazine* (7 issues per year).

## National Council for Accreditation of Teacher Education (NCATE)
1919 Pennsylvania Avenue, NW
Suite 202
Washington, DC 20006
(202) 466-7496
*Richard C. Kunkel, Executive Director*

NCATE is the sole accrediting agency of college and university programs that prepare elementary and secondary schoolteachers and other professional school personnel. It sets national standards on specific aspects of teacher preparation.

PUBLICATIONS: *Standards for Accreditation of Teacher Education, Annual List of Accredited Institutions*.

## National Council for the Social Studies (NCSS)
3501 Newark Street, NW
Washington, DC 20016
(202) 966-7840
*Frances Haley, Executive Director*

This is the professional association for teachers of social studies, history, and social sciences, as well as social studies educators. NCSS develops curriculum standards, sponsors international trips, hosts an annual conference, and provides a variety of materials to help improve social studies instruction in all grades and clarify issues that social studies teachers face.

PUBLICATIONS: *Social Education* (7 times per year), *The Social Studies Professional* (5 issues per year), *Bulletins* (3 issues per year).

## National Council of Teachers of English (NCTE)
1111 Kenyon Road
Urbana, IL 61801
(217) 328-3870
*John C. Maxwell, Executive Director*

This professional organization for teachers of English and the language arts in kindergarten through eighth grade hosts a national conference; publishes several journals, newsletters, and books; and provides other services to improve instruction in these fields.

PUBLICATIONS: *Language Arts* (8 issues per year), *English Journal* (8 issues per year), *College English* (8 issues per year), *English Education* (quarterly), *College Composition and Communication* (quarterly), *Teaching English in the Two-Year College* (quarterly), *Research in Teaching English* (quarterly).

## National Council of Teachers of Mathematics (NCTM)
1906 Association Drive
Reston, VA 22091
(703) 620-9840
*James D. Gates, Executive Director*

This is the professional organization for teachers of mathematics at all levels of schooling. It provides a range of materials to help teachers improve mathematics instruction and learning.

PUBLICATIONS: *Mathematics Teacher* (9 issues per year), *Arithmetic Teacher* (9 issues per year), *Journal for Research in Mathematics Education* (5 issues per year).

## National Middle School Association (NMSA)
4807 Evanswood Drive
Columbus, OH 43229
(614) 848-8211
*Denis D. Smith, Executive Director*

Established in 1973, the purpose of NMSA is to promote middle-grade education and serve as a voice for educators, parents, and other citizens interested in the educational and developmental needs of youth between the ages of 10 and 15. Membership is open to all interested in middle schools and includes teachers, administrators, parents, teacher educators, counselors, curriculum directors, college students, and school board members.

PUBLICATIONS: *Middle School Journal* (5 issues per year); *Middle Ground,* a newspaper (4 issues per year); and *Target,* a newsletter (4 issues per year).

## National Rural Education Association (NREA)
Office of Rural Education
230 Education Building
Colorado State University

Fort Collins, CO 80523
(303) 491-7022
*Joseph T. Newlin, Executive Director*

NREA is dedicated to improving the quality of schooling and education generally in the nation's rural communities. It represents rural schools before Congress, educational agencies, and state governments. It hosts an annual conference and has established the NREA Foundation to support specific projects in rural schools.

PUBLICATIONS: *The Rural Educator* (3 issues a year), *NREA News* (quarterly), *The Country Teacher* (3 issues a year).

**National School Boards Association (NSBA)**
1680 Duke Street
Alexandria, VA 22314
(703) 838-6722
*Thomas A. Shannon, Executive Director*

This national organization for state school board associations and local school boards seeks to improve the leadership and policymaking abilities of board members. It provides training for school board members and represents the interest of boards before Congress, federal agencies, and the courts.

PUBLICATIONS: *The American School Board Journal* (monthly), *The Executive Educator Magazine* (monthly), *School Board News* (twice a month).

**National Science Teachers Association (NSTA)**
1742 Connecticut Avenue, NW
Washington, DC 20009
(202) 328-5800
*Bill G. Aldridge, Executive Director*

This is the national professional organization for science teachers at all levels. It issues professional guidelines, offers in-service training, conducts workshops, and hosts a national conference.

PUBLICATIONS: *Science and Children* (8 issues per year), *The Science Teacher* (9 issues per year), *Science Scope* (5 issues per year), *Journal of College Science Teaching* (6 issues per year), *NSTA Report* (3 issues per year).

# Nonprofit Organizations

**American Federation of Teachers (AFT)**
555 New Jersey, NW
Washington, DC 20001
(202) 879-4400
*Albert Shanker, President*

AFT has been a integral part of the American labor movement and a member affiliate of the AFL-CIO. AFT membership tends to concentrate in large and moderate-sized cities where other AFL-CIO unions are strongest. It led pioneering efforts for federal and state legislation to recognize the rights of teachers to negotiate, bargain collectively, and strike. The AFT also works to strengthen state tenure laws, eliminate classroom overcrowding and reduce disruptions, guarantee unencumbered lunch periods, and improve teachers' pensions and fringe benefits. In recent years, the AFT has been working to bring about a restructuring of the nation's public schools.

PUBLICATIONS: *Salary and Analysis of Salary Trends* (annual) reports national and state average salaries and earnings for teachers, other school employees, government workers, and professional employees.

### Carnegie Foundation for the Advancement of Teaching (CFAT)
5 Ivy Lane
Princeton, NJ 08540
(609) 452-1780
*Ernest L. Boyer, President*

1775 Massachusetts Avenue, NW
Washington, DC 20036
(202) 387-7200
*Robert Hochstein*

The Carnegie Foundation is an education policy center established by Andrew Carnegie in 1905. It conducts surveys and analyses of aspects of the nation's schools and college.

PUBLICATIONS: *High School: A Report on Secondary Education in America* and *College: The Undergraduate Experience in America,* both written by Ernest Boyer, set forth essential educational goals to guide institutions and recommend curriculum framework. Results of CFAT's national survey of public school teachers in 1987 are reported in *Teacher Involvement in Decisionmaking: A State-by-State Profile* (free), *Report Card on School Reform: The Teachers Speak,* 1988 ($5), and *The Condition of Teaching: A State-by-State Analysis,* 1988 ($10.95). A follow-up study of teachers' views is reported in *The Condition of Teaching: A State-by-State Analysis,* 1990 ($12).

### Center for Educational Renewal
College of Education, DQ–12
University of Washington
Seattle, WA 98195
(206) 543-6230
*John I. Goodlad, Director*

The center's primary goal is to seek the simultaneous restructuring of K–12 schooling and teacher-preparation programs in colleges and universities. The National Network for Educational Renewal (NNER), which embraces school-university partnerships in 13 states, is one of the center's projects designed to achieve this goal. Another aim of these partnerships is to help elementary and secondary schools become more engaging places for learning by renewing school organizational structures, decision making, and curricula. The network works to make schools the center of change through such reforms as school-based management and reflective inquiry learning, which emphasizes learning by doing.

The center is undertaking a major project, initially in six settings, to implement the recommendations of its *Study of the Education of Educators*.

PUBLICATIONS: Three books examine the philosophical, ethical, and historical aspects of teacher preparation and teaching. John Goodlad is the author of *Teachers for Our Nation's Schools*. Goodlad, Roger Soder, and Kenneth Sirotnik are editors of *Moral Dimensions of Teaching* and *Places Where Teachers Are Taught*; all three 1990 (Jossey-Bass). Technical reports and occasional papers related to the study are published by the center.

## Center for Teaching International Relations (CTIR)

University of Denver
Denver, CO 80208
(303) 871-3106
*Ron Schukar, Director*

CTIR develops an array of curriculum materials designed to stimulate student interest and foster critical thinking skills in a variety of subjects under the rubric of international studies and global studies. These subjects include cultural and area studies, global awareness, conflict studies, ethnic studies, international relations, foreign policy, and economic development. The Center also conducts workshops for teachers and consults with school districts to help them develop international studies programs.

## Close Up Foundation

1235 Jefferson Davis Highway
Arlington, VA 22207
(703) 892-5400
*Stephen A. Janger, President*

Close Up was established in 1970 to encourage high school students and their teachers to gain a better understanding of the U.S. government and their role as citizens. Its goal is to foster informed citizens who both appreciate and become involved in their political and economic system. Throughout the year, it conducts weeklong seminars in Washington, D.C., for students, teachers, and older Americans that focus on government, economics, and world affairs. It also conducts seminars and workshops in local schools and public affairs telecast programs.

PUBLICATIONS: *Close Up Special Focus,* a series of booklets on the economy, energy, and U.S.-Soviet relations. Its other major publications are *Perspectives,* a biannual periodical of articles describing how government works, and *Current Issues,* an annual handbook that examines foreign and domestic policy issues. Both publications are designed for high school students, teachers, and other educators.

## Coalition for Essential Schools (CES)
Brown University
Box 1938
Providence, RI 02912
(401) 863-3384
*Theodore R. Sizer, Chairman*

CES is a school-reform concept that advocates schools becoming places that better help students use their minds. The coalition's framework for school redesign is based on a set of nine common principles that emphasize simplifying the goals of schools to focus on the intellectual development of students, personalizing teaching and learning by reducing the number of students each teacher works with, and helping teachers to engage students more actively in their learning. The coalition has teamed with the Education Commission of the States (ECS) to sponsor the Re:Learning project, a national effort to help school administrators and teachers redesign their school systems.

PUBLICATIONS: *Horace* (5 issues per year).

## Council for Aid to Education, Inc. (CFAE)
51 Madison Avenue, Suite 220
New York, NY 10010
(212) 689-2400
*Arnold Shore, President*

Funded by contributions from business, CFAE promotes the voluntary support of educational institutions. It sponsors public service campaigns and provides consulting and research services on voluntary support. Each year CFAE conducts a survey of colleges, universities, and private elementary and secondary schools to obtain information on the private gifts, grants, and bequests they have received.

PUBLICATIONS: The survey results are published annually in the *Voluntary Support of Education.* CFAE also publishes a number of booklets on business-school relationships including *The Corporate Handbook, Matching Gifts, Business and the Schools* and *School Restructuring.*

## Council of Chief State School Officers (CCSSO)
400 North Capitol Street, NW, Suite 379
Washington, DC 20001
(202) 393-8161
*Gordon M. Ambach, Executive Director*

The CCSSO is a nationwide organization of the 57 public school officials who head departments of public education in every state, U.S. outlying areas, the District of Columbia, and the Department of Defense Dependents Schools. In 1985 it founded the State Education Assessment Center whose purpose is to improve the monitoring and assessment of education.

PUBLICATIONS: *Directory of State Education Agencies* and *State Indicators,* an annual report on enrollment, achievement, salaries, finance, and other salient public school information.

## Council of State Directors of Programs for the Gifted
Office of Public Instruction
Room 106
State Capitol
Helena, MT 59620
(406) 444-3680
*Nancy Lukenbill, President*

This council is comprised of the individuals in charge of gifted education in each of the 50 states, the District of Columbia, and the outlying areas. It conducts state surveys to obtain a profile of gifted-education programs in the nation. Data from these reports typically is included in the educational indicators, conditions, and statistical digests published by the National Center for Educational Statistics.

PUBLICATIONS: *State of the States: Gifted and Talented Education* reports.

## Distributive Education Clubs of America (DECA), Inc.
1908 Association Drive
Reston, VA 22091
(703) 860-5000
*Frederick L. Williford, Executive Director*

DECA provides activities designed to teach secondary and postsecondary students the skills and attitudes that help prepare them for careers in marketing. Students also learn about merchandising and management. In addition, the student activities promote a greater understanding and appreciation of the United States' private enterprise system. DECA chapters are located in the 50 states, District of Columbia, Puerto Rico, Guam, the Virgin Islands, Canada, and its provinces of Ontario and Manitoba. DECA's membership numbers over 200,000 students annually.

PUBLICATIONS: *New Dimensions* (quarterly).

## Education Commission of the States (ECS)
707 17th Street
Suite 2700
Denver, CO 80202
(303) 299-3631
*Frank Newman, President*

The ECS clearinghouse collects information on laws and standards in education and about administrators, principals, and teachers. It also researches state policies on assessment and testing, collective bargaining, early childhood issues, school schedules, and other policy issues. ECS joined with the Coalition for Essential Schools (CES) to sponsor the Re:Learning project, a national effort to help educators restructure the total school organization and curriculum.

PUBLICATIONS: ECS's findings on state laws and standards in education are reported periodically in *Clearinghouse Notes*.

### Future Farmers of America (FFA)
P.O. Box 15160
Alexandria, VA 22309
(703) 360-3600
*Larry D. Case, National Advisor and Chief Executive Officer*

FFA is a high school vocational program that helps prepare students for careers in agriculture and agribusiness. Students learn about agricultural production, processing, supply and service, mechanics, horticulture, forestry, and natural resources. Its major goal is to develop leadership, cooperation, and citizenship skills appropriate for productive members of an agricultural community. FFA maintains local high school chapters, state associations, and a national office. The organization sponsors a Hall of Achievement and maintains an extensive library on agricultural education.

PUBLICATIONS: *The Natural Future Farmer* (bimonthly).

### Future Homemakers of America (FHA)
1910 Association Drive
Reston, VA 22091
(703) 476-4900
*Carol Ann Kiner, Executive Director*

Future Homemakers of America helps young people prepare for family life, vocations, and community life. The organization maintains local FHA chapters that emphasize homemaking education and HERO (Home Economics Related Occupations) chapters, which focus on preparing for jobs and careers in home economics.

PUBLICATIONS: *Teen Times* (quarterly).

### Joint Council on Economic Education (JCEE)
2 Park Avenue
Ninth Floor
New York, NY 10016
(212) 685-5499
*Stephen G. Buckles, President*

The Joint Council is dedicated to promoting, improving, and servicing economics-education programs in elementary and secondary schools. It oversees a network 50 state Councils on Economic Education and over 260 college and university Centers for Economic Education. The organization develops economics materials for use in the schools. Its centers, which typically are housed in economics departments, schools of business, or schools of education, train teachers in the principles of economics and the use of economics materials. The centers also provide films, curriculum and evaluation consulting, and a Test of Economic Literacy with national norms.

PUBLICATIONS: *Journal of Economic Education* (quarterly), *The Senior Economist* (2 issues per year), *The Elementary Economist* (3 issues per year).

### Junior Achievement, Inc.
45 E. Clubhouse Drive
Colorado Springs, CO 80906
(719) 540-8000
*Karl Flemke, President and Chief Executive Officer*

This economics-education organization provides practical, hands-on programs for students in elementary, middle-grade, and high schools. Its programs, supported by the business community, emphasize understanding how the private enterprise system works. Several of these school programs feature lessons designed for at-risk students. Junior Achievement also has an after-school JA Company program for high school–aged students, and it hosts an International Student Forum each summer. In all of its programs a business volunteer works directly with students. The national organization has over 200 franchise area offices in cities nationwide, as well as affiliates in more than 30 foreign countries.

PUBLICATIONS: Junior Achievement publishes *Partners* (quarterly plus an occasional special issue) for business organizations and educators and *Talks to Teachers* (twice a semester) for high school teachers and students.

### National Dropout Prevention Center
Clemson University
Clemson, SC 29634-5111
(803) 656-2599
*Jay Smink, Executive Director*

The National Dropout Prevention Center was created to help reduce the U.S. dropout rate by fostering public-private partnerships in local school districts and communities throughout the nation. The Center, which serves as a clearinghouse on issues related to dropout prevention, collects, analyzes, and disseminates information and provides technical assistance to those developing dropout prevention programs. The Center publishes a quarterly newsletter, conducts workshops, hosts a national conference each spring and an annual summer institute, and maintains an electronic database (FOCUS) on dropout prevention programs, conferences, resources, and organizations.

## National Education Association (NEA)
1201 16th Street, NW
Washington, DC 20036
(202) 833-4000
*Don Cameron, Executive Director*

NEA is a national organization for teachers, school administrators, and other educators. Its services include leadership training, assistance with curriculum and instructional issues, legal services, help with segregation, and lobbying with Congress, state legislatures, and state boards and departments of education. NEA also functions as a union by representing teachers and other educators in negotiations and bargaining with school districts.

NEA Research conducts surveys and studies, and annually publishes *Estimates of School Statistics* and *Rankings of the States*. These publications report school enrollments, teacher salaries, school revenues and expenditures by state, and other descriptive data. NEA also operates a National Center for Innovation designed to foster school reform.

PUBLICATIONS: *NEA Today* (8 issues per year), *Today's Education* (annual), *Doubts & Certainties*, a newsletter from the NEA National Center for Innovation.

## National 4-H Council
7100 Connecticut Avenue
Chevy Chase, MD 20815
(301) 961-2800
*Richard Sauer, President*

4-H programs offer elementary and secondary school students (ages 9–19) the opportunity to develop life skills, learn about career opportunities, and acquire attitudes that will enable them to become productive members of society. The 4-H stands for Head, Heart, Hands, and Health. Young people participate in activities that involve practical, "learn-by-doing" projects related to a variety of vocational topics and social issues.

4-H administers its programs through the nation's 72 state land-grant universities. Within the states, it also has county offices that operate local programs. Each spring the organization hosts a National 4-H Conference for youth delegates from across the country.

PUBLICATIONS: *National 4-H News* (periodically).

## Phi Delta Kappa (PDK)
P.O. Box 789
Bloomington, IN 47402
(812) 339-1156
*Lowell C. Rose, Executive Director*

PDK is a professional honorary society in education.

PUBLICATIONS: A wide range of books, monographs, papers, reports of symposia, and *Fastback,* an ongoing series of booklets on current issues and topics in education. The major journal is the popular monthly, *Phi Delta Kappan.* The September issue each year is devoted to a report on the society's annual survey of the public's attitudes toward public schools.

### Social Science Education Consortium, Inc. (SSEC)
3300 Mitchell Lane, Suite 240
Boulder, CO 80301
(303) 492-8154
*James Geise, Executive Director*

This consortium was established about 25 years ago to promote social science education. It holds workshops and provides consulting services on selecting and implementing curriculum materials, infusing new content into curriculum, and other curriculum and training services. The consortium also maintains a Resource and Demonstration Center containing more than 20,000 examples of print and nonprint social studies textbooks, games and simulations, filmstrips, teaching kits, and other curriculum resources. It publishes occasional papers and hosts an annual "roundup" each year for its members, who come from various social science disciplines across school levels.

# Testing and Accrediting Agencies

### American College Testing Service (ACT)
2201 North Dodge Street, P.O. Box 168
Iowa City, IA 52243
(319) 337-1000
*Oluf M. Davidsen, President*

### Regional offices
Sacramento, CA (916) 921-2323
Aurora, CO (303) 366-3605
Atlanta, GA (404) 231-1952
Lincolnshire, IL (312) 634-2560
Albany, NY (518) 869-7378
Austin, TX (512) 454-8694

ACT conducts and administers testing, measurement and evaluation, and research programs for a range of educational needs and audiences. It provides services for college admissions and advising, career and educational planning, student financial aid, professional licensing, and certification.

PUBLICATIONS: ACT issues several publications related to its areas of service.

## The College Board
## (College Entrance Examination Board)
45 Columbus Avenue
New York, NY 10023
(212) 713-8000
*David M. Stewart, President*

### Regional offices
Denver, CO (303) 759-1800
Atlanta, GA (404) 636-9465
Evanston, IL (312) 866-1700
Waltham, MA (617) 890-9150
Philadelphia, PA (215) 387-7600
Austin, TX (512) 472-0231

The College Board is a national association of secondary schools, colleges, universities, and educational organizations designed to assist college-bound students. It offers guidance, admissions, placement, financial aid, and other related services. It also sponsors a national forum to discuss educational issues and trends, and offers programs related to such standardized tests as the SAT and achievement tests, as well as other services for youth and adult students.

PUBLICATIONS: *College Board News* (quarterly), *College Board Review* (quarterly) plus a variety of publications related to its specific services.

### Educational Testing Service (ETS)
Rosedale Road
Princeton, NJ 08541
(609) 921-9000
*Gregory R. Anrig, President*

### Regional offices
Berkeley, CA (415) 849-0950
Pasadena, CA (818) 578-1971
Washington, DC (202) 659-0616
Atlanta, GA (404) 524-4501
Evanston, IL (312) 869-7700
Brookline, MA (617) 739-2210
Austin, TX (512) 478-8191

ETS provides evaluative instruments, research, and services related to educational testing programs such as the PSAT, SAT, GRE, and GMAT, as well as admissions, selection, placement, and guidance services. It also conducts the National Assessment of Educational Progress (NAEP), a continuing survey of the knowledge, skills, and activities of elementary, middle-grade, and high school students.

PUBLICATIONS: *Focus* (quarterly), *Proceedings of the ETS Invitational Conference* (annual).

## Middle States Association of Colleges and Schools (MSA)
3624 Market Street
Philadelphia, PA 19104
(215) 662-5600
*Cecile G. Betit, Vice-President for Administration*

MSA is one of six regional organizations that conduct evaluations and accreditation assessments of elementary and secondary schools, vocational-technical schools, and colleges and universities. Its territory encompasses Delaware, Maryland, New Jersey, New York, Pennsylvania, the District of Columbia, Panama, Puerto Rico, and the Virgin Islands. MSA also hosts an annual conference and produces accreditation materials.

PUBLICATIONS: *The Membership Directory* (of accredited and candidate schools) and *The Proceedings* (annual).

## National Assessment of Educational Progress (NAEP)
Elementary and Secondary Outcomes Division
National Center for Educational Statistics
555 New Jersey Avenue, NW
Washington, DC 20208
(202) 219-1746
*Eugene Owen, Director*

NAEP is authorized by Congress and funded by the Office of Educational Research and Improvement, U.S. Department of Education, to determine the nation's progress in education. Periodically, NAEP assesses the achievements of 9-, 13-, and 17-year-old students, and occasionally young adults (ages 25–35) in ten learning areas. The areas in which changes in educational achievement are measured include reading, writing, mathematics, literature, U.S. history, and science. These assessments are conducted by the Educational Testing Service (ETS).

## New England Association of Schools and Colleges (NEASC)
The Sanborn House
15 High Street
Winchester, MA 01890
(617) 729-6762
*Richard J. Bradley, Executive Director*

NEASC is one of six regional organizations that conduct evaluations and accreditation assessments of elementary and secondary schools, vocational-technical schools, and colleges and universities. It serves the states of Connecticut, Maine, Massachusetts, New Hampshire, Rhode Island, and Vermont. NEASC also hosts workshops and an annual conference.

PUBLICATIONS: *NEASC Notes* (quarterly) and a *Membership Directory* (annual).

## North Central Association of Colleges and Schools (NCA)

Commission on Schools
P.O. Box 18
Boulder, CO 80309
(303) 497-0261
(800) 525-9571 (outside Colorado)
*Kenneth F. Gose, Jr., Executive Director*

Commission on Institutions of Higher Education
159 North Dearborn
Chicago, IL 60601
(312) 263-0456
(800) 621-7440 (outside Illinois)
*Patricia A. Thrash, Director*

NCA is one of six regional organizations that conduct evaluations and accreditation assessments of elementary and secondary schools, vocational-technical schools, and colleges and universities. It serves the states of Arizona, Arkansas, Colorado, Illinois, Indiana, Iowa, Kansas, Michigan, Minnesota, Missouri, Nebraska, New Mexico, North Dakota, Ohio, Oklahoma, South Dakota, West Virginia, Wisconsin, Wyoming, and the U.S. Department of Defense's Dependents Schools overseas. North Central also hosts an annual conference and produces accreditation materials.

PUBLICATIONS: *North Central Association Quarterly.*

## Northwest Association of Schools and Colleges (NASC)

3700-B University Way, NE
Seattle, WA 98105
(206) 543-0195
*James F. Bemis, Executive Director*

NASC is one of six regional organizations that conduct evaluations and accreditation assessments of elementary and secondary schools, vocational-technical schools, and colleges and universities. It serves the states of Alaska, Idaho, Montana, Nevada, Oregon, Utah, and Washington. NASC also hosts an annual conference and produces accreditation materials.

PUBLICATIONS: *Accreditation Handbook* (postsecondary, biennial), *Manual of Policies and Standards for Accreditation of Schools* (biennial), *Proceedings* (annual).

## Secondary School Admissions Testing Board (SSATB)

12 Stockton Street
Princeton, NJ 08540
(609) 683-4440
*Regan Kenyon, Executive Director*

SSATB is an educational network made up of independent elementary and secondary schools, educational consultants, counselors, and educational organizations. Its primary purpose is to provide its members with the Secondary Schools Admissions Test (SSAT) that is used to evaluate, admit, and place students in private, independent schools across the country and in several foreign countries. While SSATB sponsors the SSAT, the test is developed and administered by the Educational Testing Service (ETS).

SSATB also offers opportunities for the professional growth of educators in admissions. It hosts an annual admissions meeting, admission training workshops, and regional admission workshops.

PUBLICATIONS: *Memberanda* (quarterly newsletter).

## Southern Association of Colleges and Schools (SACS)
795 Peachtree Street, NE
Atlanta, GA 30365
(404) 897-6100
*B. E. Childers, Executive Director*

SACS is one of six regional organizations that conduct evaluations and accreditation assessments of elementary and secondary schools, vocational-technical schools, and colleges and universities. It serves the states of Alabama, Florida, Georgia, Kentucky, Louisiana, Mississippi, North Carolina, South Carolina, Tennessee, Texas, and Virginia, and also evaluates school systems in Latin America. The Southern Association conducts workshops and seminars and hosts an annual conference.

PUBLICATIONS: *Proceedings* of the annual meeting.

## Western Association of Schools and Colleges (WASC)

Accrediting Commission for Community and Junior Colleges
9053 Soquel Drive
Aptos, CA 95003
(408) 688-7575
*John C. Petersen, Executive Director*

Accrediting Commission for Schools
1606 Rollins Road
Burlingame, CA 94010
(415) 697-7711
*Don E. Halverson, Executive Director*

Accrediting Commission for Senior Colleges and Universities
P.O. Box 9990
Mills College
Oakland, CA 94613
(415) 632-5000
*Stephen S. Weiner, Executive Director*

WASC is one of six regional organizations that conduct evaluations and accreditation assessments of elementary and secondary schools, vocational-technical schools, and colleges and universities. It serves the states of California and Hawaii, as well as Guam and other Pacific areas. The Western Association conducts workshops and produces accreditation materials.

PUBLICATIONS: *Directory of Members* (annual).

**Western Interstate Commission for Higher Education (WICHE)**
1540 30th Street
P.O. Drawer P
Boulder, CO 80301
(303) 497-0201
*Phil Sirotkin, Executive Director*

WICHE is a commission of states chartered to meet the needs of higher education and manpower resources in the western region of the United States. It sponsors an exchange to share educational resources and an information clearinghouse of data for policymakers in higher education and government. Membership in WICHE is restricted to the states of Alaska, Arizona, California, Colorado, Hawaii, Idaho, Montana, Nevada, New Mexico, Oregon, Utah, Washington, and Wyoming. States that are geographically contiguous to the western region may have an affiliate membership. WICHE also publishes special reports and monographs on issues pertinent to higher education.

# Private Data-Gathering Agencies

**Market Data Retrieval (MDR)**

Eastern Region
16 Progress Drive
Shelton, CT 06484
(203) 926-4800, (800) 333-8802

Midwest Region
55 West Monroe Street
Suite 510
Chicago, IL 60603
(312) 263-1623, (800) 333-8802

Western Region
1001 Bayhill Drive
San Bruno, CA 94066
(415) 871-0936, (800) 333-8802

*Herb Lobsenz, President*

This market research company compiles lists of schools and school districts, identifying school addresses, district administrators, and school principals. It publishes this information each year in a series of state directories. MDR also provides a variety of data on elementary, middle-grade, and high school; school district; college; library; and early childhood markets. It generates databases with names and addresses of administrators, teachers by subject area, college professors, librarians, and other educational markets. It also collects information on the types and numbers of computers used in schools, and reports trends in the educational marketplace through seminars and bulletins.

**National Center for Education Information**
4401A Connecticut Avenue, NW #212
Washington, DC 20008
(202) 362-3444
*Emily Feistritzer, Director*

Since 1983 the National Center for Education Information has conducted studies and surveys and published reports on a wide range of educational issues and topics. Members receive copies of its national studies and reports when they are published as well as *Education Reports,* an eight-page weekly newsletter on pertinent events from the Department of Education, the White House, and Congress. NCEI also provides documents from public and private sources, directories, charts, articles, papers, and other data to its members on a regular basis.

**Quality Educational Data (QED)**
1600 Broadway, 12th Floor
Denver, CO 80202
(303) 860-1832, (800) 525-5811
*Jeanne Hayes, President*

QED is a market research company that gathers a range of data on school districts, schools, libraries, colleges, and child-care facilities. It publishes state directories of schools, information on computer and video markets, and generates a variety of mailing lists. It offers users with Macintosh or IBM/PC-compatible computers access to Academy Online, an electronic connection to a K–12 school database. QED also helps its users design studies, draw samples, and conduct surveys.

# Government Agencies

## Educational Resources Information Center (ERIC) Clearinghouses

ERIC is a national information network for disciplines and other special areas in education. Its purpose is to gather and disseminate information gleaned from research and other scholarly inquiries. The data are obtained, organized, and disseminated by 16 subject-oriented centers, or clearinghouses, across the nation; these centers are listed by subject below.

PUBLICATIONS: This information ERIC gathers is catalogued and indexed in *Resources in Education (RIE)*. (See Chapter 8.) ERIC also publishes the *Current Index to Journals in Education (CIJE)*, an index of articles that appear in approximately 800 professional journals. Users of this information system locate entries through the *Thesaurus of ERIC Descriptors*.

### Adult, Career, and Vocational Education
National Center for Research in Vocational Education
Ohio State University
1960 Kenny Road
Columbus, OH 43210
(614) 486-3655, (800) 848-4815

### Counseling and Personnel Services
University of Michigan
Room 2108
School of Education Building
610 East University Street
Ann Arbor, MI 48109
(313) 764-9492

### Educational Management
University of Oregon
1787 Agate Street
Eugene, OR 97403
(503) 686-5043

### Elementary And Early Childhood Education
University of Illinois
College of Education
805 West Pennsylvania Avenue
Urbana, IL 61801
(217) 333-1386

### Handicapped and Gifted Children
Council for Exceptional Children
1920 Association Drive
Reston, VA 22091
(703) 620-3660

### Higher Education
George Washington University
One Dupont Circle, NW
Suite 630
Washington, DC 20036
(202) 296-2597

## Information Resources
Syracuse University
School of Education
Huntington Hall
Room 030
150 Marshall Street
Syracuse, NY 13210
(315) 423-3640

## Junior Colleges
University of California at Los Angeles
Mathematical Sciences Building
Room 8118
405 Hilgard Avenue
Los Angeles, CA 90024
(213) 825-3931

## Languages and Linguistics
Center for Applied Linguistics
1118 22nd Street, NW
Washington, DC 20037
(202) 429-9551

## Reading and Communication Skills
Smith Research Center
Indiana University
2805 East 10th Street
Bloomington, IN 47405
(812) 337-5847

## Rural Education and Small Schools
Appalachia Educational Laboratory
1031 Quarrier Street
P.O. Box 1348
Charleston, WV 25325
(800) 624-9120
(800) 344-6646 (in West Virginia)

## Science, Mathematics, and Environmental Education
Ohio State University
1200 Chambers Road
Room 310
Columbus, OH 43212
(614) 422-6717

### Social Studies/Social Science Education
Indiana University
Social Studies Development Center
2805 East 10th Street
Bloomington, IN 47405
(812) 335-3838

### Teacher Education
American Association of Colleges for Teacher Education
One Dupont Circle, NW
Suite 610
Washington, DC 20036
(202) 293-2450

### Tests, Measurement, and Evaluation
American Institutes for Research
1055 Thomas Jefferson Street, NW
Washington, DC 20007
(202) 342-5060

### Urban Education
Columbia University
Teachers College
525 West 120th Street
Box 40
New York, NY 10027
(212) 678-3433

## National Center for Education Statistics (NCES)
555 New Jersey Avenue, NW
Washington, DC 20208
(800) 424-1616
*Emerson J. Elliot, Acting Commissioner*

The National Center for Education Statistics (NCES) gathers and publishes information on the status and progress of education in the United States. NCES is a division of the U.S. Department of Education that was established and authorized by the General Education Provisions Act (1974) to "collect, collate, and from time to time, report full and complete statistics on the condition of education in the United States." These conditions include the status of student performances, achievement test scores, high school completion rates, school financial resources, staff employment and teacher salaries, student characteristics, and state graduation and teacher-preparation requirements.

PUBLICATIONS: The center publishes the information in several volumes. Indicators of trends and developments are contained in *The Condition of Education,* which is published in two volumes (one addressing elementary and secondary schooling and the other postsecondary schooling) and *1989 Education Indicators*. Each volume contains a series of illustrative tables and charts. The *Digest of Education Statistics* is a more detailed volume that contains statistical tables, plus figures and appendices. Each of the volumes is updated and published annually.

## National Institute on Drug Abuse (NIDA)
Division of Epidemiology and Statistical Analysis
5600 Fishers Lane
Rockville, MD 20857
(301) 443-6245
*Charles Schuster, Director*

The NIDA, an agency of the U.S. Department of Health and Human Services, obtains data annually on student drug use. Typically, more than 15,000 high school seniors are surveyed as part of a larger study on Lifestyles and Values of Youth conducted by the Institute for Social Research at the University of Michigan.

PUBLICATIONS: The results of the studies conducted by NIDA are published by:

National Clearinghouse for Alcohol and Drug Information (NCADI)
6000 Executive Boulevard
Suite 402
P.O. Box 2345
Rockville, MD 20852
(800) 729-6686

## Office of Civil Rights
U.S. Department of Education
330 C Street, SW
Washington, DC 20202
(202) 732-1213
*Lawrence Bussey, Chief, Surveys Branch*

The Office of Civil Rights conducts periodic surveys of elementary and secondary schools to obtain data on the characteristics of students enrolled in public schools throughout the nation. The characteristics examined in recent surveys include racial and ethnic status, gender, limited English proficiency, and conditions for the disabled. The gathering of this information is authorized by the Civil Rights Act of 1964.

PUBLICATIONS: *Civil Rights Survey of Elementary and Secondary Schools*. Data from the survey also is included in the educational indicators, conditions, and statistical digests published by the National Center for Educational Statistics.

## Office of Special Education Programs

U.S. Department of Education
Office of Special Education and Rehabilitative Services (OSERS)
Switzer Building
330 C Street, SW
Washington, DC 20202
(202) 732-1007
*Judy Schrag, Director*

The Education of the Handicapped Act (EHA) requires the U.S. Secretary of Education to provide Congress with an annual report describing the progress made by disabled children in the United States. This *Annual Report to Congress on the Implementation of the Education of the Handicapped Act* includes information on children in the public schools and those served in state-operated programs for the disabled. Data on children receiving special education and related services and school personnel providing this service are reported to OSERS by the 50 states, the District of Columbia, and the outlying areas.

# 8

# Reference Materials

THIS CHAPTER PRESENTS A SELECTED BIBLIOGRAPHY of resources for information on many educational areas and specialties. These reference materials include bibliographies, dictionaries, encyclopedias, handbooks, sourcebooks, yearbooks, digests, videotapes, and databases. The sources cover a wider range of topics than could be examined in this book. These works also present various findings and viewpoints on educational issues.

For more extensive, if not exhaustive, information on general education resource materials, see *Education: A Guide to Reference and Information Sources* by Lois J. Buttlar (Englewood, CO: Libraries Unlimited, 1989) and *The Educator's Desk Reference (EDR): A Sourcebook of Educational Information and Research* edited by Melvyn N. Freed, Robert K. Hess, and Joseph M. Ryan (New York: Macmillan, 1989). Both sourcebooks are included in this chapter.

The field of education is a rich area for fascinating books. Earlier chapters refer to many published during the 1980s and earlier, especially Chapter 4.

## Bibliographies

Ambert, Alba N., and Sarah E. Melendez. **Bilingual Education: A Sourcebook.** New York: Garland, 1986. 340p. $17.95. ISBN 0-8077-2853-5.

This sourcebook is an annotated bibliography of materials on a variety of issues related to bilingual education.

Austin, Mary C., and Esther C. Jenkins. **Promoting World Understanding through Literature, K–8.** Littleton, CO: Libraries Unlimited, 1983. 266p. $22.50. ISBN 0-87287-356-0.

This annotated bibliography describes materials of particular interest to K–8 teachers and librarians on blacks, Native Americans, and Hispanics. The materials are arranged by ethnic group, and introductions to each section describe geographic and cultural features of the country and peoples, folk literature, themes in children's literature, and the different forms of literature (e.g., poetry, picture books, biography, fiction).

Baatz, Olga K., and Charles Albert Baatz. **The Psychological Foundations of Education.** Detroit: Gale, 1981. 440p. $65. ISBN 0-8103-1467-3.

This is an annotated bibliography of books and articles on the psychological foundations of education. The sources address cognitive, affective, moral, and aesthetic dimensions of learning. The volume is arranged in six chapters devoted to broad subject areas: Education and Psychology, Intellectual Education, Moral Education, Affective Education, Poetic (Aesthetic) Education, and The Acting Person.

**Bibliographic Guide to Education.** Boston: G. K. Hall, 1979–. Published annually. 472p. $260. ISBN 0-8161-7124-6.

This is a comprehensive bibliography of publications in education that have been catalogued by Teachers College, Columbia University, as well as selected titles from the New York Public Library. It identifies books, government documents, monographs, and nonprint materials in various areas and levels of schooling.

Brewer, Deborah J., ed. and comp. **ARBA Guide to Education.** Littleton, CO: Libraries Unlimited, 1985. 232p. $26.50. ISBN 0-87287-490-7.

This guide contains over 450 reference sources that have been reviewed by the American Reference Books Annual (ARBA) since 1970. The first two parts cover bibliographies, indexes, catalogs, dictionaries, encyclopedias, handbooks, yearbooks, directories, and biographies. The third part includes specific topics such as bilingual and minority education, instructional media, reading, and special education.

Clarkson, Mary Cervantes, comp. **Mainstreaming the Exceptional Child: A Bibliography.** San Antonio: Trinity University Press, 1982. 240p. $25, $15 pa. ISBN 0-9115366-92-2, 0-939980-02-9 pa.

This bibliography includes over 3,000 books, journal articles, ERIC documents, dissertations, government documents, and pamphlets related to mainstreaming handicapped children and working with the gifted in the public schools. Entries are arranged in chapters organized by learning type: General, Gifted, Hearing Impaired, Learning Disabled and Emotionally Disturbed,

Mentally Handicapped, Physically Handicapped, Speech Handicapped, and Visually Handicapped.

**Educational Film/Video Locator of the Consortium of University Film Centers and R. R. Bowker Co.** 3d ed. New York: R. R. Bowker, 1986. 2 vols. $150. ISBN 0-8352-2179-2 (set), 0-8352-2180-6 (vol. 1), ISBN 0-8352-2181-4 (vol. 2).

This bibliography of more than 40,000 films and videos includes titles and descriptions from 52 library collections that belong to the consortium of University Film Centers.

Fagan, William T., Charles R. Cooper, and Julie M. Jensen. **Measures for Research and Evaluation in the English Language Arts, Volume 2.** Urbana, IL: ERIC Clearinghouse on Reading and Communication Skills and National Council of Teachers of English, 1985. 245p. $17. ISBN 0-8141-3101-8.

The authors describe measures for assessing student performance in English and language arts. Information on each assessment instrument includes purpose, methodology, validity and reliability measures, and norming data.

Menendez, Albert J. **School Prayer and Other Religious Issues in American Public Education: A Bibliography.** New York: Garland, 1985. 168p. $20. ISBN 0-8240-8775-5.

The books, journal articles, newspaper articles, law journal reviews, theses, and dissertations included in this bibliography cover a range of topics on religion and religious issues. The subjects include history of school prayer, Bible reading, religious teachings in the classroom, Christian music, and dramatizations. The references span from the mid-1800s to the 1980s.

Sternlicht, Manny, and Madeline Sternlicht. **Special Education: A Source Book.** New York: Garland, 1987. 431p. $50. ISBN 0-8240-8524-8.

This is an annotated bibliography of about 1,000 books, articles, chapters, dissertations, and papers on special education. The sources address mental retardation, the gifted, visual and hearing impairments, learning disabilities, brain damage, speech and language impairments, other physical impairments, emotional and behavioral impairments, and mainstreaming. This volume is a comprehensive view of the literature from 1960 to 1986.

Woodbury, Marda. **A Guide to Sources of Educational Information.** 2d ed. Arlington, VA: Information Resources Press, 1982. 430p. $39.95. ISBN 0-87815-041-2.

This annotated bibliographical listing of reference sources includes nonprint materials on educational organizations and government agencies.

# Dictionaries and Encyclopedias

Anderson, Scarvia B., Samuel Ball, Richard T. Murphy, and associates. **Encyclopedia of Educational Evaluation: Concepts and Techniques for Evaluating Education and Training Programs.** San Francisco: Jossey-Bass, 1975. 515p. $27.95. ISBN 0-87589-238-8.

This is a series of articles by authorities that synthesize the major concepts and techniques of evaluation and training programs. The writers define pertinent terms and describe evaluation models, experimental design, measurement devices, statistical tools, and related topics.

Barrow, Robin, and Geoffrey Milburn. **A Critical Dictionary of Educational Concepts: An Appraisal of Selected Ideas and Issues in Educational Theory and Practice.** New York: St. Martin's Press, 1986. 240p. $35. ISBN 0-312-00229-7.

This unique dictionary defines broad concepts that are commonly used in curriculum development, learning theory, policy studies, research, evaluation, and other areas of elementary, secondary, and higher education. The issues and ideas included are those that make up the daily language of classroom teachers and professors, as well as of educational theory and research.

Deighton, Lee C., ed. **The Encyclopedia of Education.** New York: Macmillan and Free Press, 1971. 10 vols. $199 (set). ISBN 0-02-893300-2.

This comprehensive compendium covers historical, theoretical, philosophical, and practical issues of American, international, and comparative education. The more than 1,000 articles are signed by their contributing scholars.

Dejnozka, Edward L., and David E. Kapel. **American Educator's Encyclopedia.** Westport, CT: Greenwood Press, 1982. 634p. $75. ISBN 0-313-20954-5.

This volume defines terms and phrases used in education and gives descriptions of prominent educators, educational organizations, and relevant subjects. The entries, most less than 200 words, are appropriate for elementary, secondary, and higher education.

Dunkin, Michael J., ed. **The International Encyclopedia of Teaching and Teacher Education.** Elmsford, NY: Pergamon Press, 1987. 878p. $90. ISBN 0-08-030852-X.

This volume is made up of reprinted articles from *The International Encyclopedia of Education: Research and Studies* (Pergamon Press, 1985) and is arranged in six sections: (1) concepts and methods, (2) methods and paradigms for research, (3) teaching methods and techniques, (4) classroom procedures, (5) contextual factors, and (6) teacher education. The resources are appropriate for theorists, researchers, and practitioners.

Farber, Bernard E., comp. **A Teacher's Treasury of Quotations.** Jefferson, NC: McFarland, 1985. 370p. $39.95. ISBN 0-89950-150-8.

The author has compiled a wide variety of quotations on education from people in many walks of life. The remarks, statements, and comments are arranged in 450 subject categories.

Gatti, Richard D., and Daniel J. Gatti. **New Encyclopedic Dictionary of School Law.** West Nyack, NJ: Parker Publishing, 1983. 400p. $34.95. ISBN 0-13-612580-8.

The authors describe terms related to school case law covering several hundred cases over the past century. The entries are current through the early 1980s.

Good, Carter V., ed. **Dictionary of Education.** 3d ed. Prepared under the auspices of Phi Delta Kappa. New York: McGraw-Hill, 1973. 681p. ISBN 0-07-023720-4.

This classic reference of educational terms, first published in 1945, contains about 33,000 references covering theories, concepts, methods, movements, and technologies.

Hawes, Gene R., and Lynne S. Hawes. **The Concise Dictionary of Education.** New York: Van Nostrand Reinhold, 1982. 249p. ISBN 0-442-26298-1.

This is a comprehensive dictionary of the special terms educators use in their fields, from early childhood education to postdoctoral studies and lifelong learning.

Houston, James E. **Thesaurus of ERIC Descriptors.** 11th ed. Phoenix: Oryx Press, 1986. 640p. $65. ISBN 0-89774-159-5.

This is a valuable resource for understanding the controlled terms or descriptors used by ERIC (Educational Resources Information Center). New descriptors developed since the previous edition are listed in a separate section. The ERIC system is produced and operated by the National Institute of Education, U.S. Department of Education.

Husen, Torsten, and T. Neville Postlethwaite, eds. **The International Encyclopedia of Education: Research and Studies.** Elmsford, NY: Pergamon Press, 1985. 10 vols. $1,750 (set). ISBN 0-08-028119-2.

A total of 1,448 articles covering 25 broad educational categories are included in this extensive collection. The 1,300 contributing writers represent over 100 nations. Editors-in-chief Torsten Husen and T. Neville Postlethwaite are from the University of Stockholm and the University of Hamburg.

Koek, Karin E., and Susan B. Martin, eds., for the National Organizations of the U.S. **Encyclopedia of Associations.** Detroit: Gale Research, 1989. Published annually. $295. ISBN 0-8103-4695-8.

This directory includes more than 1,100 academic, commercial, agricultural, and scientific organizations in education. Each description includes address, phone number, name and title of chief operating official, size, official publications, services offered, and date and location of annual convention.

Mann, Lester, and Cecil B. Reynolds, eds. **Encyclopedia of Special Education.** New York: John Wiley and Sons, 1987. 3 vols. $189 (set). ISBN 0-471-82858-0.

This is a compilation of terms and concepts used in special education, supported by scholarly articles. Over 2,000 articles on various aspects of special education are addressed to a wide variety of practitioners, including teachers, psychologists, physicians, social workers, lawyers, and ministers. The volumes also include information on the pioneers and significant professionals in special education. The entire Education for All Handicapped Children Act of 1975 (P.L. 94–142) is reprinted in an appendix.

Mitzel, Harold E., ed. **Encyclopedia of Educational Research.** 5th ed. New York: Macmillan and Free Press, 1982. 4 vols. $315 (set). ISBN 0-02-900450-0.

Over 300 specialists address a wide range of subjects and summarize recent research trends and findings. The first volume was published in 1941, and successive volumes are released every 10 to 15 years. Publication is sponsored by the American Educational Research Association (AERA).

Moore, Byron C., William Abraham, and Clarence R. Laing. **A Dictionary of Special Education Terms.** Springfield, IL: Charles C. Thomas, 1980. 117p. $15.25. ISBN 0-398-04009-5.

This dictionary provides terms used in special education areas including hearing, vision, speech, emotional and physical handicaps, mental retardation, and the gifted.

**1991 Deskbook Encyclopedia of American School Law.** Rosemount, MN: Data Research. Published annually. $73.50. ISBN 0-93675-21-8.

This deskbook encyclopedia summarizes education case law based on state and federal appellate court decisions. The case laws are classified according to the major subject categories including accidents-injuries-death, employment practices, faculty promotion and tenure, freedom of speech and religion, students' rights, and collective bargaining. The editorial staff of Data Research also publishes a monthly newsletter, *Legal Notes for Educators* ($89 a year).[1]

Ohles, John F., ed. **Biographical Dictionary of American Educators.** 2d ed. 3 vols. Westport, CT: Greenwood, 1978. $150. ISBN 0-8371-9893-3.

These volumes present biographical sketches of 1,665 prominent American educators who, at the time of publication, were either deceased or retired and at least 60 years old.

Page, G. Terry, and J. B. Thomas. **International Dictionary of Education.** London: Kogan Page; New York: Nichols, 1980. 381p. $13.95. ISBN 0-262-66043-1.

This volume includes more than 10,000 concisely defined terms, items of jargon, technical languages, organizations, and honor societies. Biographical information on prominent educators such as Maria Montessori, Jean Piaget, and Johann Pestalozzi also is covered.

Palmer, James C., and Anita Y. Colby, eds. **Dictionary of Educational Acronyms, Abbreviations, and Initialisms.** 2d ed. Phoenix: Oryx Press, 1985. 97p. $27.50. ISBN 0-89774-165-X.

This collection of over 4,000 organizations, tests, titles, degrees, terms, and programs is listed in two forms: one alphabetically according the acronyms, abbreviations, and initials associated with terms, and the reverse, with the terms appearing first.

Psacharopoulos, George, ed. **Economics of Education: Research and Studies.** Elmsford, NY: Pergamon Press, 1987. 482p. $85. ISBN 0-08-033379-6.

The findings of research in the economics of education are described in 12 chapter categories that include such topics as human capital, benefits of education, education and employment, analysis of earnings, distribution of educational outcomes, and financing education.

Roundtree, Derek. **Dictionary of Education.** Totowa, NJ: Barnes & Noble Books, 1982. $22.50. 362p. ISBN 0-389-202263.

This dictionary contains over 3,000 terms. The author emphasizes those that have different meanings for English-speaking persons in different countries, e.g., public school, grammar school, and gymnasium. When a term differs from one country to the next, it is followed by a symbol identifying the country. Biographies of internationally known educators and descriptions of educational organizations generally are not included.

# Handbooks, Sourcebooks, and Yearbooks

Alexander, Kern. **Public School Law.** 2d ed. St. Paul, MN: West Publishing, 1985. 817p. $48.75. ISBN 0-314-85213-1.

This is a casebook on major court decisions related to school governance, policies, and operations. The selections include excerpts from court rulings with notes on and interpretations of cases. The volume starts with an historical perspective of education in the United States, then explains the constitutional basis for the federal, state, and local governments' roles in education. The author reviews cases related to church and state, compulsory education and curriculum, students' rights, desegregation, teachers, and collective bargaining issues.

Bell, Chris, ed. **World Yearbook of Education.** London: Kogan Page; New York: Nichols, 1979–. Published annually. 300p. $48.50. ISBN 0-89397-364-5.

Each yearbook is dedicated to a significant theme or issue in international education, such as lifelong learning, minorities, research, policy and practice, health, and education for new technology. The theme for the 1990 yearbook was assessment and evaluation. A theme is examined through a series of treatises by authors from different nations. Biographical sketches of the contributing writers are included.

Buttlar, Lois J. **Education: A Guide to Information Sources.** Englewood, CO: Libraries Unlimited, 1989. 300p. $35. ISBN 0-87287-619-5.

This guide provides synopses of major sources of information in education and the related fields of sociology, psychology, history, political science, and social work. The volume offers a detailed review of bibliographies, directories, handbooks, yearbooks, dictionaries, and encyclopedias for general education reference sources, as well as reviews in more than a dozen areas within education. These areas include educational foundations, curriculum and instruction, educational administration, special education, bilingual and multicultural education, women's studies, and others.

Cohen, Sol, ed. **Education in the United States: A Documentary History.** Westport, CT: Greenwood, 1974. 5 vols. $225. ISSN 0307-9732.

This five-volume reference sourcebook includes over 1,300 significant documents in the history of American education dating to the early sixteenth century. The documents consist of letters, essays, reports, and legislation. The five volumes are divided into three books covering major educational periods: Book 1—*The Planting, 1607–1789*; Book 2—*The Shaping of American Education, 1789–1895*; and Book 3—*The Transformation of American Education, 1895–1973*.

Freed, Melvyn N., Robert K. Hess, and Joseph M. Ryan, with support from the American Council on Education. **The Educator's Desk Reference: A Sourcebook of Educational Information and Research.** New York: Macmillan, 1989. $49.50. 536p. ISBN 0-02-910740-7.

This is an extensive summary of informational resources (bibliographies, directories, encyclopedias, handbooks), journals, microcomputer software, standardized tests and inventories, research processes, and organizations in education. The entries are designed to aid scholars, researchers, writers, and practitioners in their search for information on education.

**IRA Desktop Reference 90.** Newark, DE: International Reading Association, 1972–. Published annually. 224p. $12. ISBN 0-87207-781-0.

These yearbooks describe all the events, activities, special projects, and services of the International Reading Association (IRA) and its affiliated agencies and councils around the world. They provide information on membership, committees, publications, and awards.

Miller, Elwood E., and Mary Louise Mosley, eds. **Educational Media and Technology Yearbook.** Littleton, CO: Libraries Unlimited, 1973–. Published annually. 350p. $50. ISBN 0-87287-772-8.

This yearbook contains an array of information on instructional technology and educational media including analyses of pertinent issues, listings of organizations and associations, and a directory of graduate programs. It also lists foundations that financially support media-related projects.

Nauman, Ann K. **A Biographical Handbook of Education: Five Hundred Contributors to the Field.** New York: Irvington, 1985. 238p. $16.95. ISBN 0-8290-0722-9.

This collection of biographical sketches begins with the contributions to educational thought of the ancient Greeks such as Plato and Aristotle and ends with living contemporary educators. Entries are about 100 words in length and are arranged in alphabetical order. Each sketch ends by referring to other sources of information on the educator. Several notable educators including Lawrence Cremin, John I. Goodlad, and Maxine Greene (who are discussed in Chapter 4 of this book) are conspicuously absent from Nauman's handbook.

Osborne, Chris W., ed. **International Yearbook of Educational and Instructional Technology.** New York: Nichols, 1976–. Published biennially. $39.50. ISSN 0307-9732.

This yearbook reports on international trends and events in educational communications and technology. As a companion work to *Educational Media and Technology Yearbook,* this volume includes readings on technologies in specific countries, developments in computer education, interactive video, and other instructional technology. Each volume contains a directory of databases, networks, consultants, hardware and software producers, distributors, and conferences.

Pearson, P. David, ed. **Handbook of Reading Research.** New York: Longman, 1984. 912p. $58.95. ISBN 0-582-28119-9.

This collection of scholarly articles provides an analysis and interpretation of research on reading. It includes methodologies and research findings as well as practical advice for the researcher. The articles also present a comprehensive summary of instructional practices.

Reutter, E. Edmund, Jr., and Robert Hamilton. **The Law of Public Education.** 3d ed. Mineola, NY: Foundation Press, 1985. 929p. $32. ISBN 0-88277-222-8.

This casebook is designed to provide basic information on the law that directly affects public schools in the United States. Each chapter focuses on the legal aspects of a problem area (e.g., church-state-education relationships, local school boards, teacher certification, or contracts). Excerpts from individual cases, supplemented by explanations from the authors, provide insights on interpretations and rulings.

Semler, Darrel P., and Thomas N. Jones, eds. **School Law Update, 1991.** Topeka, KS: National Organization on Legal Problems of Education, 1991. Published annually. $19.95. ISBN 0-318-23628-1.

This is a compilation of papers on the dimensions of case law that affect education that were delivered at the annual meeting of the National Organization on Legal Problems of Education.

**SIRS Crisis.** Boca Raton, FL: Social Issues Resources Series, 1986. Updated annually. $85, $17 annual supplement. ISBN 0-89777 series.

There are two titles in this most recent SIRS reprint series: *AIDS* (1986) and *Atmosphere* (1988). The series includes a variety of journal and newspaper articles on different dimensions of these two critical issues. Each topic is updated with 20 new articles annually, and a completed volume contains 100 articles. Both topics are into the second volume.

**SIRS Digest.** Boca Raton, FL: Social Issues Resources Series, 1977. $40. ISBN 0-89777-100 series.

SIRS Digests consist of stories on contemporary issues written for middle-grade students. The digests are arranged in seven volumes: *Alcohol* (1990), *Drugs* (1990), *Energy* (1987), *Family* (1990), *Food* (1990), *Pollution* (1988), and *Population* (1990), each containing 40 original articles.

**SIRS National Archives Documents.** Boca Raton, FL: Social Issues Resources Series, 1978. $40, $390 (set). ISBN 0-89777 series.

This is a series of primary resource materials reprinted from the files of the National Archives for use as teaching units. Each of the 11 units is a package of materials that contains about 50 reproductions on an era in U.S. history. The units include *the Constitution* (1985); *the Bill of Rights* (1988); *the U.S. Expands West, 1785–1842* (1990); *the Civil War* (1980); *the Progressive Years, 1898–1917* (1982); *World War I* (1978); *the 1920s* (1981); *the Great Depression and New Deal* (1978); *World War II* (1978); *the Truman Years* (1986); *Peace and Prosperity, 1953–1961* (1987).

**SIRS Science.** Boca Raton, FL: Social Issues Resources Series, 1985–. Updated annually. $80, $16 annual supplement. ISBN 0-89777 series.

SIRS Science is a series of reprinted articles in five volumes: *Earth Sciences, Physical Sciences, Life Sciences, Medical Sciences,* and *Applied Sciences.* A new volume for each title, containing 70 articles, is published annually.

**SIRS Volumes.** Boca Raton, FL: Social Issues Resources Series, 1972–. Updated annually. $85, $17 annual supplement. ISBN 0-89777 series.

This is the original SIRS program, which consists of reprinted articles on social issues from a wide range of journals, magazines, and newspapers. The 32 titles in the series are *Pollution, Population, Drugs, Energy, Food, Work, Alcohol, Money, Privacy, Family, Crime, Corrections, Women, Health, Mental Health, School, Ethnic Groups, Habitat, Transportation, Communications, Aging, Religion, Youth, Sports, Defense, Consumerism, Ethics, Death and Dying, Technology, Human Rights, Sexuality,* and *Third World.* Each issue is updated with 20 new articles yearly, and a complete volume contains 100 articles. The early titles now include at least four volumes and over 400 articles.[2]

Spodek, Bernard, ed. **Handbook of Research in Early Childhood Education.** New York: Free Press, 1982. 640p. $65. ISBN 0-02-930570-5.

This collection of articles provides an overview of issues on early childhood education along with the results of research findings. Topics include child development, developmental theories, classroom methods, early childhood educational policy, and measurement and evaluation methods.

Tashner, John N., ed. **Educational Microcomputing Annual.** Phoenix: Oryx Press, 1985–. Published annually. $39. ISSN 8755-836X.

This is a series of articles by authorities on educational computer programs and technology. The topics include hardware trends, computer languages, software development and curriculum, instructional management, and personnel management.

Thomas, Stephen B., ed. **The Yearbook of Education Law.** Topeka, KS: National Organization on Legal Problems of Education (NOLPE), 1990. Published annually. $35.95. ISBN 0-318-19549-6.[3]

This yearbook presents a summary and an analysis of case law rulings by state appellate and federal courts during a particular year. The summaries cover a wide range of educational areas and issues.

Valente, William D. **Education Law: Public and Private.** St. Paul, MN: West Publishing, 1985. 2 vols. 1,285p. $169.50. ISBN 0-314-87700-2.

These volumes summarize state and federal case law, regulations, and legislation relevant to education. A source for practitioners, they are used largely by lawyers. They cite the rulings of specific cases and state standards related to specific issues in education. In between editions, the publishers update the handbook with "pocketparts."

Wittrock, Merlin C., ed. **Handbook of Research on Teaching.** 3d ed. New York: Macmillan, 1986. 1,037p. $55. ISBN 0-02-900310-5.

This is a review of research findings on teaching, with a summary of theories underlying the teaching methods and the methods used in the studies. The handbook, a project of the American Educational Research Association, explains the relationship between the findings of studies and their theoretical foundations.

# Digests and Statistical Sources

Baker, Curtis O., Laurence T. Ogle, and Gayle Thompson Rogers, eds. **1989 Education Indicators.** U.S. Department of Education, National Center for Education Statistics. Washington, DC: Government Printing Office, 1986–. Published annually. 353p. $15. NCES 89-653.

Since 1986 the NCES has presented statistical information as indicators to augment *The Condition of Education*. This volume includes two parts: one set of indicators for elementary and secondary education and a second for postsecondary education. The data are illustrated by a series of charts that convey outcomes (student performance, high school completions, and economic outcomes), resources (fiscal and human), and context (student characteristics, learning environment, public and teacher perceptions, and state requirements).

The Carnegie Foundation for the Advancement of Teaching. Foreword by Ernest L. Boyer. **The Condition of Teaching: A State-by-State Analysis, 1990.** Lawrenceville, NJ: Princeton University Press, 1990. 330p. $12. ISBN 0-931050-39-1.

This technical report is an effort by the Carnegie Foundation to explore significant issues in education, particularly with respect to educational reforms of the 1980s. It does this by surveying the attitudes and values of teachers toward several conditions, including the behavior and attitudes of students; academic learning and instruction; school climate, building, and materials; involvement in decision making; status of the profession; and achieving excellence. The report provides a series of tables with national figures on these conditions and includes a section with state-by-state comparisons.

Many questions ask teachers to compare the condition of education in 1990 with the situation three years earlier in 1987 when the foundation conducted a similar survey. Boyer, president of the foundation, summarizes his assessment of the teachers' views in the foreword.

**Current Index to Journals in Education (CIJE).** Phoenix: Oryx Press, March 1979–. Published monthly. New York: Macmillan, 1969–February 1979. $207 (year). ISSN 0011-3565.

CIJE, which is sponsored by ERIC (Educational Resources Information Center) and NIE (National Institute of Education), contains abstracts and indexes of nearly 2,000 articles each month from about 780 education-related journals. The sections of CIJE are arranged according to the subjects of the ERIC Clearinghouses, and the entries by educational journal number, subject, and other topics. Abstracts are brief, one-paragraph summaries of the articles indexed.

**Digest of Education Statistics, 1989.** U.S. Department of Education, National Center for Education Statistics. Washington, DC: Government Printing Office, 1962–. Published annually. 462p. $25. NCES 89-643.

This comprehensive digest contains a large number of tables presenting statistical information on American education from preschool through postsecondary schools. Data cover enrollment in all types and levels of schools, employment and income of graduates, school revenues and expenditures, and national, state, and local spending levels. Much of this information is presented as national and state-by-state figures.

**Education Index: A Cumulative Subject Index to a Selected List of Educational Periodicals and Yearbooks.** New York: H. W. Wilson, 1929–. Published annually with quarterly updates. $105 (vol.). ISSN 0013-1385.

*Education Index* includes unified subject-author entries from over 350 English-language periodicals, yearbooks, and monographs in education. A listing of citations to book reviews follows the subject-author index. It also contains a list of the periodicals indexed, with addresses, frequency of publication, and subscription prices.

Elam, Stanley, ed. **The Gallup/Phi Delta Kappan Polls of Attitudes toward Public Schools, 1969–88.** Bloomington, IN: Phi Delta Kappa, 1989. 229p. $9, PDK members $7.50. ISBN 0-87367-438-3.

Each year *Phi Delta Kappan* magazine publishes a Gallup poll of the public's attitudes toward its schools. The first 20 polls are gathered in this volume, which presents a unique look at how people feel about trends, events, and issues in education. Ben Brodinsky, noted educational writer, provides a brief history for each year that examines the major developments in education as they helped shape the public's attitudes.

Ogle, Laurence T., Nabeel Alsalam, and Gayle Thompson Rogers, eds. **The Condition of Education.** U.S. Department of Education, National Center for Education Statistics. Washington, DC: U.S. Government Printing Office, 1974–. Published annually. 2 vols. $9 (vol. 1), $9.50 (vol. 2). NCES 90-681 (vol. 1), NCES 90-684 (vol. 2).

This statistical summary of the status of education in the United States is compiled by NCES for the published year. The data, conveyed through charts and figures, cover academic performances of students, enrollments, high school dropout rates, school finance, and drug and alcohol use. In recent years two volumes have been published—one addressing elementary and secondary schools (vol. 1) and the other postsecondary schooling (vol. 2).

Ratliff, L. Stanley, ed. **State Education Journal Index and Educators' Guide to Periodicals Research Strategies.** Westminster, CO: State Education Journal Index Publications, 1963–. Published semiannually in February and July. $75. ISSN 0039-0046.

*EJI* indexes all articles in state education and association publications. Many of the entries are from newsletters not included in the *Education Index* and other indexes.

**Resources in Education (RIE).** Education Resources Information Center (ERIC). Washington, DC: U.S. Government Printing Office. Published monthly. $70. ISSN 0098-0897.

RIE contains abstracts and indexes of documents (technical reports, speeches, and sources other than periodicals) that have been catalogued in the ERIC system. Many of these documents are unpublished or have had limited distribution.

Zirkel, Perry A., and Sharon Nalbone Richardson. **A Digest of Supreme Court Decisions Affecting Education.** 2d ed. Bloomington, IN: Phi Delta Kappa Educational Association, 1988. 204p. $7, PDK members $6. ISBN 0-87367-436-7.

This digest contains brief summaries of over 300 court decisions related to education during the past 150 years. The cases are organized into seven chapters according to the nature of the education issue. These issues include school district governance and finance; church-state relationships; student rights and responsibilities; employee rights and responsibilities; discrimination (handicap, national origin, race, and sex); civil rights cases; and procedural parameters. With each case, the authors summarize the facts, the judges' holding, and the basis for the decision. The book also includes a glossary of pertinent legal terms and a summary of selected provisions from the U.S. Constitution.

# Videotapes

**American Dream at Groton**

| | |
|---|---|
| *Type:* | VHS Video |
| *Length:* | 60 min. |
| *Date:* | 1991 |
| *Cost:* | $49.95 |
| *Source:* | PBS Video |
| | 1320 Braddock Place |
| | Alexandria, VA 22314 |
| | (800) 424-7963 |

The video examines the meaning and consequences of the Groton School's efforts to create opportunities for youngsters from impoverished backgrounds. Groton is a small college preparatory school, which once exclusively educated children from privileged families but today seeks to work with capable, less fortunate students. This video looks into the Groton program and its implications for a talented young Puerto Rican student from the South Bronx.

**America's Toughest Assignment: Solving the Educational Crisis**

| | |
|---|---|
| *Type:* | VHS Video |
| *Length:* | 120 min. |
| *Date:* | 1990 |
| *Cost:* | $39.95 plus $3.50 shipping |
| *Source:* | Ambrose Video Publishing, Inc. |
| | 382 Park Avenue S |
| | New York, NY 10016 |
| | (800) 843-0048 |

Charles Kuralt hosts this look into the state of education in America. In a two-hour special CBS News takes on the "tough assignment" of finding school systems where new methods are being developed and old ones retooled. The focus is on schools where the job of being scholarly is taken seriously and where parents, teachers, business and community leaders, and students are working to create a stronger educational environment. These are schools that nurture talented teachers, that know how to measure success and ensure a good education for all students. The video also features insights and comments from Ernest Boyer.

**Beginning the Conversation**

| | |
|---|---|
| *Type:* | VHS Video |
| *Length:* | 30 min. |
| *Date:* | 1990 |
| *Cost:* | Shipping and handling only |

*Source:*   Coalition of Essential Schools
          Brown University
          Providence, RI
          (401) 863-3384

This video provides an overview of the Re:Learning project's nine essential principles for school reform. It features a look at these principles as they are exhibited in different schools and classrooms. With each principle, Ted Sizer, Director of the Coalition of Essential Schools, offers a brief explanation, along with various insights and comments.

## Burning Questions: Losing the Future

*Type:*     VHS Video
*Length:*   48 min.
*Date:*     1989
*Cost:*     $250
*Source:*   Coronet/MTI Film & Video
          108 Wilmot Road
          Deerfield, IL 60015
          (800) 621-2131

*Burning Questions* explores why the United States has lost its lead to other countries in manufacturing, technology, and export. It uncovers three areas of blame: education, business, and government. The program includes historical footage with comments from experts in academia and government. In its examination of education, this film focuses on the lack of adequately trained mathematics and science teachers and explains how this deficiency contributes to a decline in innovation and technological expertise.

## From High School to College: Choice and Transaction

*Type:*     VHS Video
*Length:*   40 min.
*Date:*     1990
*Cost:*     $100 (includes shipping)
*Source:*   Videotapes
          The Carnegie Foundation for the Advancement of Teaching
          5 Ivy Lane
          Princeton, NJ 08540
          (609) 452-1780

This video is designed to help prospective students make the best college choice, with information on preparing for college testing, campus visits, and orientation. The video also includes a separate 12-minute segment, *Financing College,* that explains basic financial aid procedures.

## From Minority to Majority: Education and the Future of the Southwest

*Type:*     VHS Video

*Length:* 43 min.
*Date:* 1988
*Cost:* $30 purchase; $25 rental
*Source:* Western Interstate Commission for Higher Education (WICHE)
1540 30th Street
P.O. Box Drawer P
Boulder, CO 80301
(303) 541-0200

This video presents the concept of the "majority minority" and explores the need to improve education for minorities at all levels. It focuses primarily on the needs of Hispanic families and children and is designed for use in workshops with policymakers from business and industry, education, and state governments. Its content is enhanced with ideas from Harold Hodgkinson and Leobardo Estrada.

**Future World, Future School**
*Type:* VHS Video
*Length:* 23 min.
*Date:* 1988
*Cost:* $59.95
*Source:* IRI Group, Inc.
200 East Wood
Palentine, IL 60067
(708) 991-6300

This video takes a look at social, political, and economic trends that are affecting the nation's schools. It examines the implications of these trends on education and discusses what steps administrators and teachers can take to improve learning.

**High School**
*Type:* VHS Video
*Length:* 58 min. 15 sec.
*Date:* 1985
*Cost:* $95 (includes shipping)
*Source:* The Carnegie Foundation for the Advancement of Teaching
5 Ivy Lane
Princeton, NJ 08540
(609) 452-1780

In this video Ernest Boyer, President of the Carnegie Foundation for the Advancement of Teaching, offers viewers a look into the U.S. high school. It shows administrators and teachers at work, including their daily routine and inspiring moments. Boyer illustrates how the basic curriculum outlined by the Carnegie Foundation can be implemented in today's high schools. This program includes a core of common learning, elective clusters, a senior project, and service in the community.

### Learning in America

*Type:*  VHS Video
*Length:*  5-part series; 60 min. each part
*Date:*  1989
*Cost:*  $225 (plus $8.50 shipping); each title, $49.95
*Source:*  PBS Video
1320 Braddock Place
Alexandria, VA 22314
(800) 424-7963

This five-part documentary series, hosted by veteran journalist Roger Mudd, examines the state of American education. The series brings together many of the nation's prominent education leaders and policymakers to debate how schools in the United States should be reshaped to meet the challenges of the 21st century.

The series includes the following videos.

**The Education Race** visits schools throughout the United States and Japan and examines their differences in detail. With comments from Roger Mudd, the film looks at school curricula, teaching methods employed, attitudes of students, the role of families, and how the characteristics of these two societies affect their education systems in very different ways.

**Paying the Freight** examines the nation's educational goals in an attempt to help understand what needs to be done to reform schools in the United States. It looks at how and where the United States can spend money more effectively for its schools. Also in this program, President George Bush talks with host Roger Mudd about the future of learning in America.

**Teach Your Children** explores the issues surrounding curricula in America's classrooms. It examines what young people need to know for survival in the 21st century, textbook reform, the role of technology, and teaching of values.

**Upstairs/Downstairs** examines why some children are failing in our school systems as well as why some programs are making a difference. It looks at the disparity in funding and other resources among schools in the United States, which include wealthy public and private schools alongside poorly-financed urban and rural schools.

**Wanted: A Million Teachers** looks at the crisis in teaching today. The number entering the profession has declined, and shortages are being felt in many critical subject areas. While attracting talented individuals is a major challenge, many otherwise competent teachers are suffering from low morale and an overload of administrative duties.

### Learning in America: Schools That Work

*Type:*  VHS Video
*Length:*  120 min.
*Date:*  1990

Cost:      $79.95 (plus $8.50 shipping)
Source:    PBS Video
           1320 Braddock Place
           Alexandria, VA 22314
           (800) 424-7963

This video explores the roots of many problems plaguing elementary education by looking into schools that have overcome such problems. Hosted by Roger Mudd, it portrays four exemplary schools where staff, parents, and students have created effective partnerships that enhance learning. The key to the success of these schools is in the climate fostered and in the values and relationships nurtured. The schools featured are Northview School, Manhattan, Kansas; Columbia Park School, Landover, Maryland; City Magnet School, Lowell, Massachusetts; and Lozano Special Emphasis School in Corpus Christi, Texas.

## Standing in the Storm:
## The Story of Jan Amos Comenius
Type:      VHS Video
Length:    73 min.
Date:      1989
Cost:      $59.95
Source:    Vision Video
           2030 Wentz Church Road
           Worcester, PA 19490
           (215) 584-1893

This is story about the life of Jan (Johann) Amos Comenius and how he came to be a primary architect of modern education. It begins with the hardships and tragedy of his early life in Bohemia during the early 1600s. Comenius' travails take him to Poland, England, Sweden, and eventually Holland. Through his writings and works, modern concepts of education begin to be accepted: Girls as well as boys are educated; children are taught in age groups; illustrations are used in textbooks; and children are treated humanely. Along with its pedagogical ideas, this video provides interesting religious history.

## The Truth about Teachers
Type:      VHS Video
Length:    45 min.
Date:      1989
Cost:      $95
Source:    Pyramid Film and Video
           P.O. Box 1048
           Santa Monica, CA 90406
           (800) 421-2304

Host Whoopi Goldberg gives us a look into the classrooms of ten outstanding teachers who are working to "defeat ignorance, poverty, drugs, apathy, and

violence." These teachers, with students from diverse backgrounds, use innovative and sometimes unconventional techniques to affect the lives of their
students. They teach kindergarten through high school, and they teach spelling, reading, mathematics, history, English, the performing arts, and physical
education. The scenes and vignettes of teaching methods are interspersed with
commentary from Goldberg.

# Online Databases

**Bilingual Education Bibliographic Abstracts.** Arlington, VA: National
Clearinghouse for Bilingual Education (NCBE). InterAmerica Research Associates, 1975–. Monthly updates. BRS (BEBA).

This is a bibliographic database of citations and abstracts on the history of
bilingual education and other topics including language testing, English as a
second language, special education, and bilingual studies for adults. The
database is available through Telenet, Tymnet, and direct dial.

**Current Index to Journals in Education (CIJE).** Bethesda, MD: ERIC
Processing & Reference Facility, Educational Resources Information Center
(ERIC), 1969–. Updated monthly. DIALOG.

CIJE, which is sponsored by the U.S. Department of Education and ERIC,
is a database of indexes on more than 750 education-related periodicals. It
covers a wide range of areas and topics in education such as special education,
vocational education, guidance and counseling, science, mathematics, social
studies/social science, and rural education. It is available through Tymnet,
Telenet, Dialnet, and direct dial.

**Education Daily Online.** Arlington, VA: Capitol Publications, 1988–. Updated daily. Special Net.

This abbreviated online version of *Education Daily* includes pieces on federal
education policy, congressional hearings and other activities, press releases,
government publications, and court decisions. The database is available
through Telenet.

**Education Index.** New York: H. W. Wilson, 1983–. Updated twice weekly.
WILSON-LINE.

As in its print version, the online *Education Index* includes entries from over 350
periodicals and other publications in English from nations throughout the
world. Information may be obtained from the database by subject, author,
title, year of publication, title of periodical, and type of article. This database
is available through Telenet and Tymnet.

**Education Research Forum.** Washington, DC: American Educational Research Association (AERA), 1983–. Periodically updated.

This database contains abstracts of articles from AERA journals, conference papers, and reviews of statistical software programs. It is available through Tymnet, Telenet, Datapac, and CompuServe.

**Educational Testing Service Test Collection Database (ETSF).** Princeton, NJ: Educational Testing Service, 1950. Updated quarterly. BRS (ETSF).

This database contains descriptions of various achievement, aptitude, personality, personal interests, and other tests, as well as evaluation instruments. It is available through Telenet, Tymnet, and direct dial.

**The Electric Page.** Austin, TX: National Information Systems, 1983–. Updated daily. National Information Systems.

Through this database you can obtain electronic mail service, electronic conference capabilities, as well as abstracts of books, journal articles, newsletters, theses, and dissertations. It is available through direct dial (Southwestern Bell).

**EPIE On-line.** Water Mill, NY: EPIE Institute, 1980–. Updated bimonthly. CompuServe.

This system describes the pertinent educational information for management and instructional software. The database is available through Telenet, Tymnet, and direct dial.

**Exceptional Child Education Resources.** Reston, VA: Council for Exceptional Children, 1966–1968. BRS (ECER).

The Council for Exceptional Children provides a bibliographic database covering books, monographs, journal articles, conference papers, government documents, and dissertations on special education. It is available through Telenet, Tymnet, Dialnet, and direct dial.

**Mental Measurements Yearbook (MMY).** Lincoln, NE: Buros Institute of Mental Measurements, University of Nebraska, 1974–. Updated monthly. BRS (MMYD).

This is the online version of Buros' *Mental Measurements Yearbook*, which contains reviews of educational tests and other assessment instruments. The database is available through Telenet and Tymnet.

**Microcomputers in Education.** Darien, CT: Microcomputers in Education, 1986–. Updated monthly. NewsNet.

This database reports on public domain educational software, describes instructional uses of microcomputers, and reviews new software products.

**Resources in Computer Education (RICE).** Portland, OR: Computer Technology Program, Northwest Regional Educational Lab, 1979–. Updated quarterly. BRS (RICE).

The database describes and evaluates computer software programs designed for use in elementary and secondary school classrooms. It is available through Telenet, Tymnet, and direct dial.

**Resources in Education (RIE).** Bethesda, MD: ERIC Processing & Reference Facility, Educational Resources Information Center (ERIC), 1966–. Updated monthly. DIALOG.

This is the online version of *Resources in Education,* which abstracts and indexes technical reports, speeches, and sources other than periodicals that are included in the ERIC system. The database is available through Telenet, Tymnet, and direct dial.

**Resources in Vocational Education (RIVE).** Columbus, OH: National Center for Research in Vocational Education, 1978–. Updated Quarterly. BRS (RIVE).

This database is a bibliography of research studies (including those in progress), curriculum development projects, and career education projects on vocational education. It is available through Telenet, Tymnet, and direct dial.

## Notes

1. The deskbook encyclopedia and newsletter are ordered directly from Data Research, P.O. Box 490, Rosemont, MN 55068. Phone: (612) 452-8267, (800) 365-4900.

2. SIRS volumes may be ordered directly from Boca Raton, FL, using the toll-free number (800) 327-0513.

3. This yearbook is ordered directly from the national organization: NOLPE, 3601 SW 29th Street, Suite 223, Topeka, KS 66614. Phone: (913) 273-3550.

# 9

# Journals in Education

THE FIELD OF EDUCATION IS AWASH in periodicals and journals. A major reason is the large number of specialty areas. Each specialty, in turn, has organizations—often with national, state, and local affiliates—to help serve a variety of educational constituents. That constituency, or audience, is large: More than 8 million teachers, professors, administrators, support staff, board members, and trustees across the nation are involved in the business of education.

Unlike most other institutions, events, issues, and trends in education are often of interest to the public. And many people are inclined to participate in school affairs. Beyond the legion of people who make their living in education, about 40 million families have students in the nation's schools, colleges, and universities. The result is well over 200 scholarly and popular journals with a national audience. When the publications of state, regional, and local organizations are included, the number increases many times.

The list of education journals in this chapter is selective; it includes those with the largest circulation and a national focus on educational issues, trends, and research. The synopses accompanying these journals are intended to inform readers who are interested in public elementary and secondary school issues.

The "publish or perish" ethic that characterizes much of higher education keeps the pipeline of articles to journals well-stocked and editors busy. For professors, teachers, and other scholars interested in publishing articles in these and other journals, I recommend the *Educator's Desk Reference (EDR): A Sourcebook of Educational Information and Research*, Macmillan, 1989. EDR is edited by Melvyn N. Freed, Robert

K. Hess, and Joseph M. Ryan, and is a product of the American Council on Education. Chapter 8 contains more information on this sourcebook.

The subscription cost listed with some journals includes annual membership in the parent organization. This often entitles the member to newsletters and other materials published by the organization. Subscriptions to other journals are available without joining the organization. Single issues of a journal also frequently can be purchased from the publisher and occasionally at newstands.

### American Educational Research Journal
American Educational Research Association
1230 17th Street, NW
Washington, DC 20036
(202) 223-9485
*Quarterly. $28, individuals; $35, institutions.*

This scholarly journal includes theoretical and empirical articles based on original research. It emphasizes investigations in educational psychology.

### American Journal of Education
University of Chicago Press
Journal Division
5720 South Woodlawn Avenue
Chicago, IL 60637
(312) 702-8187
*Quarterly. $23, individuals; $41, institutions; $19, students.*

The well-documented articles in this journal examine a variety of educational topics and report on research work. Each issue also includes essay reviews and shorter book reviews.

### American School and University
North American Publishing Co.
401 N. Broad Street
Philadelphia, PA 19108
(215) 238-5300
*Monthly (12 issues). $65.*

The articles in this popular journal deal with educational administration topics such as building and grounds maintenance, facilities, purchasing, safety, and security. Its intended audience is administrators in grades K–12 and higher education.

### American School Board Journal
National School Boards Association
1680 Duke Street
Alexandria, VA 22314
(703) 838-6722

*Monthly. $46; Canada, $51; foreign, $56.*

Each issue contains 10 to 12 articles on topics related to school policymaking and administration, including school law, curriculum issues, reform trends, discipline, and program evaluation. Although topics are written for a school board audience, many of the articles have a wider appeal to educators and the public.

### Arithmetic Teacher
National Council of Teachers of Mathematics
1906 Association Drive
Reston, VA 22091
(703) 620-9840
*Monthly (9 issues). $40. Includes membership in the council and 5 issues of NCTM News Bulletin.*

The articles in this journal present new developments in mathematics curriculum, instruction, and teacher education for grades K–8. The journal serves as a way for teachers to stay updated on teaching activities, techniques, and issues, as well as to exchange ideas.

### Art Education
National Art Education Association
1916 Association Drive
Reston, VA 22091
(703) 860-8000
*Bimonthly. $50. Includes subscription to NAEA News.*

The articles in *Art Education* feature aspects of teaching the visual arts in elementary through postsecondary classrooms.

### Catalyst: Voices of
### Chicago School Reform
Community Renewal Society
332 S. Michigan Avenue
Suite 500
Chicago, IL 60604
(312) 427-4830
*Monthly (9 issues). $10.*

This publication, which first rolled off the presses in September 1989, is designed to keep educators and the public aware of happenings in Chicago's extensive school-reform efforts. Still, many of the articles are written by national spokespersons on a range of reform issues that apply to other cities and states.

## Change: The Magazine of Higher Education
Heldref Publications
4000 Albemarle Street, NW
Washington, DC 20016
(202) 362-6445, (800) 365-9753
*Bimonthly. $23, individuals; $45, institutions; foreign, add $9.*

*Change*, as its complete title declares, is a magazine, not a journal, with articles that focus on contemporary issues in colleges and universities. It features pieces that appeal to administrators in higher education including articles on innovative teaching methods, finance, professional development, admissions strategies, educational philosophy, the social role of colleges, and governing practices.

## Childhood Education
Association for Childhood Education International
11141 Georgia Avenue
Suite 200
Wheaton, MD 20902
(301) 942-2443, (800) 423-3563
*Five issues per year. $38, individuals; $65, institutions; $20, students and retirees.*

The subtitle of this journal, *Infancy through Early Adolescence*, suggests the wide range of young people's needs it addresses. In turn, the audience for the journal, in addition to teachers, includes teachers-in-training, teacher educators, parents, day-care workers, librarians, pediatricians, and other child caretakers. It contains articles on curriculum topics, innovative methods, creative projects, community issues, and educational trends as well as research on the development of children. The fifth issue is devoted to an annual theme.

## Children's Literature in Education:
## An International Quarterly
Human Sciences Press, Inc.
233 Spring Street
New York, NY 10013
(212) 620-8000
*Quarterly. $42; foreign, $50.*

The articles in this journal review new and existing literature appropriate for preschool and elementary children and discuss how teachers can effectively use literature in the classroom.

## The Clearing House
Heldref Publications
4000 Albemarle Street, NW
Washington, DC 20016
(202) 362-6445
*Monthly (9 issues). $40; foreign, $49.*

*Clearing House* is a journal for middle-grade and high school teachers and administrators that publishes short but engaging articles on a wide range of topics. These topics include curriculum development, instructional techniques, guidance and counseling, testing and measurement, computer use, school law, special education, gifted and talented, and others.

## The Computing Teacher
International Society for
Technology in Education
University of Oregon
1787 Agate Street
Eugene, OR 97403
(503) 686-4414
*Monthly (8 issues). $47.*

Classroom teachers, lab instructors, and library media specialists will find the articles in *Computing Teacher* useful. They are short and very practical pieces on teaching strategies, lesson plans, software programs, and other subjects intended for use on "Monday morning."

## Early Childhood Research Quarterly
National Association for the
Education of Young Children
Ablex Publishing Corporation
355 Chestnut Street
Norwood, NJ 07648
(201) 767-8450
*Quarterly. $35, individuals; $90, institutions; foreign, add $15.*

This relatively new publication focuses on research and other scholarly investigations related to the care and learning of children up to eight years old. It emphasizes articles that address methods and practices of working with young children.

## Education and Training in Mental Retardation
Council for Exceptional Children
1920 Association Drive
Reston, VA 22091
(703) 620-3660
*Quarterly. $28; foreign, $32.*

This journal includes technical articles, research reviews, and critical reviews of literature that relate to the education and training of the mentally disabled. The pieces address such topics as identifying and evaluating the disabled, training instructional staff, and promoting public understanding, support, and legislation.

## Education and Urban Society
Sage Publications, Inc.
2455 Teller Road
Newberry Park, CA 91320
(805) 499-0721
*Quarterly. $36, individuals; $100, institutions.*

Each issue includes about six scholarly articles on such urban educational issues as desegregation, school reform, financial resources, and equality of opportunity.

## Education Digest
Prakken Publications
416 Longshore Drive
P.O. Box 8623
Ann Arbor, MI 48107
(313) 769-1211, (800) 530-WORD
*Monthly (9 issues). $30; foreign, $35.*

Each issue is a collection of reprinted articles or summaries of key articles that have appeared in recent journals. The articles, covering topics for preschool through higher education, address major issues and trends that are appropriate for the layperson and professional scholar.

## Education Week
4301 Connecticut Avenue, NW
Suite 250
Washington, DC 20008
*Weekly (40 issues). $49.94; Canada, $72.94; foreign, $114.94 (air mail) and $82.94 (surface mail).*

*Education Week* is a newspaper-style tabloid that is published weekly during the school year. It contains a wide range of stories on government policies, state legislation, school district innovations, and educational organizations. It provides detailed coverage, including extensive excerpts, of major education reports and Supreme Court cases. Other timely features include a calendar of educational conferences, listings of professional positions available, and announcements of grants.

## Educational Evaluation and Policy Analysis
American Educational Research Association
1230 17th Street, NW
Washington, DC 20036
(202) 223-9485
*Quarterly. $28, individuals; $35, institutions; foreign, add $6.*

*EEPA* features analyses of educational evaluation and educational policy. It also examines theoretical issues of this work, as well as practical concerns in developing evaluation and policy studies.

**The Educational Forum**
Kappa Delta Pi
P.O. Box A
West Lafayette, IN 47906
(317) 743-1705
*Quarterly. $12; foreign, $13.*

This is the journal of Kappa Delta Pi, an international honor society in education. It publishes substantive articles written by educators on current trends, issues, and problems in education. The topics range from those that are pertinent to preschool through higher education.

**Educational Leadership**
Association for Supervision and Curriculum Development
1250 N. Pitt Street
Alexandria, VA 22314
(703) 549-9110
*Monthly (8 issues). $48, nonmembers; $32, members; $64, comprehensive membership; $51, regular membership.*

The main themes of the articles in this journal address curriculum, instruction, supervision, and leadership topics. They frequently involve social and political issues as related to curriculum and instruction. The journal also includes reports that interpret research findings appropriate for K–12 school administrators, its primary audience.

**Educational Researcher**
American Educational Research Association
1230 17th Street, NW
Washington, DC 20036
(202) 223-9485
*Monthly (9 issues). $28, individuals; $35, institutions. Included in AERA membership dues, $45; $20, students.*

This journal of the AERA contains scholarly articles on research trends related to classroom practices, curriculum development, and other pedagogical issues. It also includes editorials, book reviews, and federal news on education.

**Educational Technology**
Educational Technology Publications, Inc.
720 Palisade Avenue
Englewood Cliffs, NJ 07632
(201) 871-4007
*Monthly. $119; foreign, $139.*

This magazine publishes articles on innovative technology in education, including computers, audiovisual hardware and other communications media, instructional design, administration, and evaluation technology.

## Electronic Learning

Scholastic Inc.
730 Broadway
New York, NY 10003
(212) 505-3000
*Eight issues per year, September through April. $23.*

This magazine provides timely information on computer and communications technology for schools. Many articles examine software and hardware available for various instructional areas. It features reviews of new software programs.

## Elementary School Guidance & Counseling

American Association for
Counseling and Development
5999 Stevenson Avenue
Alexandria, VA 22304
(703) 823-9800
*Quarterly. $23.*

Its articles analyze research studies and evaluation measures, as well as examining issues and practices pertinent to guidance and counseling of K–8 students.

## The Elementary School Journal

University of Chicago Press
Journal Division
5720 South Woodlawn
Chicago, IL 60637
(312) 702-8187
*Five issues per year. $49, institutions; $28.50, individuals; $21.25, students.*

This journal is devoted to scholarly articles on learning skills, curriculum areas, social and cultural issues, and research work. It publishes an occasional special issue on a school or curriculum reform topic.

## Exceptional Children

Council for Exceptional Children
1920 Association Drive
Reston, VA 22091
(703) 620-3660
*Six issues per year. $35; foreign, $39.50.*

This journal covers topics on all aspects of the training and development of special-education students. Many articles focus on findings of research reports. It also contains feature articles and book reviews of interest to school psychologists, speech therapists, and administrators.

## Gifted Child Quarterly
National Association for Gifted Children
Suite 140
4175 Lovell Road
Circle Pines, MN 55014
(612) 784-3475
*Quarterly. $45. Includes membership in NAGC.*

This journal contains articles on the theory and research related to the psychology and education of gifted and talented students.

## The Gifted Child Today
GCT Inc.
P.O. Box 6448
Mobile, AL 36660
(205) 478-4700
*Bimonthly. $30; foreign, $36.*

This magazine emphasizes practical articles with an array of teaching ideas for elementary schoolteachers and parents. Each issue also includes several concise book reviews.

## Harvard Education Review
Guttman Library
Suite 349
6 Appian Way
Cambridge, MA 02138
(617) 495-3432
*Quarterly. $33, individuals; $60, institutions.*

The journal publishes substantial opinion pieces and reports of research on a range of educational topics, including those related to psychology, sociology, anthropology, economics, political science, history, and public policy. Periodically, an issue will be devoted to a specific education trend, issue, or research study. Readers can respond through its Letters to the Editors section.

## Health Education
American Alliance for Health, Physical Education,
Recreation and Dance
1900 Association Drive
Reston, VA 22091
(703) 860-4131
*Bimonthly. $85, individuals (includes membership to AAHPERD); $65, institutions. (See also Journal of Physical Education, Recreation and Dance.)*

Articles in this journal have a broad general appeal to health educators in schools, colleges, clinics, community agencies, and the workplace.

## History of Education Quarterly
School of Education
Indiana University
Bloomington, IN 47405
(812) 855-9334
*Quarterly. $47; foreign, $50.*

The first third of each issue features articles for readers interested in particular dimensions of educational history. The second part is devoted to essay reviews of major works in educational history. The final third of the journal is reserved for many brief book reviews.

## Instructor Magazine
Scholastic Inc.
730 Broadway
New York, NY 10003
(212) 505-4900
*Monthly (9 issues). $16; foreign, $40.*

*Instructor* is designed for the elementary schoolteacher and provides teaching activities in all areas of the curriculum. The activities include stories, plays, arts and crafts projects, mathematics, science, social studies projects, computer applications, work units, and lesson plans. A special section is devoted to teaching and computers.

## Journal of Chemical Education
American Chemical Society
Division of Chemical Education
1155 16th Street, NW
Washington, DC 20036
(202) 872-4600
*Monthly. $28, individuals; $56, institutions.*

This journal is intended largely for college and university chemistry instructors with a section especially for high school teachers. The articles include descriptions of innovative courses, reports on new laboratory equipment, reviews of recent advances in chemistry, explanations of classroom demonstrations, analyses of research on classroom instruction, and information on the use of computers and educational programs.

## Journal of Education
Boston University
School of Education
605 Commonwealth Avenue
Boston, MA 02215
(617) 353-3230
*Three issues per year. $16, individuals, and $23, institutions; foreign: $20, individuals, and $26, institutions.*

The journal includes scholarly articles on a range of education topics, including curriculum, pedagogy, social history, cultural politics, economics, and women's studies. The articles relate to issues relevant to schools and colleges.

## Journal of Educational Psychology

American Psychological Association, Inc.
1400 North Uhle Street
Arlington, VA 22201
(202) 955-7600
*Quarterly. $24, individual members; $60, nonmembers; $120, institutions.*

This journal features 12 or more articles each issue reporting original research and theoretical perspectives on psychological development, motivation, cognition, and learning strategies. The theory and research are related to classroom instruction.

## Journal of Educational Research

Heldref Publications
4000 Albemarle Street, NW
Washington, DC 20016
(202) 362-6445
*Bimonthly. $55; foreign, $54.*

The 12 articles included in each issue report on original research findings as they relate to classroom practices in elementary and secondary schools.

## Journal of Learning Disabilities

Donald D. Hammill Foundation
8700 Shoal Creek Boulevard
Austin, TX 78758
(512) 451-3246
*Monthly (10 issues). $45, individuals; $60, institutions; foreign, $70.*

Each issue contains eight to ten articles related to learning disabilities. The articles report research findings, describe case studies, present points of view, and review tests, materials, treatments, and books.

## Journal of Physical Education, Recreation and Dance

American Alliance for Health, Physical Education,
Recreation, and Dance
1900 Association Drive
Reston, VA 22091
(703) 476-3477
*Monthly (9 issues). $85, individuals (includes membership to AAHPERD); $65, institutions. (See also Health Education).*

The articles in this journal are written for educators in health, physical education, and dance. They are designed to show how the quality of human lives can be improved now and in the future.

## Journal of Reading
International Reading Association
800 Bardsdale Road
P.O. Box 8139
Newark, DE 19714
(302) 731-1600
*Eight issues per year. $38, individuals; $41, institutions. Includes membership in IRA.*

The journal emphasizes articles that deal with strategies and techniques for teaching reading skills to learners 12 years of age and above, including literacy programs for adults. It also contains theoretical and research articles. The journal is designed for reading teachers and professors of reading education.

## Language Arts
National Council of Teachers of English
1111 Kenyon Road
Urbana, IL 61801
(217) 328-3870
*Monthly, September through April. $35, individuals; $40, institutions; foreign, add $4.*

The articles in *Language Arts* cover all facets of language instruction and learning and are intended primarily for teachers in preschool through the middle-grade school. Each issue also is devoted to a specific theme relevant to teaching the language arts.

## Learning 90
Springhouse Corporation
1111 Bethlehem Pike
Springhouse, PA 19477
(215) 646-8700
*Monthly (9 issues). $18.*

As its subtitle reads, *Learning* provides "Creative Ideas and Activities for Teachers." It is written for K–8 classroom teachers and contains articles that present practical, hands-on activities as well as explanations of personal experiences. The magazine also includes articles from teachers that analyze or evaluate an educational theory or method in the classroom.

## Mathematics Teacher
National Council of Teachers of Mathematics
1906 Association Drive
Reston, VA 22091
(703) 620-9840
*Monthly (9 issues). $40, individuals; $45, institutions; foreign, add $5.*

This journal contains articles designed for mathematics instruction in middle-grade schools, high schools, two-year colleges, and teacher-education colleges.

## Media and Methods
1429 Walnut Street
Philadelphia, PA 19102
(215) 563-6005
*Bimonthly. $29; foreign, $47.*

As the subtitle reads, this is a magazine about "Educational Products, Technologies, and Programs for Schools and Universities." The articles provide timely information on computers, communications technology, and audio-visual equipment; describe teaching tools and techniques; and examine issues related to school curriculum and instruction.

## NASSP Bulletin
National Association of Secondary School Principals
1904 Association Drive
Reston, VA 22091
(703) 860-0200
*Monthly (9 issues). $125, individuals; $165, institutions. Includes membership in NASSP.*

This journal publishes articles on aspects of school administration, including those addressing social issues, educational trends, and curriculum innovations.

## Phi Delta Kappan
Phi Delta Kappa
P.O. Box 789
Bloomington, IN 47402
(812) 339-1156
*Monthly (10 issues). $30; foreign, $32.50.*

This is a major journal published by a national educational honorary society, with a circulation of over 150,000. The articles in *Phi Delta Kappan* address current, often controversial, topics related to major research studies, curriculum development, legal issues, and policymaking in education.

## The Physics Teacher
American Association of Physics Teachers
5112 Berwyn Road
College Park, MD 20740
(301) 345-4177
*Monthly. $61, individuals; $30.50, students.*

This journal is designed for college instructors as well as high school teachers of physics. The articles include technical pieces that address teaching new findings or knowledge and others devoted to practical teaching techniques.

## The Reading Teacher
International Reading Association
800 Bardsdale Road
P.O. Box 8139
Newark, DE 19714
(302) 731-1600
*Monthly (9 issues). $38, individuals; $41, institutions.*

This magazine is designed for preschool and elementary schoolteachers with students up to age 12. It features practical articles on the teaching of reading, but also includes reports on research findings and evaluations of instructional materials.

## Rethinking Schools:
## An Urban Education Journal
1001 E. Keefe Avenue
Milwaukee, WI 53212
(414) 964-9646
*Bimonthly. $10, individuals; $25, institutions.*

This journal is published by Milwaukee area classroom teachers and is intended to promote thoughtful discussion amd debate on educational issues. *Rethinking Schools* provides teachers, parents, and students the opportunity to offer their insights into improving schools. Its articles cover a range of topics on urban school issues and include practical classroom teaching ideas.

## Review of Educational Research
American Educational Research Association
1230 17th Street, NW
Washington, DC 20036
(202) 223-9485
*Quarterly. $28, individuals; $35, institutions.*

This journal publishes critical summaries of major studies that relate research to practice. These reviews conceptualize and interpret the studies supported by thoroughly documented analyses.

## Social Education
National Council for the Social Studies
3501 Newark Street, NW
Washington, DC 20016
(202) 966-7840
*Seven issues per year. $45, regular membership; $55, comprehensive membership; $50, nonmembers; $25, students and retirees.*

*Social Education* covers curriculum issues related to the social studies and social science disciplines, research findings, and teaching practices and methods.

It occasionally devotes an issue to the teaching and research of a particular subject and often includes a special section devoted to a timely social studies topic.

## The Social Studies
Heldref Publications
4000 Albemarle Street, NW
Washington, DC 20077
(202) 362-6445
*Bimonthly. $39; foreign, $48.*

This magazine addresses a broad range of social studies topics, citizenship issues, and classroom teaching ideas. It emphasizes articles that have practical use in elementary and secondary school classrooms.

## Teachers College Record
Teachers College
Columbia University
525 West 120th Street
New York, NY 10027
(212) 678-3000
*Quarterly. $24, individuals; $50, institutions; single issues, $10.*

This scholarly journal publishes six to eight articles in each issue on intellectual, philosophical, sociological, and historical inquiries into educational policy and teaching practices. The *Record* also includes essays and short book reviews.

## Technology and Learning
Peter Li, Inc.
2451 East River Road
Dayton, OH 45439
(513) 294-5785
*Eight issues per year. $19.95; foreign, $27.95.*

*Technology and Learning* includes articles on the research, innovative philosophies, and different uses of computers in elementary and secondary classrooms.

## Vocational Education Journal
American Vocational Association
1410 King Street
Alexandria, VA 22314
(703) 683-3111
*Eight issues per year. $25; $40 includes membership in AVA.*

The journal emphasizes articles on major trends in technology and employment that affect vocational programs and curricula. The articles, which apply to secondary and postsecondary vocational-technical education, both examine trends and provide practical solutions to problems and teaching challenges.

## Young Children

National Association for the Education of Young Children
1834 Connecticut Avenue, NW
Washington, DC 20009
(202) 232-8777
(800) 424-2460
*Bimonthly. $25, individuals; $30, institutions.*

The articles in *Young Children* include practical methods as well as scholarly reviews of teaching practices and research efforts. They are directed toward teachers, parent educators, program directors, teacher educators, and researchers in early childhood education who work with youngsters up to age eight.

# Index